Remembering
GENERATIONS

Remembering
GENERATIONS
Race and Family
in Contemporary
African American
Fiction

Ashraf H. A. Rushdy

The University of North Carolina Press • Chapel Hill and London

© 2001

The University of

North Carolina Press

All rights reserved

Designed by

Karen Schiff

Set in Adobe Caslon

by G&S Typesetters

Manufactured

in the

United States

of America

The paper in this book
meets the guidelines for
permanence and durability
of the Committee on
Production Guidelines
for Book Longevity
of the Council on
Library Resources.

05 04 03 02 01

5 4 3 2 1

Library of Congress
Cataloging-in-Publication Data
Rushdy, Ashraf H. A., 1961–
Remembering generations: race and family
in contemporary African American fiction /
Ashraf H. A. Rushdy
      p.   cm.
Includes index.
ISBN 0-8078-2601-4 (alk. paper)—
ISBN 0-8078-4917-0 (pbk.: alk. paper)
1. American fiction—Afro-American
authors—History and criticism.
2. American fiction—20th century—
History and criticism.   3. Domestic
fiction, American—History and
criticism.   4. Literature and society—
United States—History—20th century.
5. Afro-Americans in literature.   6. Race
in literature.   7. Afro-American families
in literature.   8. Slavery in literature.
9. First person narrative.   I. Title.
PS374.N4 R87   2001
810.9′896073′0904—dc21   00-062866

In memory of
my grandmother,
my Taita

I am ready
thank you for your iron thank you for your faith
I will look for you in dreams sometimes
and sometimes I'll leave you alone

tell my thank-yous to God
I have no velvet for you
to walk on only me
inside out and ready to give you home

Ruth Forman, "Homecoming"

Let then the Dreams of the Dead rebuke the Blind who think that what is will be forever and teach them that what was worth living for must live again and that which merited death must stay dead. Teach us, Forever Dead, there is no Dream but Deed, there is no Deed but Memory.

W. E. B. Du Bois

Generations do not cease to be born, and we are responsible to them because we are the only witnesses they have.

James Baldwin

i am accused of tending to the past
as if i made it,
as if i sculpted it
with my own hands. i did not.
the past was waiting for me
when i came,
a monstrous unnamed baby,
and i with my mother's itch
took it to breast
and named it
History.
she is more human now . . .

lucille clifton

Contents

Acknowledgments

This book, like so many others, was made possible because of the National Humanities Center. And, like so many other books written at the National Humanities Center, it was written there while I was supposed to be working on another project.

I would like to thank the many people who made my year at the center so memorable. The center is fortunate in being staffed by people who are as hospitable as they are efficient, who are as concerned about the social as they are the intellectual life of the fellows, and who are as generous with their time as it is possible to be. I would like to pass on my gratitude to Dot Boatwright, Sue Boyd, Corbett Capps, Linda Godowsky, Jen Horney, Linda Morgan, Mary Donna Pond, Pat Schreiber, Crystal Waters, and Michelle Weeks. I would also like to thank the director of the center, Robert Connor, who proved as entertaining a lunch companion as he was a gifted administrator. Without doubt, the library services at the center have no peer anywhere, and it would be impossible to imagine a more able set of librarians than Jean Houston, Eliza Robertson, and Alan Tuttle. Finally, I would like especially to thank Kent Mullikin, the vice-president and deputy director of the center, who is both the institutional memory of the center and an impeccable host with an endless fund of good will and good wit.

It would be unwieldy to list all the friends I made at the center, but I must mention those who kindly read parts of this manuscript and those who provided the kind of amiability and sociability you can find only among academics who have no teaching or administrative duties. Conversations with Nicki Beisel, Edward Friedman, Jonathan Levin, Nancy and Dick Lewis, Suzanne Raitt, Jonah Seigel, Tony La Vopa, and John Watanabe often inspired ideas that indirectly found their way into the book. Rochelle Gurstein and Elizabeth McHenry shared lots of meals, thoughts, and adventures with me; I treasure their humor, companionship, and affection.

A Standard Research Grant through the Social Sciences and Humanities Research Council of Canada permitted me to begin this work. My home institution, Wesleyan University, provided me with sabbaticals and leaves and research funds that allowed me to carry it on and complete it. Even more important, Wesleyan provided me with creative and intelligent students who are a pleasure to teach and learn from. I would like in particular to thank those former students and current friends whose own intellectual careers in graduate school I have followed with excitement: Casey Brown, Lauren Elmore, Tucker Foehl, Catherine Griffin, Josh Guild, Stacy Morgan, Shani Mott, Leigh Raiford, Raquel Rodriguez, Anthony Ross, Shanti Roundtree, and Ayana Webb.

I would also like to thank many people at Wesleyan for their support and their friendship. Jan Guarino and Sheila Kelleher in the English Department have been unfailingly efficient and helpful. Georgie Leone and Ginny Gumz make the Center for African American Studies as accommodating and friendly a place as any university could hope to house. My colleagues have inspired me with their work and cheered me with their company. In particular, it is a pleasure to count as a friend someone as wise and learned as Khachig Tölöyan; someone as caring and supportive as Krishna Winston; someone as generous and witty as Bill Stowe. Susan Hirsch has been a wonderful friend who has always taken time away from her own work to help me with mine. Finally, I would like very much to thank Jan Willis, who not only supported this work each step of the way but also kindly gave me a copy of her family history in manuscript that I found invaluable for this study and simply beautiful for its own sake.

People who were but are no longer at Wesleyan have remained close and dear friends. Erness and Nathan Brody continue to share with me their humor and grace. Cheryl Myers and Monique Sulle are now long-distance friends whom no distance can keep me from ador-

ing. Leah Gardiner and Jeff Kerr-Ritchie gave me a friendship filled
with radiance and laughter that I expect to enjoy for the rest of my life.

Robert Greenhill and I have been friends since we were under-
graduates together, and I would like to thank him for twenty years of
conversations that have ranged from the most heated political issues
to the most ephemeral trivia. It would be difficult to say how much his
friendship has meant to me.

William Andrews, Joseph Skerrett, Cheryl Wall, and Joe Weixl-
mann have been supporters and role models. I would like to thank
them for all the wonderful work they have produced, all they represent
as intellectuals, and all they have done personally for me.

I would like to thank the editors of *African American Review*, *College English*, and *Southern Review* for permission to reprint materials
published earlier in different forms.

It has been truly a delight to work with the editors at the University of North Carolina Press. I would like in particular to thank Sian
Hunter, the acquisitions editor, for her enthusiasm and acumen,
Pamela Upton, the assistant managing editor, for her professionalism,
and Suzanne Comer Bell, the copyeditor, for her critical intelligence
and sharp eye. They have made this a better book.

Finally, I would like to thank all the members of my family, my
mother, father, brother, uncles, aunts, nieces, and nephews. They remain the most important people in my world. This study is largely
concerned with discerning how we inherit other peoples' memories
from earlier generations, and how we begin to feel ourselves as belonging to particular families because we learn to share in those memories. For many of us, our earliest childhood memories are of hearing
stories of our elders' memories. This book is dedicated to the memory
of my grandmother. From her, from the stories she told me and the
years she nurtured me, I learned about life and love and loss. I know
she is in a better place, but I miss her every single day. I love you, Taita.

1

History Is Your Own Heartbeat

The Palimpsest Imperative in African American Fiction

In American thought, the analogies used to describe slavery almost inevitably break down and ultimately fail. In the early republic, revolutionary slaveholders used the metaphor of slavery to complain about taxation without representation; for abolitionists and other writers of the American renaissance, slavery was the nation's original sin; for late nineteenth-century intellectuals, it was what Henry Adams described as a cancer in an otherwise healthy body; for our liberal contemporaries, it is America's great crime or her terrible shame. Yet in each case the analogy tends to fall apart. The early republicans could not see the material reality of their metaphor, those whose unfree labor produced the wealth the British monarchy sought to tax; the transcendentalists imagined an original sin for which the American Adam apparently did not lose his innocence; the American

Adams himself could imagine a state of health in an organism other-wise riddled with cancer; and contemporaries who willingly call slav-ery a crime and a shame refuse to consider reparations a justice or even an apology appropriate.[1] Such a long history of failed metaphors leads one to suspect that more is at issue here than an ineptitude in analog-ical thinking. What is at issue is that American intellectuals have con-sistently employed terms, narratives, and conceptual devices that hide what they are trying to reveal. Slavery, in American intellectual dis-course, is not only or merely a metaphor, a sin, a cancer, a crime, or a shame, although it is also all of those things. Slavery is the family se-cret of America.

It is not secret in the sense that it is hidden from view or unknown. It is, after all, an institution that arose almost simultaneously with the founding of the nation (about a dozen years after the establishment of the first permanent settlement at Jamestown), an economic system that proved to be one of the most crucial sources of wealth for the growing national economy in the expansion of the global market from the Enlightenment to the Industrial Revolution, and a social system the nation debated from the Revolutionary to the Civil War. There are material residues that attest to its existence, governing documents that hint at its importance, and contemporary analyses that prove its enduring relevance. So, it is not secret in the sense of being inaccessi-ble or the object of knowledge of a confidential few. It is secret in the sense that it haunts the peripheries of the national imaginary because it is "what we think we know, what we can never forget, and what seems continually to elude our understanding."[2] Slavery is the event we need to rationalize in order to credit the democratic vision of the errand into the wilderness, the institution we need to explain as a cen-tral paradox in the creation of American freedom, the social system that thwarted the ideals of the nation's founding statements. Slavery, in other words, functions in American thinking as the partially hidden phantom of a past that needs to be revised in order to be revered.

Contemporary American intellectuals are more aware of how slav-ery is the American family secret. Two metaphors that resonate effec-tively in the current dialogue draw on haunted imagery: the American slave past is "*that* ghost which we have not entirely faced," and the memory of that institution is "a haunted house" we fear to inhabit.[3] These are telling figures. A domestic space haunted by a liminal ap-parition beyond the grave indicates the ways the past is not dead, but likewise not seen or acknowledged by all. What makes the nation's slave past a secret is precisely that it is something, like a miracle, that can be denied even by those who witness it or its effects. Consider another historical atrocity that haunts a different national imaginary. Intellectuals writing about the Holocaust have also argued that it "functions as a cultural secret, a secret which, essentially, we are still keeping from ourselves, through various forms of communal or of personal denial."[4] These cultural secrets, these haunted national memories, are symptoms of a malaise, if not an actual illness, that comes of an inability to comprehend the function of the past. What does the past mean in the formation of what we call the present? What can the past mean for a contemporary society founded upon or the product of the horrors of slaughter and dehumanization in the effort to exploit labor, torture people, and recreate race? Even more basic, how do we understand the past — not practically, as in what materials and sources of information best generate narratives faithful to the times represented, but, existentially, as in what is this past that made possible the present, that gave form and structure to the society we live in, that produced the inequities we either recreate or try to amend, that, in fact, created our sensibility to be alert to a past and our epistemology to understand it *as* past?

These questions, in many ways, are ancient and can be found at the heart of enduring philosophical dilemmas about the nature of time and human thought. More pertinent for our purpose, they are also questions that get reformulated in specific ways in different and differently defined ages. At an epochal level, these are questions that come to us from an Enlightenment problematic about the constitution of the human subject and its relationship to time. As Richard Terdiman argues in his meditations on a broadly defined modernity, Western civilization's "preoccupation with history" emerges from a "massive disruption of traditional forms of memory . . . and thereby of history" and resolves itself in an "attempt to master the crisis of diachronicity, the new and disorienting opacity of the past."[5] At another level, in the twentieth century, these questions about the meaning of the past assume an urgency that comes from a different kind of rupture and crisis. World wars and international struggles that disrupted local and national traditions also led to different historical sensibilities in those who would explore the meaning of a past that existed before genocide, before colonization. From the end of the second world war to the domestic revolutionary and reform movements of the 1960s, there arose both cultural and institutional forms for exploring that past through a new social history that came to value again what Terdiman referred to as "traditional forms of memory."

Contemporary intellectuals who ruminate on historical crises, like American slavery or the Jewish Holocaust, return to those traditions of memory and oral history in order to ask from a different angle what the meaning of the past is for a present social order. For Toni Morrison, author of the 1987 novel on slavery, *Beloved*, for Claude Lanzmann, producer of the 1985 film on the Holocaust, *Shoah*, the point of such return, the impetus behind asking such questions, is to give voice to the victims of the past, to "resurrect" the dead so that they haunt the living.[6] *Beloved* and *Shoah* examine an episode, institution, or practice in the past that in many ways feels like a rupture, like an event that makes the present incomprehensible because it is an event that constitutes a break, a fissure, a tear in the fabric of history. To think carefully on these things is to wonder how it is possible to live in a world or society where such systematic horror occurred, where what human beings did to each other so far exceeds our imagination and our language that we can contain it and represent it only as a historical moment (an "episode," "institution," "practice," or "event"), even as we are aware that these events constitute a break with the past and these practices have perduring effects on the future. What *Beloved* and *Shoah* demonstrate is that there are moments when the past abruptly stops, where the idea of historical continuity becomes impossible, because we remain haunted by what Shoshana Felman calls a "history that has not ended . . . [a] historical occurrence of an event that, in effect, *does not end*."[7]

Having said this, though, let me add that it is equally important for us to recognize the ways life does and did go on, particularly for those who suffered but survived the institutions described in these works. There is a danger of neglecting the dailiness of the lives of the people who lived through slavery and the concentration camps, the danger that arguing for a historical break means either denying the small joys and recurring sorrows of those individuals who lived through it or forgetting what, to appropriate a phrase by Hannah Arendt, we can call the "banality of evil," the terrifying normalcy of human suffering wrought of human desires for hierarchy, cruelty, supremacy. In other words, there must be some way for us to value aright the grotesque depth of depravity these events exhibit, what we can think of as their history-rupturing profundity, without denying that they are culminations of consistent and altogether too common historical patterns. They are events that make us think of the stoppage of history, while they are very much the results of history, the accretions of daily events and regulating structures that construct a world we can make sense of because its social divisions appear natural. The texts I am referring to here try to achieve this double vision of the unbelievable misery and the believable daily events that make it miserable. *Beloved*, for instance, forces us to look at both the enormity of the "sixty million dead" whose bones litter the bottom of the black Atlantic and the particular specificity of a colored ribbon for a little black girl's hair attached to a bit of her skull. She compels us to see the meaning of each in the other, and the relationship of both to the present we occupy.

The subject of this book is a set of texts written prior to *Shoah* and *Beloved*, but ones that are equally involved in the same Enlightenment problematic about the meaning of the past for the present. These texts ask questions about cultural and family secrets, explore the idea of a memory repetitively haunted by a historical event, and meditate on what the past means, can mean, should mean, for a present American subject tortured by a recollection of the past in an ahistorical society. These texts — Gayl Jones's *Corregidora* (1975), David Bradley's *The Chaneysville Incident* (1981), and Octavia Butler's *Kindred* (1979) — each represent an African American person in late-twentieth-century America haunted by a family secret involving an antebellum ancestor. Each asks us to meditate on the social, psychic, and material effects that slavery has had and continues to have for individuals, families, communities, and nation-states. Together, these *palimpsest narratives*, as I am calling them, ask us to consider the profound relationship between the past and the present, between a national history of slavery and the contemporary nation and peoples it produced.

My primary argument is that the palimpsest narratives address the social problems, political issues, and cultural concerns of their moment of production by generating a narrative in which an African American subject who lives in the 1970s is forced to adopt a bitemporal perspective that shows the continuity and discontinuities from the period of slavery. After first defining the form of the palimpsest narrative and its constituent properties, I will discuss the basic economic, cultural, social, and political developments that gave the seventies its particular cast of mind. I will then examine the national discourses on family and race that largely set the terms, defined the parameters, and created the conditions for African American intellectuals to return to slavery as both the historical cause of and a meaningful analogy for the inequities and injustices of their own time.

The Form and History of the Palimpsest Narrative

The most general political statement that texts like *Beloved* and the palimpsest narratives of the 1970s make is that historical events have enduring afterlives. These texts generate different artistic and conceptual devices for making that point artistically. Morrison, for example, has one of her characters theorize what she calls "rememory," in which individual experiences of suffering continue to exist at the site where the suffering happened. "Rememory," then, becomes a mental-spatial structure where what happened in one place at one time to one person becomes experientially available at another time for another person. Morrison has the ex-slave Sethe Garner describe the idea to her freeborn daughter Denver:

> I was talking about time. It's so hard for me to believe in it. Some things go. Pass on. Some things just stay. I used to think it was my rememory. You know. Some things you forget. Other things you never do. But it's not. Places, places are still there. If a house burns down, it's gone, but the place — the picture of it — stays, and not just in my rememory, but out there, in the world. What I remember is a picture floating around out there outside my head. I mean, even if I don't think it, even if I die, the picture of what I did, or knew, or saw is still out there. Right in the place where it happened.

These "rememories" not only exist outside the agent's mind, but they are available to anyone who enters the sphere where that action occurred. There are times, Sethe says, when "you be walking down the road and you hear something or see something going on. So clear. And you think it's you thinking it up. A thought picture. But no. It's when you bump into a rememory that belongs to somebody else."[8]

A "rememory," then, is a way to understand how we can share in the prior experiences of others. One way of describing this magical anamnesis available to one not involved in the original act is to say that it is a Kantian noumenon substantiated into what Freud calls "psychical reality."[9] Another is to say that it is a form of intersubjectivity where subjects differently placed in time and situation can intimately "have" the same experience. The most important point about "rememory," though, is that Morrison forces us to see in what ways the past melts into the present (time, we recall, is something Sethe has trouble believing in). In *Beloved*, "rememory" becomes that conceptual device for understanding the sometimes direct, sometimes arbitrary relationship between what happened sometime and what is happening now.

The palimpsest narratives develop other rhetorical and narrative strategies for raising precisely the same question about a past that, like the ghost in *Beloved*, will not die. Each of the authors of a palimpsest narrative, as we will see, does this in his or her own way. Jones proposes that hearing familial narratives and singing the blues allows one to experience a genealogical past in significant ways. Bradley develops a theory similar to Morrison's "rememory" in which the spirits of past historical events continue to haunt the places where those events took place; and he has his narrator travel to local sites in order to make meaningful his narration of those events. Butler makes the same point by having her narrator be literally transported from her own time to an antebellum plantation to which she then traces her family line and the origins of her own psychic troubles. Each of the authors, then, conceives of a novel strategy by which to make the point that the past influences a present that can be modified and made better only by returning to and understanding that past, that personal and national family secret of slavery.

Palimpsest, I am suggesting, provides us with a useful concept for understanding the impetus behind what these writers are collectively doing. A *palimpsest* is defined as either a parchment on which the original writing can be erased to provide space for a second writing or a manuscript on which a later writing is written over an effaced earlier writing. The *Oxford English Dictionary* gives examples for the first use from the seventeenth century and for the second only from the nineteenth, when the term began to assume a more metaphorical set of connotations. Thomas Carlyle, for instance, used the term when he criticized the type of historiography produced by those he derided as "cause-and-effect speculators" unable to discover the deeper, more spiritual connections between the past and the present. Such historians were thereby disabled from seeing history as what Carlyle calls that "Palimpsest" or "Prophetic Manuscript" of a continuity in which every historical event is interrelated to "all other events, prior or contemporaneous."[10]

At least one of the writers of these palimpsest narratives has considered the possibilities opened up by the literal figure of the palimpsest. In a recent work-in-progress, Gayl Jones has her narrator write her story on an actual palimpsest. In this case, a seventeenth-century fugitive slave of African descent living in a New World nunnery writes her experiences over those of a sixth-century Spanish nun. The idea of having "new documents written over old ones," where sometimes the "old ones show through," makes clear at the level of the material text the symbolic nature of the documentation of the slave experience. The palimpsest shows the complexity of representation, where different historical periods are marked on the same textual space, and highlights the multiplicity of writing subjects within a given text. In this work, Jones toys with the potential that a palimpsest literally provides an artist who wishes to explore how the present is always recorded over a past text. For our purposes here, the palimpsest also provides us with a fruitful metaphor for the intricate ways that contemporary lives and life stories are inscribed on parchments through which the slave past always shows.[11]

What the authors of the palimpsest narratives do is figuratively make the same point, that the present is always written against a background where the past is erased but still legible. In addition, they take the opportunity in their narratives to explore the political underpinnings of racial identity by showing how the original markings of "race" in antebellum America continue to exert deleterious power over people of African descent in contemporary American society. The palimpsest effect here, then, is, as some postmodernists have suggested, that the subject in a politically oppressive society can be thought of as a "tablet, a parchment or stratum that is overcoded, decoded, and once again recoded" by and within the repressive and ideological apparatuses of the state.[12]

For our purposes, then, a palimpsest narrative can be defined as a first-person novel representing late-twentieth-century African American subjects who confront familial secrets attesting to the ongoing effects of slavery. Sometimes these novels are premised on a contemporary subject's dealing with the discovery of an ancestor's narrative, while in other cases these novels deal with the destructive effects of an individual's or a community's attempts to forget a slave past. In either case, they always represent a modern black subject who describes modern social relations directly conditioned or affected by an incident, event, or narrative from the time of slavery.[13]

Although I am here primarily concerned with those palimpsest narratives that emerge in the wake of the Black Power movement, those novels begun at the height of the 1960s and published between the mid- and late seventies, it is worth noting that there is a long history of African American writing that takes slavery as its "pre-text."[14] In the 1890s, the period Rayford Logan referred to as the "nadir" of African American history, a decade characterized by rampant lynching and other vigilante violence, the legalization of social segregation, and the political disenfranchisement of black citizens, authors like Frances Harper, Charles Chesnutt, and Pauline Hopkins examined their present political circumstances in light of the epoch of slavery. These writers traced in both periods the ways white Americans policed black family life, social mobility, and sexual choices, while revealing, most insistently, the biological and social connections between black and white families from slavery to the turn of the twentieth century.[15] The form emerged anew between the 1930s and 1950s, with Zora Neale Hurston and Ralph Ellison showing us the ways a twentieth-century black subject deals with a slave ancestor's life story, while Richard Wright and Ann Petry described the enduring effects of slavery in creating the social inequities fracturing given communities. In the late sixties, Paule Marshall gave the form renewed vigor in her remarkable book *The Chosen Place, the Timeless People* (1969), which represented the ways that the political activity of a black community was both modeled on and inspired by a historical act of slave resistance.[16]

The form flourished and found its most complete expression in the seventies, in the three palimpsest narratives that constitute the subject of this study. Each of these novels represents the effects of a slave past on a personal present by showing how ancestors' lives act as a palimpsest on the lives of their contemporary progeny. *Corregidora* is about a familial history of oppression which causes the narrator as much pain as it provides her psychic resources in her two marriages; *The Chaneysville Incident* is about a son's search for the meaning of his father's apparent suicide and his discovery of family connections that could potentially destroy or promote his sense of connection with his white fiancée; *Kindred* is about an orphan's painful struggle to reconstruct kinship with historical family members and to construct new kinship bonds with her white husband. Each of the palimpsest narratives is concerned with representing families whose sons and daughters struggle to generate historical narratives that would produce for them new albeit refracted relations.

These novels raise several topics germane to the understanding of slavery and its representation, questioning the ways that voices of slaves can be commodified, asking how writing can show the tensions between the constraining and freeing of subjectivity, and demonstrating the destructive nature of personal relationships cast into the terms of property relations. What is particularly striking about the palimpsest narratives as a whole is that they contemplate the nature of memory in the creation and transmission of a family secret, meditate on the significance, dangers, and necessities of employing the idea of "family" itself in political contexts, and, especially, signal the importance of "race" as the most salient of those past social structures daily reproduced in contemporary life. In practice, the palimpsest narratives are structured around a partially hidden family secret that allows the authors to explore the role of generational memory in transmitting and repressing that secret and the function of the nation-state in creating and recreating the ideologies of family and race that promoted the conditions for the formation of that secret. What the narratives insistently suggest, I argue, is that the family secret of an individual family is symptomatic of the family secret of the nation — slavery itself. They argue that point, as did the novelists of the 1890s, by showing that present political circumstances are both echoes and results of a slave past premised on structures of American thinking most evident still in the reproduction of particularly deleterious discourses about family and about race.

The Discourse of the Family in the 1970s

The palimpsest narratives flourished in the seventies, a decade characterized as both culturally stagnant — one critic noted the perfect symbol for the decade was "the Pet Rock, which just sat there doing nothing" — and deeply significant as the decade witnessing the completion of postindustrialism and ushering in the rise of postmodernism. Prompted by earlier demographic shifts and technological developments, faced with a declining steel and automobile industry in a globally more competitive market, and confronted with the first peacetime oil shortage in its history, the country completed a shift from a manufacturing to a service economy, with the attendant social dislocations. Union membership sharply declined, as did jobs in the manufacturing industries. Meanwhile, "stagflation" and the "fiscal crisis of the state" combined to erode consumer confidence and expose the flaws in Keynesian economic policies (although it was Nixon's departure from Keynesian liberal practices following his 1972 reelection that largely spurred the economic crisis of 1973). In addition to the economic failures, the nation went through a period of traumatic political crises as the lies about Vietnam, Cambodia, Kent State, Jackson State, and Watergate produced a skeptical and apathetic citizenry with little faith in its elected leaders and only slightly more in the system they represented. The country's military fiascoes and diplomatic embarrassments in Southeast Asia, Nicaragua and Iran diminished Americans' sense of the nation's role in the international community.[17]

The social dislocations produced by these economic and political conditions were most poignantly felt along racial lines. Although the 1970s' "literature about postindustrial America" tended to focus on the "changes wrought in the more comfortable quarters of white America," black and white intellectuals continued to assess the precise ways that the economic stagnation and social meanness of the seventies combined to affect African American labor and life. The ratio of black to white income declined from a postwar high of 62 percent in 1972 to 59.7 percent by 1974 and 57.1 percent by 1978. As Michael Harrington noted, stagflation had "racist consequences" because of the "structural racism of the economy."[18] Neoconservative intellectual attacks and judicial decisions on affirmative action weakened and left virtually powerless one of the few government efforts to correct the structural racism of the American labor market. Reactionary popular uprisings and court mandates against busing threatened to undo the meager gains in school desegregation. Redlining and other forms of real estate chicanery left the country as residentially segregated as if protective covenants had not been made illegal. All these factors, amidst the general climate of right-wing backlash to black political gains in the sixties, left African Americans in a state of tightly contracted and strictly policed labor pools, educational opportunities, and residential options.

What the nation seemed to feel most of all, political analysts and cultural workers agreed, was a general sense of malaise, a "revulsion against politics" that produced social "passivity and quietism." What Christopher Lasch brilliantly called a "culture of narcissism" was marked by a "self-absorption and political retreat," a turn to "purely personal preoccupations," and the triumph of a "survivalist mentality." Whether it was viewed as a specifically antithetical response to the turbulence of the sixties or a more general result of "long-term shifts in the structure of cultural authority," the seventies was a decade best characterized as the second "Gilded Age," a period of widespread political disengagement and solipsistic patterns of consumption. This state of affairs had particularly significant implications for American family life, as both Lasch and Stephanie Coontz noted. In a society and era of rampant self-absorption and diminished social conscientiousness, human relationships of all kinds, especially those of kinship and domesticity, tend to fail. When identity is viewed as a personal accomplishment and the result of consumer inventiveness rather than meaningful and committed social and communal bonds, we find an increasing delay in marriage and an inclining divorce rate (from 2.2 per thousand in 1960 to 5.2 in 1980). In the early 1970s, economist George Gilder diagnosed this erosion in family patterns as a pathological development threatening the stability of Western civilization. The unmarried man, he wrote, "is disposed to criminality, drugs, and violence, . . . irresponsible about his debts, alcoholic, accident prone, and venereally diseased." "Unless he can marry," Gilder concluded, "he is often destined to a Hobbesian life — solitary, poor, nasty, brutish, and short."[19]

This sentiment, published almost a decade after Daniel Patrick Moynihan issued his infamous report on African American lower-class family life, echoed and supplemented what Moynihan had implied, which, essentially, was that men, particularly black men, required states of patriarchal authority to be effective citizens.[20] In places where women ruled (as in Moynihan's matriarchal black family) or men roamed (as in Gilder's Hobbesian world of bachelors), the society was destined to break down. Both Moynihan and Gilder advocate the need for particular institutions, sites of dominance as it were, to rein in the potential pathology of undomesticated men. Where Gilder urges marriage as a way of preventing crime, drug use, and violence, Moynihan had suggested the military as a place where black men might find the strength to govern their women. What is striking, but perhaps not so very striking, is that Gilder's prescriptions about the perils of American bachelorhood so closely echo Moynihan's discussion of black family life while seeming not to be about any specific racial group. The reason it is not so particularly striking, of course, is that the seventies also witnessed the development of a coded system of political talk where "racial" topics could be signified in an apparently race-neutral but truly race-determined language. The famous memo Moynihan sent to Nixon — "the time may have come when the issue of race could benefit from a period of 'benign neglect'" — was a signal that the time had equally come when the "language of race" had developed to the point where social dislocations were so coded as to be "understood *racially*."[21]

The discourse of the "family," then, assumed a form in which the intended racial referent was hidden in the coded transracial language of social science and public policy. In the seventies, Moynihan's critique of black family life was carried on through manifestoes and journalistic essays that appeared to be race-neutral but read as racialist discourse. Robin Kelley has in fact traced to the kind of discourse associated with Moynihan the whole gamut of social deceits that traffick as a "living, vibrant racism" under the guise of social science writing and public policy decisions concerning the "culture wars" that began in the conservative backlash of the seventies. And the culmination of that discourse, as Wahneema Lubiano has carefully shown, involved the state's co-opting of black nationalist ideology. The "black nationalist family project that projects strong ideas of responsible black male fathering and subordinate black female mothering," which Lubiano traces to Moynihan and aligns with "an intensification of the state's policing of certain segments of the country," ironically leads back to the very institution Moynihan had argued was responsible for the pathologies of black family life — slavery. Like the other forms of policing the black population (control of labor, residence, and educational mobility), the combination of "aesthetized disciplining within the black nationalist family narrative" and the state's apparatus for manipulation and regulation lead to what Lubiano calls an "evolving control over black Americans that rivals slavery and segregation for its efficacy."[22] Two conclusions are to be drawn here. The first is that in the seventies race was being "coded" into market practices and political discourses. As the overt racism of the 1950s gave way to the covert racism of the 1970s, there were new ways of talking about and reproducing racist oppression in seemingly race-neutral ways. The second is that the metaphor and idea of slavery, the original form of policing African American life, proved apt for describing the resurgent forms of structural racism that survived and defied the civil rights acts of the mid-sixties.

But the seventies also saw a massive response to the Moynihan Report and the politics it represented —first in the form of a challenge to the historiography of slavery on which the report drew, and then in the production of familial narratives attesting to the strength of the black families Moynihan had maligned. Histories of slavery began for the first time to draw on the slaves' own testimonies and accordingly reported in more detail the precise nature of black family life in the peculiar institution. In 1972, George Rawick's *From Sundown to Sunup* and John Blassingame's *The Slave Community* set new standards for the attention they paid to the social life of the slaves themselves. In 1974, Eugene Genovese's *Roll, Jordan, Roll* took seriously its subtitle, "The World the Slaves Made," and explored the familial bonds slaves created to give meaning to their world. In 1976, Herbert Gutmann produced the massive and magisterial work *The Black Family from Slavery to Freedom*, begun in the mid-sixties as a direct response to Moynihan and completed in the mid-seventies as a more nuanced and balanced study of generations of black family life in the transition from rural indenture to urban migration. The general reformation of the professional study of slavery in the 1970s brought not only new attention to the underused resources of slave interviews and narratives, new consideration of the multiple forms of slave resistance, and new delineations of the richness and importance of slave cultural practices, but also a novel respect for the vitality of the slave family.[23]

Easily the most significant seventies intervention into the discourse on the African American family was Alex Haley's *Roots*, which captured the imagination of the nation as a book, selling one million copies in its first six months, and, especially, as the most-watched television event in the history of the miniseries (with between 85 and 135 million Americans watching one or more of the eight episodes aired in January 1977).[24] *Roots* was part of and helped promote even further a surge of interest in genealogy in the 1970s. The Afro-American Historical and Genealogical Society was founded in New York in the 1970s, with branches in Chicago, Washington, and Philadelphia. Jeane Westin's *Finding Your Roots*, F. Wilbur Helmbold's *Tracing Your*

Ancestry, Dan Rottenberg's *Finding Our Families*, and Charles Block-son and Ron Fry's *Black Genealogy* were a few of the popular manuals to appear in 1976 and 1977. The National Archives, which houses census manuscripts necessary for genealogical research, reported that after the airing of *Roots* the number of letters they received tripled, and applications to use the research facility rose by 40 percent. The cover story of *Newsweek*'s Independence Day issue in 1977 was "Everybody's Search for Roots." A New York department store sponsored a May 1977 "roots week" with lessons in genealogy and ethnic heritage for its shoppers. *Roots*, then, clearly provided a crucial point of convergence for what one contemporary called the seventies' "fascination with family and the ethnic group." The book was, as one reviewer put it, "at bottom a story about the family," but it was also about the family as a historical institution clearly part of a larger ethnic identity. It was, as many have since punned, a novel about roots and routes, a story about beginnings and an ethnic "coming-to-America" success narrative. It gave African Americans what Gerald Early called "a mythic origin in an Edenic Africa" as well as an "immigrant history of overcoming adversity through the story of a great and enduring family."[25]

Haley's *Roots* and the genealogical and ethnic identity movements it inspired and drew on in many ways exemplify the palimpsest imperative. Haley demonstrated the relationship of the past to the present by showing us a saga of transnational deracination, labor exploitation, and familial survival over the course of generations. One way to understand the ways the past formed the present is to trace the contours of a particular familial line. This strategy raised three issues particularly salient for the authors who wrote palimpsest narratives before and after the publication of *Roots*. The first concerned the records capable of providing information about a familial past and the value one could give to oral tales about family ancestors. The second concerned the difficulty of confronting the fact that these tales did not circulate freely within families because they were charged with the peculiar form of shame attached to having slave ancestry. The third concerned the possible or proper ways of dealing with the particular form this shame sometimes took — the family secret. I would argue that one of the major reasons *Roots* is now recognized as a "historically symptomatic text" of "the American 1970s" is that it raises precisely those questions that defined the discourse on the African American family: finding the historical sources to tell the story of the family from slavery to freedom, and responding to the shame and secrecy of that part of the American past.[26] These are the issues that the palimpsest narratives equally confront: family tales, family shame, family secrets.

In an essay in *The Black Seventies*, one contributor notes that black children of her generation received a kind of double education. While African Americans were "reading the lies in the history books at school we were learning our true history at home from our parents," implying that part of what she sought in a "foundation for a new educational system" could and should include the versions of history told within African American families. But in our culture, American families do not appear especially well suited to act as agents of truth telling about the past. Family tales are oral productions in a society where orality is a diminished skill for recollecting the past, and many families are invested in generating narratives of their origin purified of the stains of criminal or base behavior. African American families provide an especially significant case study for this problematic. For one thing, the history of black family life in America reveals a quite different dynamic about the place of and respect accorded orality. Since slave families were persistently denied the skills of literacy, and since the media apparatus provided few venues for publication of black family histories after the end of slavery, black families were forced systematically to rely on oral forms of transmission in a way families of European ancestry were not. As African American intellectuals have long pointed out, there is a significant tradition of folklore and historical information passed on by "great-grandparents and grandparents"—what Ralph Ellison called "our familial past"— that provide supplementary and often subversive versions of the past. "This record exists in oral form," noted Ellison, "and it constitutes the internal history of values by which my people lived even as they were being forced to accommodate themselves to those forces and arrangements of society that were sanctioned by official history."[27]

Because those hegemonic social arrangements also regulated the thought and intellectual practices of all people in the nation, even those African American intellectuals who deeply believed in the value of oral testimony had to overcome internalized self-doubts about forms of historical information not sanctioned by "official history" or credited by professional historians. Those African American writers who produced narratives about slavery have especially felt the need to turn to the "old documents" of official history in order to "substanti-ate" and "to authenticate" the stories they acquired from their families. Even Margaret Walker, who asserted the truth value of familial his-tory in her essay in *The Black Seventies*, felt compelled to use "literary documents to undergird the oral tradition" she had received "from [her] grandmother's lips." By the time he was writing in the late six-ties, Ernest Gaines was enough the beneficiary of the new social his-tory that sought to report the past "from the bottom up" so as to be able to value both the "truth" of "what Miss Jane [Pittman] and folks like her have to say" and draw on "the other sources, the newspapers, magazines, the books in the libraries." Pauli Murray talks about how she took her familial oral tales, compared them to the "historical record," and found that she was "able to confirm enough of the fam-ily stories to trust the credibility of our oral traditions." She describes her elation when she finds "stories I had heard at home confirmed by documents." And in the most famous of these anecdotes of discover-ing the truth of an oral-familial tale, Alex Haley describes how he underwent a kind of conversion experience while doing the research for *Roots* and discovered that the stories he had heard on the porch of his grandmother's house in Henning, Tennessee, could be confirmed through both written records and through the oral performance of Kebba Kanga Fofana, the griot of the Kinte clan. In the end, Haley proclaimed: "I trusted oral history now better than I trusted the printed page." [28]

Another reason oral histories have been dubious sources of infor-mation is that American families generally desire to invent a glorious rather than report a notorious past. In the case of African American families, that desire has been spurred by a prevalent feeling of "shame" attached to slave ancestry. A "slave heritage," Derrick Bell notes, is a most forceful "symbol of shame," one that black families historically attempt to hide, ignore, mute, or deny. Alice Walker noted in a BBC documentary that her family spoke in "whispers" about certain parts of their history. Margaret Walker's father was less subtle; when he found his mother-in-law telling young Margaret "stories of slave life in Georgia," he would cast aspersions on her "harrowing" fables and try to counter the effect they had on his daughter by calling them "tall tales." Dorothy Spruill Redford recalls that "[s]lavery was never men-tioned around our house," and the "first time [she] heard the word, [she] thought some shame was attached to you if you even uttered it."[29] Jan Willis reports that her family never talked about slavery, and would employ ambiguous language when talking about that period of their family's past, using such terms as "deeded" to refer to the selling of ancestors from one plantation to another. Doing research for her family history project, she found herself first grieved and then "ashamed" to discover a receipt showing the sale of her kin. Even though it was whispered, muted, disclaimed, imaginatively reworked, and circumscribed in neutral terms, an ancestral slave past nonetheless caused these families and these individuals a poignant sense of shame.[30]

Eventually, each of these individuals and families worked through their shame and came to the same conclusion as the narrator of Ralph Ellison's *Invisible Man*: "I am not ashamed of my grandparents for having been slaves," he declares at the end of twenty years of searching for his identity. "I am only ashamed of myself for having at one time been ashamed." For instance, after much maturing, living through the aftermath of *Brown*, the ordeal of Montgomery, the struggles in Selma, the advent of Black Power, and, finally and most important, the televising of *Roots*, Dorothy Spruill Redford found herself no longer ashamed of the idea of a slave ancestry. In 1977, she went to her mother and asked the questions she had kept to herself as a child because she had always "assumed that [her] parents' silence stemmed from some secret sorrow — all somehow linked to slavery and the South." Asking the questions twenty years after the end of her childhood, Redford found her mother eager and proud to respond to questions that would initiate her daughter's decade-long search for a "lost heritage." Implicitly, as Redford notes, shame often leads to secrecy; and family shame produces family secrets.[31]

When Carole Ione began to research her family history in 1973, she found shame and fear underneath the "pride of family that kept secrets and told lies." As she dug into a past her mother and grandmother refused to talk about, she ended up discovering "another family secret, so unpleasant that [she] wanted to forget it." But she continued digging deeper in order to "heal the awful thing that happened to us all." Never are these family secrets more powerful and more potentially disruptive than when they are about the greatest source of family shame — slavery. Pauli Murray's great-grandfather Thomas Fitzgerald had long told his family that he was born a free person of color in Delaware. When Murray set out to discover more about her ancestor, she accidently stumbled across a manumission paper signed by Thomas Fitzgerald's former owner, George Lodge, on August 8, 1832, when Fitzgerald was twenty-four years old. Because her family had "gloated privately" that there was "no hint of slavery" in the "Fitzgerald branch" of the family tree, Murray's discovery left her feeling as if one hundred years of "family tradition cultivated so carefully through four generations of Fitzgeralds" had "crashed down" on her head. Slavery, she realized, had "done such violence to the human spirit that the very memory of it was intolerable long after people had outlived it." Even in her own adolescence and adulthood, Murray continues, "many were trying to grow without roots at all, plucking their sustenance from the air about them" rather than accept a slave past. These are the family secrets that a nation in denial about slavery produces.[32] I will discuss in the next section how that national discourse operates in the construction of race as well as the production of family secrets.

First, though, we need to discern a method for reading and determining the multiple significances of family secrets since each of the palimpsest narratives has at its heart the problematic of contemporary subjects who need to discern a sometimes unknowable, always hidden, past in order to live a fuller and healthier present. We need, as Frederic Jameson says of another body of fiction, a "different type of narrative theory" that will allow us "to identify the psychic center of gravity of a narration whose surface categories and representational tactics are not demonstrably or symptomatically distorted by it," especially when that fiction has in it "traces and symptoms" that refer to a "fundamental family situation which is at one and the same time a fantasy master narrative."[33] In other words, we need a theory to read those texts that are not representing a psychotic or schizophrenic subject but rather showing the hidden socialized illness in particular aspects of family life that are themselves symptomatic of a national disorder caused by slavery. Because the palimpsest narratives demonstrate the ways that family secrets are products of a history of enslavement, they constitute precisely the kinds of texts and body of fiction that would be best served by an elegant theory enabling us to understand the narrative structure and representational strategies of family secrets.

Drawing on the psychoanalytic theories of Nicolas Abraham and Maria Torok, Esther Rashkin has formulated just such a theory and produced a set of protocol for just such a reading method. In her recent study *Family Secrets and the Psychoanalysis of Narrative*, she describes a "reading process" which is a "kind of 'archaeology' in which buried fragments of infinitely regressive and symptomatic family histories are disinterred and used to reconstruct unspeakable sagas concealed in the past." The purpose of such a reading process, she suggests, is to "demonstrate how and why it is possible to treat the 'lives' of certain fictional characters as narratives — composed of symbols — of the traumas they have surmounted." These characters reveal the traumas they have suffered, but of which they cannot speak, by producing symptomatic acts of "secret" discourse. According to Abraham and Torok, whose work provides Rashkin with her theoretical model, this kind of discourse consists of "cryptonyms," that is, words that "hide within themselves."[34]

There are two especially notable features about what Abraham and Torok call their "cryptonomy" that suggest the affinity of this theory for reading the palimpsest narratives. First, they argue that the subject who develops a trauma disabling him or her from speaking about the family secret at the heart of the trauma is usually dealing with a dead family member. In his foreword to Abraham and Torok's study of the Wolf Man, the subject of Freud's most famous case, Jacques Derrida notes that a "crypt" means both 1) the "cipher" or "symbolic or semiotic operation that consists of manipulating a secret code" and 2) the "topographical arrangement made to keep (conserve-hidden) the *living dead*." As Abraham and Torok show in their discussion of the phenomenon of "incorporation," the Wolf Man, whose sister had allegedly seduced him when he was three and a half years old and she five, and who had thereafter committed suicide when she was about twenty, "had been the bearer of a shared secret." After "his sister's death, he became the bearer of a crypt." As the bearer of such a crypt, the Wolf Man is able to reveal his trauma only cryptically. The reason he is unable to resort to explicit or direct discourse is that his sister and her discourse are effectively lodged within him as a psychic blockage. In a more general sense, as they write elsewhere of this psychic phenomenon as a family situation, the "buried speech of the parent becomes (a) dead (gap), without a burial place, in the child."[35]

Second, the phenomenon of what they call "cryptophoria" is not only familial, but it is also transgenerational. "Its effect," they write in "A Poetics of Psychoanalysis," can "persist through several generations and determine the fate of an entire family line." In their analysis of the Wolf Man, for instance, Abraham and Torok note that for the analysis to succeed, it would have "to extend to the paternal grandparents and even to the great-grandparents, so that the Wolf Man could be situated within the libidinal lineage from which he was descended." In the more general theoretical formulation of Nicholas Rand, the "phantom," which is a "delusion of the living provoked by the tormenting unconscious suspicion that something had been left unsaid during the life of the deceased," represents "the interpersonal and transgenerational consequences of silence."[36] Abraham and Torok's cryptonomy theorizes a way of reading that allows us to determine how departed spirits or phantoms from generations long dead occupy present subjects in a manner that "silences" those subjects and forces them to reveal their trauma cryptically.

Something like a cryptonomy provides a useful way to approach the palimpsest narratives, since these are texts where the family secret is a "generative force," and the subjects of the novels are "psychic products of . . . infinitely regressive family histories" who recapitulate in their individual lives their "ancestors' sagas, all the while expanding those sagas with the stuff" of their own lives.[37] In *Corregidora*, the narrator is inhibited from speaking freely because she is haunted by a family secret that deals with issues of desire and the propriety of desiring which her family history has taught her to devalue; in *The Chaneysville Incident*, the narrator is forced to confront the specter of death as a personal, familial, and cultural loss as he attempts to resolve a set of family secrets connecting black and white families in the American past; and in *Kindred*, the narrator literally suffers the effects of a psychic transgenerational phantom when she finds herself untangling a family secret about the racial makeup of her own family line. We see, then, how something like a cryptonomy would serve us in discerning the deeper meaning of the family secrets embedded in each of the palimpsest narratives.[38]

The important thing about family secrets in general is that they are transgenerational, that they originate in previous ancestral traumas but haunt those in the present who make up the remembering generations. Carole Ione, for example, is grieved by the combination of sorrow and secrecy in her mother's life. "As the only daughter of an only daughter of an only daughter, I have all my life felt the pure lineage of my mother's childhood sorrow as my own. I was never able to separate it from myself and could do nothing to assuage it." Yet she recognizes that her mother's sorrow is itself an inheritance and her mother the pained "recipient of an accumulation of sorrows, the secret shadowy heritage of the women who came before her." There is a remarkable moment when Ione sits in a room in Saratoga and intuits the presence of the "spirits of all the women in [her] family past and present." In that moment, she says, "I felt only their loss there." That "loss," what Ione describes as shame, a family secret masquerading as family pride, is the result of two wholly interrelated institutions in American life: slavery and race. In the case of Ione, we see this in her struggle to deal with a family secret — that her family had a history of slaveholding — while she simultaneously attempts to understand the function of race in her own life, what she describes as her "longing to assuage the painful and confusing aspects of blackness." [39] For, finally, the important thing about family secrets in African American life is that they are the result of one historical American institution, slavery, and the ongoing social institution it created, race. It is to that discourse of race that we now turn our attention.

The Discourse of Race in the 1970s

The most important intellectual development for the discourse of race in the seventies was the emergence of "ethnicity," which, as a word, was first defined in the *Oxford English Dictionary* supplement in 1972, and, as a concept, assumed unprecedented influence in American cultural studies. At the beginning of the decade "ethnicity" was "the neglected dimension in American history." By the middle of the decade, intellectuals were complaining about the proliferation of studies of ethnicity and alerting those scholars producing them to what one 1977 article called "the limits of ethnicity." "Ethnicity," for some, was a social identity that threatened identifications based on "class," while for others it endangered a shared sense of American citizenship. The seventies ultimately turned out to be what Michael Novak called "the decade of the ethnics." For the advocates of ethnicity, the concept was crucial to understanding new forms of human identity, given what Nathan Glazer described as the "trends of modernisation." In an essay tellingly entitled "Univeralisation of Ethnicity," Glazer argues that the formation of ethnic identity (what he also calls "ethnicisation") was a response to the disruptive features of the modern world: "urbanisation, new occupations, mass education transmitting general and abstract information, mass media presenting a general and universal culture." In the face of these developments, the individual in a given mass society seeks out replacements for lost "traditional and primor-dial identities." For the individual in America, that means finding "some kind of identity — smaller than the State, larger than the fam-ily, something akin to 'familistic allegiance.'"[40] Ethnic identity proved to be just that.

Critics on the left generally focused on the fact that ethnicity was a symbolic system in which one could choose to pledge "allegiance." It was, in other words, not an integral identity growing out of the mate-rial conditions of concrete experience and therefore not a source of so-cial change. Some saw and lamented the connection between the "rise of ethnic identification" and the "reduction of class sentiment," while others felt that the new ethnicity was a "conservative" and indeed "re-actionary" movement precisely because it promoted "ethnicity" as a "semantic substitute" for "class." Those who defended the idea of eth-nicity against the charge of its being necessarily conservative argued that ethnic groups were in fact "new social forms," not just groups of people who shared religious, linguistic, or cultural habits. They maintained that ethnic groups recreated their distinctiveness because these groups were in fact "interest groupings whose members share some common economic and political interests and who, therefore, stand together in the continuous competition for power with other groups."[41] Like class, then, ethnicity could be a motor to mobilize groups of people in political activism and social change.

The other major criticism of ethnicity came from those who were troubled by the idea that ethnic identity was comparable to or able to subsume racial identity. Ethnicity scholars argued that "'race' and 'ethnicity' form part of a single family of social identities," and, fur-ther, that ethnicity was the larger concept able to include race within it. The most vigorous early critic of this belief was Pierre van den Berghe, who argued, with some qualifications, that an ethnic group could be "socially defined on the basis of cultural criteria," whereas race could be defined on the "basis of physical criteria." Since then, few have defended the idea of "race" as a meaningful sociological cat-egory, many finding deeply flawed the very idea of "physical" criteria, and most uneasily choosing to use "ethnicity" in the broadest possible sense or creating neologisms like "ethnoraces" to accommodate what-ever difficulties they had with the loss of "race" as a category. Some scholars of African descent have seen this idea of ethnicity as liberat-ing. Stuart Hall, for instance, charged that the task for cultural studies was to reclaim a "new conception of ethnicity" in order to challenge and expose the older idea of race. Since "ethnicity acknowledges the place of history, language and culture in the construction of subjectivity and identity," it serves as a perfect vehicle for demonstrating that the "black subject and the black experience are not stabilized by Nature or by some other essential guarantee."[42] Ethnicity, then, like other developments in the general liberal environmentalism of postwar intellectual life, became part of the machinery used to dismantle essentialist thinking and the concept of race on which it fixated.

In the United States, though, this was less easily done, primarily because of the historical fact of slavery. When those scholars who choose to employ "ethnicity" as a broadly conceived term covering all social groups living in America come to the case of African Americans, they usually add a caveat of the following sort: "This choice does not represent an attempt to gloss over the special legacy of slavery and racism in America. Slavery has posed a special problem to interpretations of America and poses special problem to our enterprise." In the end, however, that enterprise tends to work its way around rather than through the problem. Slavery becomes what some have cleverly called "ethnicity theory's version of black exceptionalism," that point where the theory shows its seams most clearly.[43] What often happens is that ethnicity scholars tend to do three things: 1) they ignore the historical role of slavery and segregation in the distribution of wealth and social capital in this country and assume that African American economic success ought to proceed along the same paths as those followed by other groups who immigrated to America; 2) they deny the various ethnicities within the population of people of African descent in the United States, implying that there are several white ethnicities but only one black one; and 3) they fundamentally avoid acknowledging the ways that slavery was the institution that played the most formative role in creating not only the basic divide in this country (black/white) but also in historically providing a primary definition for each of these social identities.

This last point is especially important, since many ethnicity scholars tend to downplay the way that race in the case of African Americans is not an "achieved" but an "ascribed" identity; and even more scholars discount the depth to which the idea of slavery remains most resonant in the ascription of African American identity; and almost all fail to acknowledge the foundational role slavery played in creating and giving meaning to white identity. Let me draw on a series of political episodes that will demonstrate these points. Trying to explain why a white supremacist like David Duke would support the nomination of Clarence Thomas to the Supreme Court, Manning Marable found it useful to remark on the difference between "race" and "ethnicity." Thomas, he argued, was "racially black," by dint of both "governmental definition and societal recognition," that is, he "belongs to a specific racial group characterized in part by physical appearance and political condition." "Ethnically," however, Thomas ceased to be African American because he feels "no active ideological or cultural obligations to the dispossessed, the hungry and homeless who share the ethnic rituals, customs, and traditions of blackness." Thomas's ethnic identification is a matter of choice, while his "racial identity is essentially passive, a reality of being within a social formation stratified by the oppressive concept of race."[44] No matter how hard he struggles against his racial identity, Thomas cannot break free of it because both the official institutions that define social divisions in this nation and the unofficial understanding of "race" in this society remain bound to many of the structures of thought inherited from, or, more accurate, produced through slavery.

Consider, for example, another commentary on the case of Clarence Thomas. At a Skidmore College conference entitled "Race and Racism," Jim Sleeper maintained that the Thomas-Hill hearings meant that "the culture of slavery is dead, because no longer do whites bring to such an event the expectation that race will be the dominant motif. It evaporated before thirty million people." Sleeper's argument at Skidmore is a harbinger of what he would later articulate as his hope for an end to "liberal racism," where liberals would let the idea of race fade into oblivion and begin the work of creating a fundamentally fair nation where race was no longer "the organizing principle of our polity and civic culture." But Sleeper's Skidmore comments suggest precisely the reason race remains the most salient organizing principle in that polity and civic culture. For one thing, "race" in Sleeper's formulation is only what inheres to nonwhite people. What he means when he says "race" is not the dominant motif in the Thomas-Hill hearings is that the two players in that drama didn't act "racial," which means "black," by which is implied that their behavior didn't support any of the still too-prevalent and too-powerful stereotypes about African American mores and modes of conduct that, as historians

Winthrop Jordan and George Frederickson so convincingly showed, developed in the course of American slavery. Moreover, "race" is precisely what white people recreate when they gaze on and judge black people. It is highly telling that Sleeper argues that the "culture of slavery is dead" only when and because "whites" don't bring their expectations about race when they attend a black legal battle royale. Race is what black people have; the power to eliminate race by their thinking is what white people possess. That dialectic is in many ways precisely the same one that defined the "culture of slavery."[45]

There are dangers to prematurely jettisoning "race" as a category of social discourse when the historical effects of that category remain potent. And while "ethnicity" is surely a more useful term to designate different forms of generationally reproduced group life, "race" is not likely to disappear until more of the material inequities on which it is based dissolve. One of the lessons of the 1970s was not only that "ethnicity" was a term threatening to subsume "race," but that ethnics (almost always meaning whites of European descent) found in their rediscovered religious, cultural, and linguistic heritages the sources for a new group identity around which they organized their political interests and through which they entered into "competition for power with other groups." The decade that began with ethnicity as the "neglected dimension" in American history ended with ethnicity as an organizing principle in the struggle for limited resources in the polity. The 1979 conference "Civil Rights Issues of Euro-Ethnic Americans," hosted by the Civil Rights Commission, for example, gave European American "ethnics" an opportunity to voice their criticisms of "race-based" affirmative action programs. Until the "culture of slavery" is truly dead — and the rumors of its demise are greatly exaggerated — it seems both historically conscious and politically conscientious not to forget the impact slavery had on the formation of American populations and the economic distributions among them. It seems not only wise but moral to remember that African Americans, as Barbara Fields noted at the Skidmore conference, were regularly identified as "people who [were] slaves" and now as "people who are descended from slaves." "There's no way you can separate those two identities," she concludes.[46]

The final point I wish to make here about ethnicity studies concerns the status of "whiteness." Jim Sleeper's belief that the culture of slavery dies when whites give up a certain intellectual predisposition seems to me symptomatic of political discourses about race in general, that is, the failure to comprehend the fact that the culture of slavery gave birth to whiteness and to appreciate the deep meaning of that fact. Winthrop Jordan noted in his magisterial study of the emergence and development of racial thinking in America that European settlers of the first mainland colonies called themselves "Christians" when they landed at Jamestown in 1607, used the terms "English" and "free" to talk about themselves at midcentury, and began to employ the term "white" around 1680. They were Christians when they first met the non-Christian Native Americans, became free nationals when they started codifying in law the permanent and inheritable indenture of people of non-European descent, and became white when slaves became black. Understanding the role slavery played in the creation of whiteness helps ultimately to show us two things: first, that slavery was an institution that "calibrated values in other core institutions" (like patriarchy, religion, and white skin privilege), and, second, that whiteness, like any other social identity, is not a genetic identity but a historical one that emerged in certain social conditions. Recognizing the ways whiteness historically came into being does not mean we then understand the continuing role it plays in contemporary struggles, for it is certainly true, as Barbara Fields notes, that if "race lives on today, it does not live on because we have inherited it from our forebears of the seventeenth century or the eighteenth or nineteenth, but because we continue to recreate it today." On the other hand, it is certainly the case that the ways we recreate race are deeply, almost indelibly, affected by the history of its original creation; and that is why the dialectic of slavery continues to have so forceful a meaning for us now.[47]

That is exactly one of the key points raised by the palimpsest narratives — namely, that, in more general terms, the past influences the present, and, in more specific terms, the institutions that first created the social meaning of blackness and whiteness continue to exert influence on the contemporary significance of those categories. Indeed, I think it even fair to say that the palimpsest narratives are part of a larger program of inquiry into the meaning of whiteness that also effloresced in the seventies, and, by the 1990s, would develop into the field of "whiteness studies." It is true that there is a notable difference between some of the sociological work of the 1970s on white attitudes — like *Whitetown, USA* (1970), *Portraits of White Racism* (1977), and *White Awareness* (1978)—and the studies of whiteness in the 1990s as a socially located political position with a history in the making of American laboring classes (*The Wages of Whiteness* and *Love and Theft*) and a crucial dimension in the construction of personal identity (*White Women, Race Matters* and *Beyond the Pale*). It is also important, though, to see in what ways the work of the nineties is a continuation of that of the seventies.[48] For one thing, the rise in ethnic consciousness in the seventies was certainly a necessary prelude to the critical exploration of the whiteness that previously united these now-ethnic groups. In addition, when the civil rights movement with its trajectory of seeking parity and equality gave way to the Black Power movement with its emphasis on celebrating black racial identity, white activists in the movement were forced to consider anew their own racial identity and examine in what ways they had an investment in both the race they had previously not claimed and unconsciously shared the racism they had located only regionally (in the South) and incarnated only in political reactionaries (George Wallace, "Bull" Connor). Finally, it is important to note that the interrogation of whiteness is a long-term intellectual project in which African American writers have played the most significant role, from the study of white habits of mastery in the slave narratives to the exposition of whiteness that marked so many of James Baldwin's essays from the mid-sixties on.

The palimpsest narratives are part of that intellectual enterprise, and their analysis of the construction of whiteness is an important contribution to the most advanced version of 1970s "whiteness studies." There are two ways that the palimpsest narratives engage in their inquiry into whiteness. First, they implicitly ask questions about the meaning of whiteness as a social category by presenting us with racially mixed narrators. In *Corregidora*, we are told the story of the effects of the master's forced raping of Corregidora women from Ursa's great-grandmother, the "darkest woman in the house, the coffee bean woman," until four generations later, when Ursa feels herself "[s]tained with another's past, . . . [t]heir past in my blood." In *The Chaneysville Incident*, the narrator seeks knowledge of his father who sought knowledge of the racially mixed fugitive slave, light enough to pass, and "whose blood, he believed flowed in his veins," raising implicitly the question of "blood" as a metaphor for the impossible complexity of race in America. And *Kindred*, as I noted earlier, is premised on Dana's discovery of her family secret that her great-grandfather is white. Second, each of the palimpsest narratives also examines the precise process through which whiteness was invested with certain social powers in the course of slavery. In fact, part of what these novels do is show how whiteness itself is a palimpsest, the parchment that pretends to be original, the identity that passes as natural, and the "power that secures its dominance by not seeming to be anything in particular."[49] By returning to slavery in order to make these two points — that "racial" identity is a matter of denying the widespread traffick in white blood, that "white" itself is a category historically formed and socially recreated — the palimpsest narratives expose the family secret of America, that is, that race is the product of the system of indenture and is based on hiding biological kinships, on literally making secret the family connections that give the lie to the system of race itself.

Family and Race in the Two Gilded Ages

Near the end of his 1972 book *No Name in the Street*, James Baldwin writes: "It has been vivid to me for many years that what we call a race problem here is not a race problem at all: to keep calling it that is a way of avoiding the problem." The problem, he continued, is instead "rooted in the question of how one treats one's flesh and blood, especially one's children. The blacks are the despised and slaughtered children of the great western house — nameless and unnameable bastards. This is a fact so obvious, so speedily verifiable, that it would seem pure insanity to deny it, and yet the life of the entire country is predicated on this denial, this monstrous and pathetic lie." For Baldwin, this situation in which a nation was founded on a form of slavery that produced a valued whiteness and a devalued blackness was pathological, and the lie that continued to reproduce those values and deny the crucial blood ties among all the children in the great western house was equally pathological. A liar, he wrote, "always knows he is lying, and that is why liars travel in packs: in order to be reassured that the judgment day will never come for them. They need each other for the well-being, the health, the perpetuation of their lie. They have a tacit agreement to guard each other's secret, for they have the same secret."[50] It is, as I hope I have shown, a family secret in every sense of that term — a secret within a family, a secret about family, and a secret denying the possibility of family.

Family is a social unit and political metaphor many find suspect, and for good reason. As Stephanie Coontz has shown in her brilliant studies of the histories, the myths, and the realities of American family life, "family" has long been and largely continues to be an idea and political concept used by cynical public officials and rabid religious zealots to mandate unfair distribution of civic benefits, to control the life options of women, and generally to foster homophobia and racism. In recent electoral campaigns, the term "family values" was employed by politicians and promoted by interest groups who wanted both to validate the government's intrusion into private life and to urge citizens to limit their view to private life. This has been the trend for the past century in the United States. Historians noted that the election of 1896 marked a shift from a public concern with "economic justice and social morality" to "personal issues and abstract patriotic posturing." By the 1970s, the language of "private relations and family values" emerged to counter the ideas of "beloved community" that had animated the civil rights movement and consequently led to a contraction and deformation of the public sphere. The language of family infiltrates and replaces the language of public commitment, as relations that used to be premised on shared political goals are transformed into enclaves of people who share "similar private motivations" and "personal activities as leisure and consumption." In addition, the language of family becomes divisive as these enclaves view with suspicion people who are perceived as "different" and attempt to exclude them from "the family circle."[51] "Would you want your daughter to marry one?" is the kind of question asked by a society that values only racially homogeneous families.

But "using family as a model for public life" need not produce an "unrealistic, even destructive, definition of community." Progressive causes in American history have used the language and concept of familial belonging to argue for a more inclusive and just society. The abolitionist motto —"Am I not a man, and a brother?"— can be faulted for its sexism and the picture of the chained beggar that accompanies it, but the point it made about a "human family" proved an important intervention into a society debating slavery at the same time as its scientists debated theories of monogenesis. The point is not that family is inherently a flawed concept that must recreate the patriarchal values of sexism, homophobia, and racism. The point is that family is the concept ideologues of patriarchy employ to organize their anxious constituents to hate free women, gay people, and people of color; and they do so by valuing and promoting only one form of nuclear family life and denigrating and positing as a negative foil all other forms of what they call "dysfunctional" behaviors and family structures. We could, I suppose, take a lesson from the abolitionists of the nineteenth century and challenge those ideologues by generating a discourse of family that is neither homogeneously uniform nor motivated by fear and the accompanying desire to exclude. Family, if freed of its popular definition as a social unit organized around a patriarchal authority whose role is to regulate the intellectual and practical activities of its members in the interests of maintaining a larger social order, could conceivably serve as a model for public life and might provide an inspiring vision for communities of socially conscientious people desiring to create the widest possible base of justice and fairness. But since "family" might be unable to bear that burden of meaning, perhaps it is just as well to dispense with it and challenge those ideologues with the idea of a broadly defined "kinship." That, I think, is the social vision that has consistently inspired many African American intellectuals, who have often used "family" in a politically oppositional way with the features and characteristics and values we now think of as associated with "kinship."[52]

This is especially true of those who have produced palimpsest narratives, both that first generation of 1890s writers who represented slavery as a pretext for contemporary social life and those who followed their example in the 1970s. The political situation and debates of what Coontz calls the two "Gilded Ages" are similar in many ways. In both the post-Reconstruction and post–civil rights eras, reactionary American politicians challenged black political and social gains, while American courts used the activist language of the earlier struggles to pass judgments misserving African Americans. The Fourteenth Amendment was interpreted to give corporations rights individual black people were denied, and the beautiful terms Martin Luther King Jr. used to describe his dreams for a fair future became fodder for those who fought affirmative action and other programs of remediation and redistribution. What was most important was that in both ages black Americans were blamed for their economic ills and black families demonized as inadequate socializing agents. In 1889, Philip Bruce presented a portrait of African American family life that was as pathological as the one Moynihan produced in 1965.[53] So, as a result, in both the 1890s and the 1970s, family became both a politicized entity and a subject of entry into political debates about larger social issues.

Black intellectuals responded to this mobilization of public opinion, and criticized the political context in which it occurred, by returning to slavery in order to assert the integrity of African American families, show the biological connections to white Americans, and argue for the social basis of family life in America. Consider the novels of the 1890s. The eponymous heroine of Frances Harper's *Iola Leroy* is an octoroon who declines a marriage offer from a white doctor because, first, she desires to reconstruct her nuclear family by finding her mother, brother, and uncle, and, then, she wishes to affiliate herself with the larger African American family by both marriage and political commitment to uplift. The daughter of a slaveholder, Iola becomes the self-defined black woman of Reconstruction. Likewise, in *Contending Forces*, Pauline Hopkins shows us the ways that history repeats itself at the same time as she shows us the fluid lines of biological descent between white slaveholders in Carolina and black social activists in Boston. Charles Chesnutt's *The Marrow of Tradition* tells the story of two families, the black Millers and the white Carterets, descended from the same patriarchal figure. In each of these novels, we are shown that "black" people share the blood of their "white" antebellum slaveholders and Reconstruction oppressors. Who is black, who is white, what is family, when the connections are so plentiful and consistent and complex? These novels argue, from two distinct angles, first, that black people and white people are biologically descended, in the title of another Hopkins novel, *Of One Blood*; and, second, that "family" like "race" is a matter of socially meaningful actions and public choices, as each of the characters, white and black, must struggle to decide whether and how to create a racial identity that might recreate the color line and claim a kinship that challenges it.[54]

The palimpsest narratives of the 1970s are engaged in the same issues and responding to a similar political ethos. They, too, are about family as deeply contested terrain. Their authors attempt to alter the debate about family as a restrictive and exclusive social unit by shifting the terms of debate to include systems of kinship that are inclusive and more accurately reflect the ties of "blood," even while they argue for the importance of dispensing with biological connections as less meaningful than socially symbolic ones. They are also engaged in challenging the dominant discourse of race in which political enemies and rival interest groups share a version of race that misserves those who have traditionally had their social opportunities and political options foreclosed because of their race (that is, people of color). These books of the 1970s adopt this particular form, the palimpsest narrative, in order to challenge the myopia and parochialism that comes from ahistorical analyses of contemporary social arrangements, most evident in the racial essentialism shared by both the cultural nationalists in the waning period of the Black Power movement and the neoconservative writers generating the social science documents and public policy statements that defined and limited the material opportunities for African Americans in the post–civil rights era.[55]

My argument is that the palimpsest narratives, which flourished in the mid-seventies, constitute a response to those discourses exhibiting a historical amnesia about the enduring effects of past social systems. By representing a contemporary subject whose psychic health, romantic success, and even physical survival depend on an ability to comprehend the role of the past in the production of the present, the palimpsest writers emphatically assert the fundamental part played by American slavery in the making of the modern world, particularly, they insist, its effects on familial structure and the creation of an American grammar of race that first defined and continues to recreate social and material inequities. What I am examining in the chapters that follow is how these writers all represent the processes of transmitting and resolving family secrets as a way of showing the perduring effects of slavery on contemporary subjects. The primary issues explored in the palimpsest narratives are family and race, and the debate in which these texts are engaged is about how these institutions were created and recreated by the generations of the past and those generations in the present who fail to remember them.[56]

2

The Sexual
Is Historical
The Subject
of Desire

Narration in Gayl Jones's work, particularly the narrating of the experience of New World slavery, constitutes an act of intersubjective communion, the creating of a sensibility that the hearer
is an equal sharer in the story to the degree of being as involved in its
events as the teller, of believing oneself to have lived out what another
experiences. Although Jones has dealt with how and to what ends narrative creates intersubjective bondings in virtually all her writing, she
has made the dynamic of intersubjective relations central to her narratives of slavery, those poems and fictions about the experiences and
long-term psychic effects of New World slavery. In her poem about
the aftermath of the second Palmares *quilombo* (a Brazilian community of several villages of fugitive slaves), Jones has the character
Bonafacia describe the intersubjective effects of hearing Diamantino's

narrative: "When he told me his story / it was as if I'd experienced it myself." In *Song for Anninho*, her earlier narrative poem about the destruction of the original Palmares in 1695, Jones's narrator Almeyda recalls hearing her grandmother's story and the sense of connection it created between them. Learning that she is "the granddaughter / of an African" and has therefore "inherited a way of being," Almeyda feels her grandmother's "words and memories / and fears and the tenderness" run through her "like blood." That "was the moment," she says, "when I became / my grandmother and she became me."[1] Jones's characters listen to others' stories so attentively as to feel that they are living out the experiences they describe, hearing with such intensity that they assume an intersubjective communion with their narrators.

In her drama, her poetry, and especially in her 1975 novel *Corregidora*, Jones has made an original contribution to contemporary narratives of slavery, by focusing on the intersubjective relations that talking about slave experiences can produce. She employs a form she traces to Zora Neale Hurston's *Their Eyes Were Watching God*, in which an ancestral narrative of slavery is "framed within a novel that dramatizes a modern version of it," in which the "grandmother's slave narrative" prefaces, foreshadows, and "provides the dramatic and revelatory pattern" for the granddaughter's own life. Jones demonstrates in *Corregidora* that the ancestral slave narrative is the site of both enabling and constricting intersubjective relations which are themselves derived from and dramatically restructure the function of remembering in individual psyches, extended families, and the ideological apparatus of the modern nation-state.[2]

Jones's revision of the palimpsest narrative form is significant because *Corregidora*, like the other palimpsest narratives, challenges the idea of rugged individualism and signals the ways attention to ethnicity since the late sixties spells a "partial retreat from the traditional idea of the self-made man." In addition, Jones traces the specific and complex ways that an ancestral slave narrative works on the terrain of family as the family produces and reproduces the modern subject.[3] Jones focuses on the subject of desire as constituted historically in order to show how both the spectacular and the hidden experiences of slavery, especially the historical subjection of desire, operate in the formation of contemporary African American subjectivity. Jones's focus, then, is twofold, her vision, one might say, bi-temporal. She demonstrates how historical forces continue to inform modern social relations, first, by dwelling on the ways an ancestral slave narrative causes unhealthy deviations in the psychic and sexual lives in one family descended from slaves, and, second, by attending to the ways that these historical forces are subtly transmuted in contemporary political debates regarding the politics of identity and racial formation in the Black Power era. Jones, in other words, explores how memory operates in both the creation of family and the recreation of a black community, exposing, though not always critically, the connections amongst race, family, and nation in the debate over Black Power that marked the moment of production for her 1975 novel.

Recent critical work on *Corregidora* has been richly suggestive in exploring the novel's profound treatment of black women's sexuality as a product of both historical oppression and cultural productivity, as formed and transformed through American slavery and African American blues expressivity. These works range from readings diagnosing the reproduction of trauma in the text to those emphasizing how the blues allows black women to reclaim their bodies and sensuality as their own.[4] In addition, critics have begun to explore how African American women's novels are "historical" not only in the sense of making history their subject but also in making their own significant intervention into history, especially in the post–civil rights era.[5] Here, I will be arguing for the important connection between Jones's representation of the slave past and the Black Power present, particularly focusing on the ways she shows how *performance* is both a means of historical recovery and a strategy for creatively resisting the patterns of identity formation in which are inhered the residues of slavery in both the family and the nation.

The Lessons of the Foremothers

The first and most prominent site for negotiating subjectivity in *Corregidora* is the family, in this case one haunted by a transgenerational set of historical tales that dramatically affect the final descendant's forty-seven-year search for rehabilitation. By recollecting and working through the mixed messages of the oral-familial tales of her childhood, Ursa Corregidora is able to define the limits that a slave past can and should have on her, learning both the value and the dangers of remembering generations. In one of her first comments on the process of remembering family history, Ursa reveals how tales suffer by the accretion of narrators and by the distance of those who tell from those who experienced the events: "My great-grandmother told my grandmama the part she lived through that my grandmama didn't live through and my grandmama told my mama what they both lived through and my mama told me what they all lived through" (9). By the time Ursa herself becomes the teller of these stories, she finds that they have become an "'epic,' almost impersonal history of Corregidora," lacking the intimacy that familial tales require to become part of and give value and meaning to "personal history." Because Ursa recognizes the importance of her family history, accepting it "as an aspect of her own character, identity and present history," she "wants to make sense of that history in terms of her own life." Yet she "doesn't want to be 'bound' by that history" or told "how she must *feel* about that past."[6] Here, Jones shows us the tension informing the family story as a site of subject formation. The oral-familial tale in which the past is remembered and offered as a resource for the formation of contemporary identity — a place where "voices that carry through time" produce both "history and personal life memory" — is also a place where one's identity can be "[b]roken on the edge / of family memory." In *Corregidora*, Jones casts into a generational framework a dilemma she expresses elsewhere: "I am burdened by memory when I desire to be."[7] Ursa's negotiation of her familial tales reflects precisely that anxiety and antagonism between believing in the impossible idea of a rootless identity unburdened by historical memory and the equally impossible idea of an identity wholly suffused with the past.

The past as she knows it does not give Ursa much freedom because she is resolutely told how to feel about her Great Gram's experiences on the Corregidora plantation. Almost completely controlled by the coercive language Great Gram uses to describe the persistent sexual assaults she suffered in Brazil, Ursa finds herself falling into a formulaic and impersonal discourse, using "Corregidora" as a germinal word that triggers off a set of complex associations which ultimately form an established narrative she is indeed "bound" to tell. She is compelled to repeat the story she has inherited because she's been taught not to doubt its veracity or to challenge its authority (8–9). When five-year-old Ursa asks, "You telling the truth, Great Gram?," Great Gram responds by slapping her. "When I'm telling you something don't you ever ask if I'm lying. Because they didn't want to leave no evidence of what they done — so it couldn't be held against them. And I'm leaving evidence. And you got to leave evidence too. And your children got to leave evidence. And when it come time to hold up the evidence, we got to have evidence to hold up. That's why they burned all the papers, so there wouldn't be no evidence to hold up against them" (14). Ursa is taught not to doubt the truth and the function of the Corregidora legend. Skepticism toward the truth of the legend is rewarded with physical violence and a remarkably repetitive insistence on the importance of "leaving evidence." Any feeling of spontaneity Ursa might have possessed in her five-year-old sense of proportions, in her childhood inquisitiveness, is stunted by her Great Gram's physical and formulaic responses. Ursa learns that any act of communication becomes a vehicle only for rehearsing the crimes of Corregidora.

Even as a child, though, Ursa was aware of the formulaic quality of her Great Gram's stories, cognizant that those stories were losing their emotive strength. As the young Ursa recalls, Great Gram seemed rapt by the words she used to describe the crimes committed against her body and soul. "It was as if the words were helping her, as if the words repeated again and again could be a substitute for memory, were somehow more than the memory. As if it were only the words that kept her anger" (11). What Great Gram exhibits in her attitude toward the "words" she uses to express her emotional valence regarding her personal past is an example of what Kristina Minister called the "dissipation of the original reflexive function" of the oral performer's tale. Writing about this process as it afflicted the famed storyteller Ila Harrison Healy in her declining years, Minister noted that Healy's "originally reflexive personal narratives grow impersonal because performances originally constitutive of self fade into portrayals of reflexivity."[8] The danger Ursa perceives is that words can overtake feelings, becoming containers more than vehicles of emotion. One of the reasons for this effect is that the stories have become reified; they have lost their very sense of being "generational" tales. Consider Pauli Murray's use of generational memory. Murray asserts that in "telling [her] grandmother's story [she] had to embrace *all* the tangled roots from which [she] had sprung, and to accept without evasion [her] own slave heritage, with all its ambivalence and paradoxes." Her own text of her grandmother's story became a "resolution of a search for identity and the exorcism of ghosts of the past." In Ursa's memories of Great Gram's slave heritage, there's no ambivalence (since Great Gram had ensured that there would be no questioning of her version of the past), no paradoxes since the tale is of pure victimage and equally pure evil, and little feeling that Ursa was supposed to be searching for her own identity at all. The ghosts are not being exorcised; they're being embalmed. The Corregidora story has become a *legend*, assuming the status of an immutable, inflexible, mythical artifact. When a generational memory stops changing, growing, and circulating, that story becomes dead.[9]

What Ursa has inherited from Great Gram is a formula she rehearses without a requisite amount of revisionist energy, without a sufficient investment of herself and her personal identity, to give that formulaic story a renewed and animated circulation. As Trinh Minh-ha has pointed out, what "is transmitted from generation to generation is not only the stories, but the very power of transmission." From Great Gram Ursa acquired the power of transmission without the concomitant respect for the dialogic nature of those transmissions. Ursa's attitude toward her family history is one of "monological steadfastness," and the logical corollary to a sense of history transmitted through formulaic discourse, estranged from a connection to her own life, is a historical narrative composed in monological and authoritative discourse, a discourse, notes Mikhail Bakhtin, that "permits no play with the context framing it, no play with its borders." The context framing Ursa's memories is her life; and that is precisely what is ignored in her recollections of the formulaic conversations with Great Gram. Elsewhere, Jones states that the oral tradition should provide the storyteller with the resources to reinforce as well as "complement" and "act on" the reality the tale represents.[10] Ursa, however, does not act on the tale; she repeats it, and is thereby disabled from realizing the pragmatic benefits of narrating an oral-familial tale.

Only later, after she hears the stories from her Gram, who lived a generation later but not entirely removed from the original atrocities of the Corregidora plantation, does Ursa come to appreciate the inevitable slippage of memory and the healing process an unstable memory can provide. Unlike Great Gram, Gram does not focus exclusively on the need to "leave evidence." She notes that the act of leaving evidence has its own dangers to those doing the leaving: "They burned all the documents, Ursa, but they didn't burn what they put in their minds. We got to burn out what they put in our minds, like you burn out a wound. Except we got to keep what we need to bear witness. That scar that's left to bear witness. We got to keep it as visible as our blood" (72). Gram suggests that because they didn't burn what they put in "our minds," the former slaves were and the descendants of slaves are still subject to the indoctrinations and psychic injuries of slavery. Here Ursa learns the possibility of both "bearing witness" and surviving the ordeal by not dwelling on it to the exclusion of her own life, by not making herself a monument to the sufferings of the past but by healing herself and leaving only the scar tissue and not the open psychic wound as evidence of the horrors of history.

One of the reasons Gram is able to do this and able to counsel Ursa to follow her lead is that Gram is aware of the treachery of memory, of its sliding, unstable, constructed quality. She reveals to Ursa that one cannot always distinguish between a memory of one's own experiences or those of an earlier ancestor. She says she doesn't remember abolition because she was too young, but she feels "sometime it seem like I do too" remember abolition because her own mother may have told her stories that have assumed experiential value in her mind (78). Indeed, Gram goes so far as to talk explicitly not only about how memory is a construct of earlier narratives, but to suggest that memories change because feelings are indeterminate and liable to be transformed. It's "hard to always remember what you were feeling when you ain't feeling it exactly that way no more," she tells Ursa (79). What is absolutely remarkable is that Gram is here describing how she feels about Corregidora, who had been represented without any ambivalence in Great Gram's memories. No matter the poignancy of the painful experience that originally wrought them, Gram suggests, feelings and the memories of feelings do not always remain constant or clear.

Unlike Great Gram's inflexible and resolutely unambivalent tales, Gram's story is about the difficulty of recollection, the fluid quality of experience, the changing nature of feelings. Great Gram's narratives had been constricting because they constituted an arrested and monumental discourse (relying on "words" to remove the indeterminateness of memory), serving only the purpose of "leaving evidence." Gram's narratives are liberating because they are motivated by both the need to bear witness and the need to heal the mind and recuperate from slavery; and Gram's discourse is open to changing contexts and altered conditions, not monumental or legendary but intimate and therefore "able to reveal newer *ways to mean*." "A story is *not* just a story," notes Trinh. "Once the forces have been aroused and set into motion, they can't simply be stopped at someone's request. Once told, the story is bound to circulate; humanized, it may have a temporary end, but its effects linger on and its end is never truly an end."[11] The effects of the Corregidora story clearly do linger on; what Ursa has to do is humanize the story by *experiencing* it rather than *rehearsing* it, investing by discovering herself in the oral-familial tales.

Like Hurston's Janie, then, Ursa lives her life in the shadow of those overpowering ancestral narratives of enslavement, trying to discover what she herself desires through the filter of tales insistently reiterating what she should want. The intersubjective relations these familial tales make possible are problematic because they contain both healthy and dangerous possibilities. They are healthy because they define the self in broad historical terms, providing a rich and sustaining context for contemporary subjects to gauge their actions. They are also dangerous because they can overwhelm and submerge the contemporary subject, producing deleterious historical patterns profoundly inadequate for contemporary social relations. In *Corregidora*, Mama represents how dangerous those intersubjective relations can be. Although she is able to produce a coherent narrative of her "private memory" (104), that she had always hidden from Ursa, and tell her daughter the complete story of her own courtship and stormy marriage with her husband Martin (111–23), she finds herself unable to produce a likewise coherent version of the Corregidora past. She either falters in her storytelling — she sounded "as if she were speaking in pieces, instead of telling one long thing" (123) — or is utterly consumed by the narration: "Mama kept talking until it wasn't her that was talking, but Great Gram. . . . [S]he wasn't Mama now, she was Great Gram talking" (124). The story is so overpowering that "the memory of all the Corregidora women" had become "her memory too, as strong with her as her own private memory, or almost as strong" (129). Mama's example reveals to Ursa the ultimate danger of the intersubjective relations that occur in familial narratives of enslavement, when the oral-familial tales assume such prominence in the psychic life of the subject as to cause her to submerge her identity and lose her own to the dominant ancestral voice. Like Almeyda in *Song for Anninho*, Ursa's mother can say, "I became / my grandmother," but because the relationship between her "private memory" and the "memory of all the Corregidora women" is not dialogic, she cannot say, as Almeyda can, "and she became me." A freed voice, Jones has written, is neither solipsistic nor self-negating. While a freed voice does not deny the place of the other in self-discovery, it is also insistently "self-defining."[12] Mama does not have that freed voice; Ursa learns to strive for it.

Ursa learns different things from each of her maternal ancestors. From her Great Gram, she learns to produce a ritual, formulaic account of her Great Gram's experiences as a way of "leaving evidence" or "bearing witness." From her Gram, she learns that it is important to heal her mind as well as to bear witness, and she also learns that feelings are not static entities; they are transformed by the passage of time and the accumulation of wisdom and experience. This serves Ursa two ways. It helps her break out of the formulaic discourse that had "bound" her earlier; and it also helps her in her thinking about her relationship with Mutt. Finally, from Mama Ursa learns that the epic, impersonal tale of a family's travails in slavery can threaten to consume the teller and alienate the listener unless it is supplemented with personal, intimate tales that incorporate the teller's and her more recent ancestors' experiences into that epic structure and thereby promote in the listener a more empathetic feeling for the tale. What Ursa has to learn, then, is how to develop within herself the capacity to act on all the lessons she acquires from her maternal ancestors: to pass on the narrative of Corregidora's horrible crimes without losing her own voice and sense of her own historical placement.

The Family Secret of Slave Resistance

For most critics of the novel, Ursa learns to do this by singing the blues, and her singing the blues is likewise a sign that she has learned to overcome the horror of being bound to the past or, better, that she has found a way to translate into a cultural artifact the oppressive history of the Corregidora women, to create from her ancestors' and her experiences a "song branded with the new world" (59).[13] With this reading I have no real disagreement. I would only add that the blues is but one communicative form serving to facilitate Ursa's development. She translates the oral-familial tales into blues songs only after she engages in other mediating oral forms, especially the imagined future conversations with Mutt, or what Jones calls "ritualized dialogue," those italicized portions of the novel in which Ursa and Mutt engage in an imaginary conversation where the meaning is wrought out of "the language, the rhythm of the people talking, and the rhythm *between* the people talking."[14] Moreover, and more important, I would argue that what Ursa produces in terms of a cultural form (the blues) depends intimately on her diagnosing the root cause of Mama's and her own inability to talk about Great Gram's history without succumbing to possession or falling into rote repetition. She can do that only by discovering the hidden family secret at the heart of the Corregidora legend because Ursa's and Mama's arrested discourses are in many ways ultimately a product and consequence of that family secret.

As we saw in Chapter 1, the foremost psychoanalytic theorists of family secrets, Nicolas Abraham and Maria Torok, argue that there is a "phantom" at the heart of a particular kind of psychic trauma. This phantom is a result of the "unconscious suspicion that something had been left unsaid" during the life of the deceased relatives in the family line. This "gap" or "silence" affects the later generations who find themselves haunted by this ancestor's "secret." The phantom, then, represents "the gap that the concealment of some part of a loved one's life produced in us." In some unexplainable way, the phantom — the psychic result of the ancestral family secret, the "transgenerational consequences of silence" — passes "from the parent's unconscious into the child's," and continues to haunt that child and his or her children. In effect, Abraham and Torok conclude, family secrets produce "encrypted" phantoms that "persist through several generations and determine the fate of an entire family line."[15] This fascinating theory helps us understand how the present is connected to the past not only materially (because the injustices and inequities of earlier times persist in the present distribution of resources and power) but also psychologically. What happened to an ancestor has both social and psychic consequences for the generations that follow.

It is also a theory that perfectly describes *Corregidora*, a novel very much about how the later generations of a family line suffer psychic and discursive dysfunctions as a result of the traumas that pained an earlier ancestor. And at the heart of the novel resides the family secret of the Corregidoras. As a child, Ursa learned that Great Gram had done "something that made [Corregidora] wont to kill her," forcing her to flee and leave her daughter on the plantation (79). Nobody is told what Great Gram did to Corregidora. Gram admits that Great Gram "never would tell me what she did. Up till today she still won't tell me what it was she did" (172). And Corregidora also "never said nothing about what it was she did to him" (173). This secret, then, haunts the later generations who insistently wonder: "What is it a woman can do to a man that make him hate her so bad he wont to kill her one minute and keep thinking about her and can't get her out of his mind the next" (173)? In this secret is contained crucial information about the destiny of the Corregidora women. Because Great Gram's departure after this secret act left Gram to be "raised" and then raped and impregnated by Corregidora (172), this act is responsible for both the extension of the Corregidora maternal line and for hinting at the strategy of procreative "bearing witness" the Corregidora women use to hold up his crimes. Also, in this secret reside the complex of issues affecting the Corregidora women. What act can a woman perform on a man that incites both hatred and persistent desire? What is the nature of desire and its relationship to pain and hatred? Finally, this secret inhibits the later generations' productive inquiry into the past, thus creating a stultifying and incomplete narrative and giving the Corregidora legend its "epic" quality. The silence, the phantom, haunts not only the Corregidora family line but also the family narrative.

At the end of the novel, Ursa disrupts the "epic" narrative by deciphering the family secret, which opens up a historical space for her to manifest her stunted desire. Most readings attempt to resolve the ambiguous dynamics between Ursa and Mutt, her first husband, by determining whether or not they are "reconciled" at the end of the novel. Agreeing with Jones herself that the "open-ended" conclusion of the novel points "toward a kind of redemption," I would like to explore how Ursa and Mutt's reconciliation is premised on the solution of the family secret, which Ursa uses to exorcise the past that would possess her and gain instead a qualitatively different and more liberating intersubjectivity from the family narrative she completes.[16]

In the final scene, Mutt returns after a twenty-two-year absence to tell her he wants her to "come back" (183). Mutt tells Ursa how after the American courts took his great-grandfather's slave wife away from him for unsettled debts, his great-grandfather "went crazy" and started eating "onions so people wouldn't come around him," then eating "peppermint so they would" (183–84). Responding to the loss of Ursa, Mutt tries to do the same thing as his great-grandfather; "but it didn't do nothing but make me sick," he informs her (184). What Mutt is saying to Ursa is that he appreciates the power of the past but he also cannot live according to its regime, that he cannot replicate what his ancestor did in an attempt to deal with his modern problems.

In other words, this brief relation shows us that Mutt is no longer demanding of Ursa that she "forget" the past, as he had earlier asked her to do, since he himself has attempted to act out a historical incident in order to determine what knowledge it could give him. His answer, therefore, is that the past needs to be recalled but not relived, at least not relived in the register in which Ursa has been reliving it.

Following Mutt's lead, Ursa also attempts to reenact her own great-grandparent's historical act, showing that she, too, has learned to distinguish between a healthy ability to remember the past and a disabling imperative to remain fully immersed in it. While doing so, she solves the family secret. Thinking it "had to be something sexual that Great Gram did to Corregidora," while she herself performs fellatio on Mutt, Ursa concludes that Great Gram had bitten Corregidora's penis during an act of fellatio and produced that unspeakable tension between hatred and love, desolation and desire, exquisite pleasure and excruciating pain (184).

Ursa approaches this act of sex as an act of historical archaeology and genealogy, in the Foucauldian sense of genealogy of beginning a historical "analysis from a question posed in the present."[17] As a genealogical study, this final sexual encounter provides Ursa with a chance to determine her place and her displacement as a Corregidora woman, to define her selfhood and her salvation in familial terms that include her mother as part of the "family romance," and, finally, to see in what ways there is some kind of mutual responsibility involved in the lives of the Corregidora women and their men. Here it is imperative that we be careful in assessing what Ursa is saying. While recognizing that what Corregidora had done to Great Gram was no worse than what "Mutt had done to me, than what we had done to each other, than what Mama had done to Daddy, or what he had done to her in return," Ursa is also not "blaming the victim" or assuming that the victim plays as active a part in the victimization as does the oppressor (184). Rather, what she seems to be suggesting is that the tale of the Corregidora women is not one of pure victimage, but one in which the women have some degree of agency despite the historical and social inequities under which they become subjects of their own lives. After all, the answer to the family secret is an act of one slave woman's resistance, however meager and insufficient that expression of agency and resistance may appear. What Ursa's interpretation of the family secret does is open up for her a set of associations that help her realize the connections between Great Gram's sexual act of resistance against Corregidora and the potential power Ursa has over Mutt. In addition and more important, it teaches her and allows her to reveal to us how both Great Gram's and Ursa's acts are historically resonant and part of a collective endeavor of redefining the role of sexuality and desire in acts of resistance and of producing desire out of resistant activity.[18]

First, though, we need to appreciate what "resistance" means in a patriarchal institution. Discussing the effects of slave "disaffection" and their response to the "paternalism" of slavery in the Old South, Eugene Genovese argues that slaves simultaneously exhibited "accommodation and resistance to slavery." Accommodation offered the slaves a way of "accepting what could not be helped without falling prey to the pressures for dehumanization, emasculation, and self-hatred." Resistance, meanwhile, falls into either "prepolitical nonrevolutionary self-assertion" — including forms of day-to-day resistance such as lying, stealing, dissembling, shirking, murder, infanticide, suicide, and arson — or "political responses" to enslavement such as flight or collective violence against the system. Challenging this binary distinction, Barbara Jeanne Fields has argued that resistance "does not refer only to the fight that individuals, or collections of them, put up at any given time against those trying to impose on them." Instead, she suggests, resistance "refers also to the historical outcome of the struggle that has gone before, perhaps long enough before to have been hallowed by custom or formalized in law."[19] Resistance, in other words, is not only a given set of actions premised on transcendent principles but also a complex of possibilities emerging from and responding to historically specific conditions and occurring in particular social spaces. In order accurately to represent historical acts of resistance we need to examine the context within which resistance is rendered necessary and the avenues through which it is made possible, exploring carefully how resistance entails acts that produce anxiety and danger for the oppressors in specific sites or spheres of activity.

In the case of New World patriarchal slavery as it affected the lives of slave women, the site or sphere of activity was sexuality. In Brazil, in particular, slave women were especially subject to the sexualized commodification of their bodies. As happened in other slave societies, slave masters in Brazil were afforded limitless opportunities to "live in a state of fornication" with their slaves, as Padre Fernao Cardim noted during his sixteenth-century tour of Brazilian plantations. In addition, though, and uniquely, slave masters in Brazil prostituted slave women. While the prostitution of "slave women as a source of income is virtually unknown in the history of slavery in the United States," Brazilians time and again reported the practice, from the Jesuit Joao Antônio Andreoni's 1711 account of slave women selling "their own bodies" to the 1871 report of Judge Miguel José Tavares, who ordered 186 women freed in accordance with the Roman law stating that any master who prostituted a slave woman had to manumit her.[20] Given the particular historical circumstances of Brazilian slavery, then, we should expect that resistance would involve that site of activity where oppression was most pronounced: sexuality. As William Andrews rightly observes, "when the sex act becomes politicized, as patriarchal power inevitably makes it, it can be best interpreted as a weapon, either of oppression or rebellion."[21] And because slave women suffered a "dual form of oppression," having to resist their commodification as both economic and sexual beings, their acts cannot fairly be characterized as "nonrevolutionary self-assertion." Rather, as Darlene Clark Hine points out, the "slave woman's resistance to sexual and therefore to economic exploitation posed a potentially severe threat to paternalism itself, for implicit in such action was the slave woman's refusal to accept her designated responsibilities within the slave system as legitimate."[22]

Readings of *Corregidora* have rarely recognized that there is much of a representation of resistance in the novel.[23] Most critics focus on Great Gram's narratives which are, after all, fully and thoroughly imbued with the horror and suffering of enslaved Brazilian women who lived out "[d]ays that were pages of hysteria" while bowing down to a slave master's "genital fantasies" (59). But there are important representations of slave women's resistance and they play a crucial role in Ursa's final assay on the Corregidora family secret. The final scene, in fact, is a point of convergence for several reasons. It is the site where Ursa reenacts her Great Gram's actions of sexual resistance, and the point where Ursa literally converges with her great-grandmother ("It was like I didn't know how much was me and Mutt and how much was Great Gram and Corregidora"). It is also the space where several interrelated stories of slave resistance come to bear. And in the moment Ursa is attempting to read the family secret, she draws on not only her psychic capacity to "become" her grandmother but also the tales she has heard about the possibilities for resisting enslavement or, in her case, neoenslavement.

At the moment of her possession or convergence with Great Gram and the moment of her ambivalent epiphany ("in a split second of hate and love I knew what it was"), Ursa is offered a choice of what sort of action she could perform on Mutt. Aware of her power over him ("I could kill you," she repeats), she is likewise aware of the dangers of wielding that power.[24] And the dangers are not only immediately pertinent — few men would passively watch as their penis was bitten off, as Ann duCille correctly notes ("a sleeping John Wayne Bobbit notwithstanding")—but also historical, for this scene of possible emasculation as personal empowerment resonates with an earlier scene of emasculation as futile slave resistance.[25] Immediately after she spells out for Ursa the "two alternatives" to enslavement, resistance or submission, Great Gram tells her the story of a slave woman "over on the next plantation" who responded to her master's attempted rape by cutting "off his thing with a razor she had hid under the pillow." After the master bled to death, the state's police "cut off her husband's penis and stuffed it in her mouth, and then they hanged her. They let him bleed to death. They made her watch and then they hanged her" (67). If one didn't take the alternative of accommodation, Great Gram notes, one had "to suffer the consequences," which included the "physical cruelty and beatings" attendant on women's efforts to "protect their sexual integrity and resist white men," and risking the lives of their own families.[26]

Ursa, then, knows the extreme cost of a resistance exercised through the kind of power a woman can possess in a sexual act. A slaveowner may be vulnerable during an act of forced sex, but he is nonetheless empowered by the social arrangements existing outside and supporting the plantation. Ursa knows not only the danger of Mutt's response to an attempted emasculation but also, and, more significant, the history of black men who suffered emasculation and castration at the hands of white slaveowners. After all, the story Great Gram tells is about a black woman who does end up with her husband's severed penis in her mouth but only because of the violent state apparatus defining him as "slave" and "black." Great Gram's story, then, defines sexuality as a site of oppression in several ways. The state not only permitted white slave masters to rape the bodies of their African slaves, but they made black sexuality itself a spectacle in the punishment of slave resistance. As Great Gram noted, "what happened over on that other plantation" served as "a warning, cause they might wont your pussy, but if you do anything to get back at them, it'll be your life they be wonting, and then they make even that some kind of a sex show" (125). Finally, sexuality is also a primary site of oppression because masters determined the quality and direction of their slaves' desires. Corregidora, for instance, would not allow sexual relations between black men and women, oppressing his slaves by deflecting their desires and corrupting their romantic relations (124). And Great Gram's story is finally like so many others in the novel: it reveals the historical damage done to the romantic relations between black men and women during slavery, and makes clear that the social arrangements policing slave resistance also police black desire.

Under these conditions, then, sexuality for enslaved peoples assumes a different value, no longer only a domain of personal self-assertion or the terrain of accommodation, but rather a site for resistance to the system of slavery itself. Since acts of overt resistance, such as emasculating a slave master, prove more destructive to the agents of resistance than the purveyors of oppression, slaves on the Corregidora plantation do take a lesson from "what happened over on that other plantation" and attempt to configure their own forms of resistance to the situations in which they find themselves. These take two forms, both of which Ursa alludes to in the final scene as she attempts to solve and interpret the significance of the family secret. First, there is the personal revenge of the sort Great Gram had when, after the state stopped supporting and policing slavery, she finally imitated the woman on the next plantation and bit Corregidora's penis (but without emasculating him).[27] Second, there is the kind of communal activity of creating social relations beyond slavery and fostering sustained personal relations outside of the master-slave dialectic. This form of resistance is figured in the idea of Palmares, the fugitive slave society in seventeenth-century Brazil. As Ursa hovers over Mutt's midsection, then, she most likely has in her mind *two* different scenes, two different "moments" that come to her in a split second. The text signals that Ursa is thinking of both scenes by having her recollect the exact words Gram had uttered when she wondered about Great Gram's mysterious action — "What is it a woman can do to a man that make him hate her so bad he wont to kill her one minute and keep thinking about her and can't get her out of his mind the next?" (184, 173)—and by having her also recall "Mama when she had started talking like Great Gram," which is the moment when Ursa is told the story of the slave woman on the next plantation and the story of Palmares (184, 125–28).

The person who dreams of Palmares is a young slave boy who flees the Corregidora plantation when he is caught talking to Great Gram about his dream of "running away and joining up with them renegade slaves up in Palmares" (126). It is crucial for us to appreciate the significance of this reference to Palmares, perhaps the single most meaningful collective act of slave resistance in Brazil and the most long-lasting and complete African maroon community in the Americas, because it establishes the terms of resistance in the novel. Palmares, in effect, is an event that, to use Barbara Fields's terms, "refers . . . to the historical outcome of the struggle that has gone before" and therefore provides resources for future acts of resistance.

Palmares is the most famous and longest-standing Brazilian *quilombo*. Beginning probably before but certainly by 1605, when forty African slaves from Pôrto Calvo took refuge in Palmares, the *quilombo* grew to a population of 20,000 and survived almost constant attacks from 1640 to its eventual destruction in 1697. During its ascendancy, Palmares provided its fugitive slave population with a stable sociocultural existence based on a syncretic but largely Angolan-Congolese political, economic, and social system. Predicated on an "African political system which came to govern a plural society and thus give continuity to what could have been at best a group of scattered hideouts," Palmares stood as a resplendent example of continued resistance in its defense against scores of attacks by Dutch and Portuguese armed forces. As an African social system, Palmares represented "the resistance of a civilization that refused to die (a struggle in which African religion played a key role) as much as a direct protest against the institution of slavery." As an African-based economy, Palmares was both generally a rejection of the "Portuguese economic and social order" and specifically a "reaction to a slave-holding society entirely out of step with forms of bondage familiar to Africa." The Palmares community eventually developed its own complex economic support system, not only producing its own food and tools but also developing a class of skilled mechanics and craftsmen.

As a successful act of communal resistance and socioeconomic stability, Palmares stood as a self-supporting community that could inspire and draw on the slave population of neighboring plantations and thereby deplete the slave-labor force of Pernambuco. In a 1671 letter, Governor Ferna de Sousa Coutinho noted that the "example and permanence" of Palmares "each day induces the other Negroes to flee and escape from the rigorous captivity which they suffer." In fact, it was even more than an inspiration to slave populations on neighboring plantations; it was a system of perpetuating freedom through a methodical attack on slavery and slavishness. According to a contemporary report, the citizens of Palmares were considered free if they fled the plantations of their own accord; but they remained slaves in Palmares if they were "stolen" from their plantations. They would remain slaves in Palmares until they earned their freedom by going back and stealing another slave from the plantation. In other words, because Palmares provided its citizens (called *palmaristas*) with an opportunity to free themselves by freeing another, they effectively created a genuine sense of collective being. That, perhaps, was the greatest psychological accomplishment of this, the most famous of the New World maroon societies. Before and after its final destruction in 1697, highlighted by the turning point of the suicide of 200 *palmaristas* in the late night and early morning of February 5–6, 1694, after forty-two days of siege, Palmares provided the slave population of Pernambuco and other parts of Brazil with a sparkling and edifying example of slave resistance that translated itself into a countercultural formation. It was a lesson not soon, and not yet, forgotten. When Arthur Ramos made a search for oral traditions of Palmares legends in the late 1930s, he found an annual stage play in the township of Pilar that recalled the "sequence of events as it persists in the memory of the people." And recently, in 1995, the 300th anniversary of the end of Palmares was marked by concerted efforts to create celebratory monuments on the site, attempts by the Palmares Foundation to win land titles for the contemporary descendants of escaped slaves, and continued research into the materials uncovered by the Palmares Archeological Project.[28]

Palmares has certainly remained a profoundly important memory in Gayl Jones's work from her earliest play, "The Ancestor: A Street Play" (1975), to her latest narrative poem, *Xarque* (1985). For the most part, Jones uses Palmares as a symbol of a heroic and continuing heritage, a point of psychic communion with the past, and a site representing the historical possibility of healthy loving relations between black women and men. For latter-day Americans of African descent in Jones's works, Palmares provides both a legacy — "we are a continuance / of their flesh and voices" — and a place where twentieth-century individuals feel an intersubjective connection with the seventeenth-century past, feeling as if they "were there." Most of all, though, Jones uses Palmares the way Paule Marshall uses slave resistance in *Daughters*: to signify "a time when black men and women had it together, were together, stood together."[29] Palmares is the real and mythical place where love "[b]etween men and women" flourished as it had in the "old country," a place where former slaves could begin to shed their servitude by creating love and leaving not only a heritage of heroic resistance but also a "legacy of tenderness."[30] And the connection between an unfettered desire and an unfettered body is crucial. Palmares represents a revolutionary potential in Jones's work, as it had in history, because it was predicated on the connection between personal and collective freedom (one freed oneself by freeing another) and between domestic and public space (between where people loved and where they labored, or, to be more precise, the social arrangements of their labor).

In *Corregidora*, Palmares likewise operates as a symbol of the possibility of a "free" love in that place where it has "always" been possible for men and women to commune.[31] In Palmares, in the condition of freedom and a social system based on African societies ("like the old country"), men and women of African descent can live and love without the pernicious presence of either a Corregidora or the political system supporting him. Even though the woman and man on the next plantation suffered horrific deaths, and even though their murders acted as spectacles of "warning" for the slaves on the Corregidora plantation, so long as slaves kept alive the idea of Palmares they had reason to hope for freedom and autonomy and they had sufficient incentive for them to perform acts of resistance toward gaining their freedom. The dream of the young slave boy on the Corregidora plantation was not only to join the society of "Palmares, where these black mens had started their own town, escaped and banded together," but also to create a space where it was possible to love, to "have him a woman, and then come back and get his woman and take her up there" (126). For him, Palmares was not just the historical place where, as Great Gram tells him, "way back two hundred years ago" white men had killed all of the *palmaristas*. Palmares for him remains a symbol, both the hope for and the possibility of a place where a man and a woman are free if they create the time and space for their love. Palmares, he pronounces, was not "way back two hundred years ago." "Palmares was now" (126).

For Jones such a history of resistance represents a means for present African American subjects to produce narratives of temporal disjunction in order to appreciate the legacy of their own history (of both resistance and tenderness) and thereby create the conditions for continuing that legacy. The slave boy who wishes to escape the Brazilian plantation in the mid-nineteenth century in order to join a community destroyed in 1694 gives us a sense of how an idea of a resistant community exceeds its historical placement. So, too, does Ursa's final act of reconciliation with Mutt attest to her using the past to construct the present, of using an act of historical resistance to create the conditions for a contemporary love. And it is a *choice*, Jones makes clear, by showing us the conscious effort Ursa makes to construct a version of the past in the final scene. After stating that the answer to the family secret came to her in an epiphany—"In a split second I knew what it was, in a split second of hate and love I knew what it was"—Ursa gives that answer in a highly ambiguous way: "A moment of pleasure and excruciating pain at the same time, a moment of broken skin but not sexlessness, a moment just before sexlessness, a moment that stops just before sexlessness, a moment that stops before it breaks the skin" (184). Ursa does not describe a "moment." She describes, in the style of a gradation, a set of options. A moment of "broken skin . . . just before sexlessness" is not the same thing as a moment that stops "before it breaks the skin." It is important to note that Ursa casts this epiphany into a gradation, describing various options from emasculation to harmless nibbling, because it alerts us to the fact that Ursa is *choosing* among possibilities, not only as a model for her own present activity (to bite or not to bite) but also as a way of asserting what kind of past she imagines and what role that past will play in her present life.

If there is a "moment" in this scene, it is the moment when Ursa has to choose among the resonant historical scenes of resistance she has available to her—to imitate the woman who emasculated her master, to imitate Great Gram who broke the skin on Corregidora's penis in biting it, or to set her own course based on the imperatives associated with Palmares. In the end, Ursa does not follow the example of the woman on the plantation and emasculate Mutt, nor does she emulate her Great Gram and bite Mutt's penis enough to break the skin. She stops before breaking the skin. Just as Mutt had discovered that he was not made healthier by emulating his great-grandfather, so does Ursa discover that she would not achieve wholeness by imitating her great-grandmother. Choosing instead to pursue a course of action in which she would initiate the possibility for Mutt and her to create the space and time for a loving relationship, Ursa essentially chooses to believe that "Palmares was now." Palmares, then, provides Ursa with a way of understanding how most effectively to use the past and it is therefore a story that helps her overcome the part of the education she received from her Great Gram about the more destructive ways of replicating the past. In the final scene, recalling the time Mama "had started talking like Great Gram," Ursa is able to discern the meaning of the story Great Gram passed on to Mama who then passed it on to Ursa. At the end of her rendition of this story to Ursa, Mama notes: "They just go on like that, and then get in to talking about the importance of passing things like that down" (128). "Things like that," it turns out, are stories about options for resistance and the connections between different kinds of resistance. And as Ursa discovers, these stories, even when they are told by someone in a state of possession, retain their residual potential for liberation. The story of Palmares, which Great Gram passed on to Mama without believing, which Mama passed on to Ursa without understanding its significance, becomes for Ursa an opportunity to discover and use in her own life another version of the multiform past.

Unlike Gram and Mama, and even Great Gram, Ursa is able to solve the family secret, complete the family narrative, and resuscitate the voice she had lost to history because she is the beneficiary of several advantages her foremothers did not have. Ursa sees the connections among her great-grandmother's act, other acts of slave resistance, and her own actions in the present, transforming the family narrative from one of pure victimage to one of agency. She simultaneously changes her own position within the family narratives from a state of debilitating possession, entailing the loss or arresting of voice, to a state of healthy intersubjectivity.

Ursa is able to reinterpret the family story because of a shift in the historical discourse of slavery from the 1940s, when Ursa first begins to meditate on the past, to the late 1960s, when she is able to decipher the family secret and reinvigorate her own life with the possibilities for her own resistant acts. When in 1947 she recollects the events of Great Gram's life, Ursa discovers tales of slavery as overwhelmingly oppressive and slaves as unalterably slavish; when she recollects those events in 1969, she sees resistant slaves who form communities and provide useful models for the present. The point Jones is making, I think, is that to keep alive the memories of slavery is to keep them available for interpretation and reinterpretation so that they can serve each passing generation in the particular ways that generation chooses to view the slave past of the New World. And because the generation of the sixties chose to focus on resistance and community and cultural productivity in the slave past, an interpretive framework that was largely a product of the Black Power movement's influence on American historiography, Ursa was able to recreate a version of her familial narrative that emphasized the possibility for more productive social and romantic relations.[32] What is important, then, is that the answer Ursa finds for the family secret and likewise the interpretation she makes of her family narrative are not necessarily "correct" (witness the inherent ambiguities and incoherent contradictions), but they are the appropriate ones, the ones that work best within the spirit of the late sixties and the ones most suitable for Ursa's present life.

By creating this history, by acting on her Gram's knowledge of the past as a flexible entity and memory as an unstable tool for discovery, Ursa is also able to alter her relationship to the family narrative so that it is no longer the space where she loses her voice and becomes instead a site for her recovery, allowing her to see how her life is in dialogue with the past, not merely reflective of it or the container of its meaning. Because of the different historical sensibility she brings, because of her creative impetus in recreating the past, Ursa finally does not remain confused in her convergence with the past — "I didn't know how much was me and Mutt and how much was Great Gram and Corregidora" — but emerges from that intersubjective moment to enter a "blues duet" with Mutt in which they together work at defining the relationship between the past and the present as it affects their relationship. By reenacting an event from each of their great-grandparents' lives, Ursa and Mutt come to a knowledge about the confused desires produced out of enslavement, as Mutt imitates an enslaved ancestor who wants people simultaneously to love and abhor him, and Ursa an ancestor who feels both "hate and love" (184). But out of this knowledge, out of a remarkable series of narratives about historical failures at coupling, Mutt and Ursa gather together the lyrics of a blues song that will in turn provide them with the resources for understanding and producing a desire less fraught with anxiety and confusion.

The Performance of Race

A fact that goes unstated in the criticism because it is understated in the novel is that the final reconciliation scene takes place in 1969, which strikes me as being important not only because it marks the twenty-two years since Mutt and Ursa have last spoken. It also suggests the considerably different social circumstances in which that reconciliation takes place and signals the political dialogue Jones is having with the historical moment of her novel's production, the moment of Black Power. Written in the early seventies, published in 1975, coinciding, that is, with the crest and waning of the Black Power movement, *Corregidora* challenges the "reading codes of Black Aesthetic ideology" and engages in a debate with "black nationalist discourse." Indeed, the novel deeply questions the very bases of Black Power as a movement partly premised on valorizing one quality of "blackness" and partly premised on dismissing various "outdated" black cultural ideas and formations.[33] Taking up the tenets of black identity and racial formation in the post–civil rights, Black Power era, Jones critiques the ways Black Power intellectuals, particularly some of the cultural nationalist camp, employed "blackness" as a weapon against other black people. Some cultural nationalists articulated a "new consciousness of Blackness" that repeatedly drew attention to the "social division within the black populace," attempting to establish a positive black subjectivity "not on any sense of inclusiveness with respect to the black community" but rather by producing a "negative foil" in "intraracial division."[34] Simultaneously, she challenges the facile assertions of those cultural nationalists who dismissed and proscribed cultural forms like the blues as "invalid" and "not functional" because these cultural forms "do not commit us to the struggle of today and tomorrow, but keep us in the past."[35]

Critiquing what she calls the "new strictures of exclusion" and the "new hegemony" established by the Black Power intellectuals and Black Aesthetic theorists, Jones complicates the racial formation operative in Black Power by exposing its historical roots, by dwelling on the ways that contemporary concepts of authenticity in black communities are connected to historical master discourses on plantations.

She also uses the proscribed cultural form of the blues to structure and give force to what she refers to as the "blues relationships between black men and women," showing that the blues is a site for the serious examination of the complicated interplay of identity and desire.[36] Troubled by the ways black cultural nationalists eschewed cultural forms (blues), downplayed the importance of formative historical periods (slavery), and argued for rigid regimentation of racial identity (black is, black ain't), Jones used her palimpsest narrative to explore how the complex of desire, sexuality, and racial identity, like the intersubjectivity created in family narratives, offers both enabling and constricting options. And, as was the case with family narratives, Jones is again showing us the ways performance is at the heart of the strategy she outlines for challenging the constricting parameters of racial formation.

Recognizing the limited hold the past can have on her, negotiating between the imperatives of a historical legacy of enslavement and the demands of lived experience in the present, Ursa discovers another feature of genealogy, namely the specific ways that her body is "totally imprinted by history." Genealogy, since it is primarily "an analysis of descent," writes Foucault, is also therefore a discourse of the situation between "the body and history," of the processes through which historical episodes mark the body as "the inscribed surface of events."[37] Ursa feels distressed at the knowledge that she is "[s]tained with another's past," having "[t]heir past in my blood" (45). Although the past she knows is the product of family narratives, her body, she also comes to recognize, is literally formed of that history — she thinks of her veins as the place of "centuries meeting" (46) — and transformed by it, particularly in its capacity for desire and its embodiment of sexuality. Indeed, the family secret she solves by understanding the connection between resistance and sexuality and the primal scene she reenacts as a site of confused desire shed light on the national secret regarding the historical creation and recreation of racial schemas through the formation and manipulation of sexuality and desire.

Aware of having been early educated to desire reproduction for the sake of keeping alive the history of Corregidora's horrors — to "make generations" is what "all Corregidora women want. Have been taught to want" (22)—Ursa is yet unaware of how the rest of her desiring function is also fraught with the weight of the past. When she looks at her great-grandmother and her grandmother, she sees "[h]ate and desire both riding them" as they try to deal with the persistent effect Corregidora's sexual regime has on their present lives (102). When she looks at her mother, Ursa realizes that all she ever saw was a well of "[d]esire, and loneliness," another life left desolate by the plantation culture at its roots (101). Yet Ursa does not readily see that her own life is also deeply imbricated into the sexual politics of the Corregidora plantation, her own desires likewise frustrated because of the social relations that the plantation culture inaugurated and yet maintains. For her, the fact that Mutt denies her sexual intimacy or even temporary release when she is "exhausted with wanting" appears unrelated to the past relations between black women and men in the time of slavery (64–65). Nor does Ursa see how she recreates this pattern and the social relations on which it is based when she herself learns to use sex as a weapon in her battles with Mutt. After Mutt starts using sex to get Ursa to quit her singing career — "[w]henever he wanted it and I didn't, he'd take me, . . . [b]ut those times that I wanted it, and he sensed that I wanted it, that's when he would turn away from me" — Ursa gets to the point where she "tried to learn from him, play it his way" (156). The results of this sexual warfare are comic as well as tragic. They are comic in that each spouse acts on what she or he thinks the other does not want. Mutt decides to have sex with Ursa because he thinks she is unwilling. Acting on his misperception, Ursa decides to withhold sex from Mutt because he is acting on what he perceives to be her unwillingness. This comedy of misperceived desires does have its dire consequences, though. Having repelled his advances, Ursa believes she has emerged victorious — "it was the first time I hadn't given it to him when *he* said yes" — only to discover she has confused herself about her own desire: "Maybe it was because I *did* want it" (157). By acting on what she believes to be Mutt's lack of desire, Ursa is left to wonder about the precise state of her own desire.

This state of confused and frustrated desires in the realm of sexuality has its basis, of course, in the patriarchal, capitalist order where "heterosexual coupling functions as a domain of male power," where "legitimate compensation for man's labor is the conspicuous consumption of the surplus value of women's leisure: her female sexuality"; and male "ownership" of women's bodies "extends to the abstract ownership of what women produce in such relationships: desire."[38] Moreover, in the case of African American heterosexual coupling, this specific state of confusion about desire and sexuality has its roots in the slave past, where a master class had organized a method of simultaneously policing the desire of slaves, commodifying their sexuality, and racializing their bodies.

The stories of plantation life in Brazil in *Corregidora* focus on the ways that slave women's bodies were subject to a particular kind of discipline which commodified their bodies at the same time as it policed their desires. Forced into plantation prostitution, the slave women on the Corregidora plantation were transformed into objects of sexual labor. At the same time, Corregidora defined the range of their sexual activity along racial lines. While white men could purchase access to black women, black men were not allowed to have any kind of sexual activity with black women. As Great Gram recalls, "he didn't wont us with no black mens. It wasn't color cause he didn't wont us with no light black mens" (124). Simultaneously, then, Corregidora was creating the boundaries of racial definition and racial privilege — who was black, who had access to black women's sexuality — while regulating the sexual desire in the social relationships he was promoting. Black women were prohibited from having sexual relations with black men and prohibited from developing anything but sexual relations with white men since Corregidora forced his slaves to "make love to anyone, so they couldn't love anyone" (103–4). As was the case in the United States in the seventeenth century, this racial schematic was meant not only to produce "blackness" as a virtual absence but also simultaneously to create "whiteness" as a state of privilege and power.[39] Black men denied access to black and white women were forced to see how their thwarted desires and the limitation on their sexuality were defining characteristics of their "blackness," while black women were racialized by being made subject to sexual domination and losing whatever subjectivity they could exercise in directing their own desires. By having open access to black women, meanwhile, white men were able to ascertain the unlimited range of their forceful desires and to see sexuality as a form of racial domination, thus defining the imperial power of "whiteness." It is worth noting that Corregidora would get "mad and beat" anyone who doubted his authentic whiteness by suggesting that his dark complexion made him look "like one a them coal Creek Indians" (11, 23). The point Jones is making by showing us the historical connection among the governing of desire, the patrolling of sexuality, and the racialization of the populations of the New World is that "color" is a register and not a cause in the production and distribution of power. Corregidora denied sexual access to "light black mens" as a way of defining the privileges of "whiteness" along lines of power, not color. The slaves who might have been tempted to think of Corregidora as "colored" were quickly disabused of this notion, just as they learned to define as "black" even those slaves who were "as light as [Corregidora] was" (124).

Having set the historical conditions of racial formation in relief, then, Jones asks pertinent questions about the ways the contemporary state and the descendants of slaves continue to recreate this policing of desire, commodification of sexuality, and racialization of lived experience. She traces how this reenactment of the disciplines of plantation culture occurs in both the legal institutions of the white state and the discourses of the black community. We saw how Corregidora was able to inscribe race onto the bodies of his slaves by governing their desires and defining their sexuality in commercial terms. He is supported in this strategy by the state's police and legal apparatus. When a black woman attempts to resist her commodification, refuses to prostitute herself, determines that her desire for her husband is more important than her subjection to her master, the police punish her by viciously reasserting the sexual claims of the state on her body and the governance of her desire. When a black man frees his wife by purchasing her, the law makes that relationship one of commercial ownership and reclaims as property what the man thinks of as romance (150–51). The novel shows us also how in the present the state's legal and police apparatus continue to reinscribe race onto the bodies of people of African descent, but it is less through the institutional channels than the informal discourses of the society that this reinscription occurs. It is true that when a crime occurs involving the body of a black woman, the police "put it in the nigger *woman* file, which mean they ain't gon never get to it" (134); but Jones attends less to ways the formal state apparatuses define sexuality, desire, and race in contemporary America and concerns herself more with how these ideas get rearticulated within black community discourses.

It was the state that had auctioned off Mutt's great-grandmother as a piece of property, but it is Mutt who threatens to auction off Ursa as a sexual commodity (159–60). It was the master Corregidora who prostituted his slave Great Gram, but it is her husband Martin who makes Mama "walk down the street looking like a whore" (120–21, 184). In the past, the state and slave masters defined the parameters of racial identity (who was white, who was not); in the present, black communities deploy color as a gauge to determine inclusion. Ursa recalls poignantly those scenes where she is called out on account of her coloration and her long hair. In Bracktown she is called a "red-headed heifer" trying to take "everybody's husband away from them" (73). In Hazard, Ursa "feels resentful" when people suggest that she is not black enough, that she could "pass" or that she is racially "mixed up every which way" (70, 80). Certain people befriend her only after she marries someone darker than herself (69). The point Jones is making here is that black community discourses, relations between black women and men, and among black women alone, have bought into the racial schemas formed on the plantation and reenacted in contemporary state apparatuses. It is this kind of black communal thinking that Gram says is the "wound" slavery "put in our minds" (72). This is the "wound" Jones holds up by showing us how contemporary social relations continue to recreate debilitating ideas about racial identity by regulating black women's desire and commodifying black women's sexuality. After all, Mutt threatens to auction off Ursa as a "piece a ass for sale" immediately after he has tormented her by denying the demands of her desire (159). Like Corregidora, then, Mutt controls Ursa's sexual desire at the same time as he commodifies her sexuality and rearticulates the site of her racial identity. The auction block, in this novel as much as in the first African American novel, *Clotel*, is a point of the convergence of discourses about sexuality, desire, and race.[40]

It is crucially important to note that Jones does not demonstrate how white hegemonic values established in plantation culture infiltrate and pervade black community discourses in order to argue that black men have replaced white men as the immediate oppressors of black women, as some of her earlier critics believed and criticized her for believing. Rather, Jones shows that "the past" which some cultural nationalists had facilely dismissed as having nothing to do with the present and the future is and remains an integral part of the ongoing search for African American liberation.[41] Not to acknowledge the "wounds" of slavery would be to leave them festering; not to address the ways subjections of the past get rearticulated in the present is to let them retain their force. For that reason, Jones dwells on the ways the past forms the present, demonstrating the overt and hidden ways that those mores created in slavery continue to be refurbished and refined as part of the lexicon of "race" in modern America. By exposing these complex historical continuities that have both psychic and institutional manifestations, Jones draws the connection between the "secret" of the family and of the nation. Having shown how what she calls Black Power's "new strictures of exclusion" have become part of the black community's ways of defining race, and demonstrated how this racial formation is intricately involved in the regulation and policing of sexuality and desire, Jones posits for us a solution to the "national secret" akin to the solution Ursa had employed for her "family secret."

The ways a contemporary descendant of slaves can contest this process of subjection, of being subject to a prohibitive racial formation with rigid definitional boundaries circumscribing sexual desire, is to perform as a subject of desire. The way to heal the wound is not to ignore but to cauterize it; the way to deal with the effect of the past is likewise not to transcend or forget or even to continue to speak incessantly about it but to reenact it, to perform it with a difference. Drawing on Gram's hints regarding the instability of memory, Ursa had solved the family secret by reliving it, by drawing on other episodes from history to recontextualize it, and ultimately allowing herself to perform that scene in a new and liberating way. Drawing on her recognition of the historical basis and therefore the pliability of racial identity, Ursa likewise shows us that the solution to the national secret is neither to accept nor to deny the strictures of the past but to flaunt them in a different kind of reenactment that simultaneously accentuates the performed quality of desire, sexuality, and racial identity. For Jones, the blues — with its "strategies of remembrance," its connection of "individual and group experience," and its capacity for "carrying us beyond the apparent stereotypic"— constitutes the cultural form best suited to that performance.[42]

Critics of *Corregidora* have early and long noted that the novel is a compelling portrait of a "blues relationship," an intensely profound representation of a "blues life," and a remarkable set of observations about the generational creation of one family's blues song. Ursa uses the blues to compensate for her inability to "make generations" by producing "generations in song" and using "her mouth as her mother and grandmothers used their wombs," creating in effect in the blues a "surrogate daughter who bears witness" to Corregidora's legacy. The blues also allows Ursa to go through a process of reconciliation both for herself, by making "the necessary claims of kinship with her past" while achieving "a degree of separation from it," and with Mutt, by learning that "justice is not a blues solo of ambivalence or alienation, but a healing communication between reconciled lovers." [43] Given the various functional roles the blues plays in the novel, then, what seems most striking about the representation of the blues is that the "new world song" that adequately captures the sufferings of the Corregidora women and allows Ursa to achieve for herself what Jones calls "whole and consummate being" is largely nondiscursive (59). While the songs help Ursa "explain" what she "can't explain," the blues do this "without words, the explanation somewhere behind the words" (56, 66). The blues Jones represents in *Corregidora*, it seems to me, is functional not so much because it is expressive or communicative through verbal facility but because it is performative. "What's a life always spoken, and only spoken?" Ursa asks (103). For her, life is not to be cast into a discursive narrative form but to be lived, history not to be answered with another verbal construct but to be rendered suspect through an extravagant performance. The blues, for Jones, is performative because it is a cultural form generated less for reflection and more for change. The "internal strategy of the blues," she approvingly quotes Sherley Anne Williams, "is action, rather than contemplation," and, we may add, for Jones its mode appears to be performance, not articulation. [44]

First, it is important to note that blues is *work*; in other words, not just expressive as a form of communication, but performative as labor. Jones makes a crucial point concerning the ways the blues operates in the social and economic arrangements of a nation whose primal labor arrangements are based on slavery. Blues singing as a career represents Ursa's financial independence from Mutt, who insists he married Ursa "so he could support" her (3). As a form of social production and means of gaining access to a salary providing her with economic autonomy, singing is Ursa's way of challenging the conditions produced by slavery, especially the processes through which black women's labor capacity was exploited and their sexuality commodified. The African American women in *Corregidora* realize that American culture provides twentieth-century women with few socioeconomic opportunities that don't replay that plantation dynamic. For them, prostitution, real or symbolic, is one of the few things "you can do to keep your own hours" (30). Nobody better understands that than Cat Lawson, who most clearly sees the ways that the American labor market prostitutes black women who are either subject to sexual harassment as domestics or physical hazards as factory workers (29–30, 64–66, 176–77). Because singing the blues is Ursa's career, her form of cultural production and thereby her form of contributing to the social and economic market, it is a talent providing her with an alternative to the dangers of factory labor and the frustrations of domestic labor, giving her a degree of freedom in controlling her labor and her body in a way that other women don't have.

But the blues in this novel does not simply free Ursa and leave other black women subject to the forces of American institutional life. What is most important in the blues, Jones argues, is that they contest primary ideological premises in the national narrative that make sex into commerce and black women's bodies into fungible items. In performing the blues, Ursa challenges the dominant racial formation and its inherent process of subjection inherited from slavery and rearticulated in contemporary social relations. Having shown that the enracing of black women largely occurred through the commodification of their sexuality and the coercion and control of their desires, Jones goes on to demonstrate how the performance of an unfettered sexuality and a liberated desire provides an answer to and a way of undoing the historical legacy of that enracing process. The blues performance gives Ursa what it had given black women singers historically — an opportunity to produce a "truer sexual self-image," explore the historical "black female sexual experience," and become the "primary subject of her own being." As several black feminist critics have noted, the classic women's blues singers of the twenties used their performances to contest the "objectification of female sexuality within a patriarchal order" and reclaim "women's bodies as the sexual and sensual subjects of women's songs."[45] Following in their footsteps, Ursa also uses her singing to reclaim her sexual subjectivity and express the range and breadth of her desire. In one particularly resonant moment, she uses the blues to resist the fetishistic way Mutt commodifies her sexuality when he talks about "*his* pussy" as the "center of a woman's being." She performs for him and informs him that "I sang to you out of my whole body" (46). Her desire, her sexuality, is not centralized and not subject to his control, his fetish, or his possession, and she informs him of this by performing with her whole body, not just singing with her voice.

It is in the final scene, though, that we see how the blues most explicitly contests the racial formation that emerged out of slavery and gets rearticulated by those who continue to commodify black women's sexuality. At the end of the novel, after the final scene in which Ursa alludes to the ideal of Palmares as a social space where black women and black men had positive healthy relations, after both Mutt and Ursa reenact but creatively deviate from an ancestral scene of enslavement, the two lovers "replace the ambiguity of language and the pain of violence with a direct exchange of feeling" as "both characters sing" a blues song of reconciliation.[46] This song, the only time Ursa sings a duet, is about the connection among desire, sexuality, and racial identity. In the final blues duet, Mutt claims, "I don't want a kind of woman that hurt you" and Ursa responds, "I don't want a kind of man that'll hurt me neither" (185). This exchange signals the beginning of reconciliation between Ursa and Mutt, while raising questions about the historical source of desire (who "wants," how are we taught to want) and the pain (the "hurt") of coupling both historically and in the present. Most important, it also raises the dilemma of identity (what "kind" of man or woman a particular history and social circumstances produce for romantic coupling). In this blues duet about a "blues relationship" between a black women and a black man in 1969, the culminating moment in a final scene that had been insistent about the replaying of the past in a different measure, we see how performance, especially the blues performance that demonstrates the historical connection among desire, sexuality, and racialization, enables or at least promises the possibilities for undoing that racial formation.

The blues performance, like Palmares as a symbol of resistance, also promises the positive consequences of resisting and undoing that racial formation, for the blues performance is a cultural form that likewise provides a forum for the creation and sustenance of the same kind of healthy intersubjective relations produced by those familial narratives about slavery. Ralph Ellison had remarked on the "feeling of communion" that emerges when the "spirit of the blues" is able to "evoke a shared community of experience." Jones, too, notes that "the blues and blues vocabulary" of African American life produce, or can produce, a "unifying effect, which brings a sense of wholeness to the individual, not in solitude . . . but in communion." As Jones asserts, the blues "pulls together and asserts identity (self and other) through clarification and playing back of experiences and meanings." It is a process neither seeking a static end-product nor a form of communication premised on the idea that what is communicated is some tangible thing, some identity that is complete. The "playing back" is the constant state of performance on which experience and the search for identity are premised; the fact that "self and other" are imbricated in this search tells us that the blues performance is capable of producing a state of "intersubjective" communion, providing a forum for the "'I' voice of the blues" to merge with that of the ancestral "other," producing what Houston Baker calls the blues's "energizing intersubjectivity."[47]

The blues performance, then, like the performance of history, challenges the codes and categories through which one can understand the experiences of the past and the politics of the present. The sexual and racial categories inherited from plantation culture can be contested through the blues because it is a productive cultural formation. Like the family narratives, to which it is so closely aligned throughout *Corregidora*, the blues performance produces an enabling version of the past and reproduces a healthier set of resources for the reconstitution of the desiring subject, because the blues also follows the practice of the family narratives in contesting the representations of a desiring subject either utterly freed from or utterly imprisoned by the past. Both forms of oral narration and self-representation attest to the palimpsest imperative in Jones's work, the desire both to share the story of enslavement and to demonstrate the strong but not disempowering hold the slave past has on contemporary social relations.

In the case of *Corregidora*, the palimpsest imperative serves Jones's intent of creating a work that challenges the nostalgia and amnesia Americans conventionally exhibit toward the past. Slavery is neither unrelentingly a series of horrors effected on unresistant victims, nor is the time before slavery ("the old country") or those places of respite from slavery (Palmares) spaces where patriarchal black men ruled over submissive black women. Slaves could be resistant and people of African descent could form relationships premised on parity and equality, freed from both the slavery of European masters and the master-slave dialectic that governs those social relations. But Jones also shows us how that master-slave dialectic is pervasive and enduring, how it occupies too central a place in contemporary social relationships, and how it still structures both inter- and intracultural intimacies. Jones's achievement, it seems to me, is to have reformulated the form of the palimpsest narrative in order to raise questions about the performative nature of identity, both for the individual who learns to tell stories of family and sing songs of desire in order to recognize but not become defeated by the brutality of the past, and for the community which Jones would have become more inclusive (dispensing with what she calls those "new strictures of exclusion") by undergoing an honest reassessment of those institutional forces that continue to exert power over social relations in contemporary America.

3

The
Stillness
That
Comes
to All
The Subject
of Death

About to undertake a history of the local black community for the Bedford county bicentennial in 1969, Harriette Jackson Bradley asked her husband, a trained historian, how she should proceed. He told her to "go to the graveyards and the courthouses," the courthouses because they "preserve everything" as repositories of historical documents and the graveyards because they are literally where the bodies of history are buried. When David Bradley recalls this exchange between his mother and father, he notes that graveyards and courthouses are "the two places that people don't lie."[1] It is a funny comment, of course, delivered in Bradley's typically wry way, because in courthouses people are in fact prone to lie and in graveyards they lie prone. At a deeper level, though, the Bradleys, father, mother, and son, are all making a serious and crucial connection between sites of archival documentation and sites of burial. We can think of each of these sites as a "domain," that is, a "particular site of production of discourse, a specific semantic field."[2] The courthouse is a domain of privileged official records and data, while the graveyard is a domain of unofficial and subterranean information. Both are places that contain varying qualities of knowledge from which to generate narrative accounts of the past. In *The Chaneysville Incident* — which has at its heart the story of the thirteen fugitive slaves whose graves Harriette Jackson Bradley discovered in her historical research — David Bradley meditates on the problematic of producing historical knowledge respectful of variously valued domains, the official and the unsanctioned, while exploring the deep and complex relationship between historical inquiry and death.[3] Death, in Bradley's novel, is a subject affecting verbal and narrative representation, an event conditioning and demanding familial reconstruction, and an idea defining cultural and racial differences.[4]

The Chaneysville Incident is literally structured around and suffused with scenes of and ideas about death and burial. The novel begins with the historian John Washington called back to his hometown to attend his dying surrogate father, Old Jack Crawley, whose death about midway through the novel gives impetus to John's familial-historical research into the death of his biological father, Moses Washington. The rest of the novel has John seeking to understand the meaning of his father's death, who, it turns out, committed suicide in 1958 on the same spot his own grandfather, C. K. Washington, committed suicide in 1858. The novel is structured to begin with John's memory of his father's funeral, attended by everyone "old enough to respect death and young enough to walk to meet it," and end with John's narrative of the deaths of the twelve other fugitive slaves who commit suicide with C. K. Washington to avoid recapture and to escape enslavement when they come to understand that "the Stillness That Comes To All, that they called Death, was not an ending of things, but a passing on of spirit, a change of shape, and nothing more."[5] Burial likewise plays an important structuring role in the novel, which begins with the funeral of John's father, has the burial of John's surrogate father at its center, and ends at the graveyard of the twelve fugitive slaves and John's great-grandfather. In addition to showing the significance of burial sites to familial reconstruction, Bradley also makes clear the connection he is drawing among death, burial, and history. According to the historian

John, each individual's death has a history (about his brother's death, he comments: "It goes back a long way. Most murders do"), and history itself is a process, as he describes it, of finding out "where they hid the bodies" (279, 186). And, finally, Bradley likewise makes clear the connection among death, burial, and race. John shows how graveyards are sites of final racial marking ("in my home town, white people and black people aren't buried together"). Indeed, the very idea of racial difference, emerging in and through the African slave trade, is ultimately about "something so basic, so elemental, so fundamental that it can be faced only if one is forced to face it: death" (75, 208).

Death is not only basic, elemental, and fundamental in this novel. As it is in other cultural representations, death is also always about "something else," as Kenneth Burke wrote in a thesaurus of "the 'deflections' that the idea of death reveals as a literary topic."[6] In *The Chaneysville Incident*, Bradley uses death as the subject around which he organizes and through which he negotiates the relationship amongst three interrelated symbolic systems — narrative, family, and race. In terms of its representational strategies, then, *The Chaneysville Incident* is about the role death plays in what we can call *symbolic relations* — that is, systems of communication, systems of kinship, and the interconnectedness of these two systems of relation. Bradley is concerned with showing us the role death plays as a signifier in the primary symbolic systems we use to communicate (language and narrative). He is also concerned with showing us that family itself is a symbolic entity necessarily reconstituted and rearticulated in the event of death and in the social act of burial. Since death, as represented, is a "deflection" of language and a destabilization of families, or, to put it another way, since death occasions and produces a social and discursive *refraction*, the act of burial becomes a stabilizing strategy of using that refraction in the structuring of family narratives and the reconstruction of families. Finally, Bradley also exposes the ways cultural ideas about and attitudes toward death and burial are part of the apparatus of racial formation in the American state.

The main objective in Bradley's representation of death and burial in *The Chaneysville Incident*, then, is to explore how death — as term, idea, and representation — operates in cultural and personal narratives concerning the symbolic nature of families and the performative quality of racial affiliation. Bradley gives a nice finishing touch to his meditation on death and historical narration by having his narrator respond to the discovery of his great-grandfather's emancipatory suicide and his father's sympathetic suicide by committing a "symbolic suicide"—an apt ending for a novel so thoroughly concerned with the social and cultural meanings of death and the performative quality of cultural identities. John's symbolic suicide, which I will describe and discuss more fully in the final section, aligns him with his paternal line, and, by implication, his racial community because of its implied attitude toward death ("not an ending of things, but a passing on of spirit"), while simultaneously communicating to his white fiancée, Judith Powell, that he has related her presence into his familial narrative. In the end, John's symbolic suicide shows how transgenerational family secrets require of their would-be inquisitor the capacity for understanding the essentially symbolic nature of familial ties and racial identities. To see how death in *The Chaneysville Incident* operates on the three symbolic systems Bradley chose to explore, then, we need to begin by examining in what ways death and burial have been understood as significant discursive events in the lives of individuals, families, and societies.

A Cultural Grammar of Death and Burial

Even though death is about as "universal" a phenomenon as one could possibly hope to locate—Hegel says that the "universality which the individual *as such* attains is *pure being, death*"—ideas about death are as diverse as ideas about any other phenomenon in a multicultural world system. Despite multiple beliefs about death in different societies, most social historians have generally noted two distinct attitudes about death in world cultures. Phillipe Ariès has argued that although there are five main themes in the evolution of Western attitudes toward death—the tame death, the death of the self, remote and imminent death, the death of the other, and the invisible death—the major distinction marking "ways of not thinking about death" occurs between "traditional" and "technological" societies.[7] In either kind of society, death creates a crisis in discursive and narrative representation, which is closely related to and necessitates a burial that allows the family of the deceased to reconstitute itself.

Although, as Frederic Jameson notes, the "idea of death in a fragmented and individualized society" is "far more frightening and anxiety-laden than in a genuine community, in which dying is something that happens to the group more intensely than it happens to the individual subject," in both societies discourse about death involves various forms of subterfuge.[8] In a "technological civilization," there is a denial of death and a refusal to talk about it. In "traditional civilizations," there is "not a denial but a recognition of the *impossibility of thinking about it directly or for very long* because death is too close and too much a part of daily life." In either kind of civilization, the attitude toward death involves a certain kind of willed ignorance and a distinct strategy for avoiding direct thinking or talking about the subject — strategies for indirection or refraction, we might call them. As Vladimir Jankélévitch notes in his study *La Mort*, death inspires modesty because of the "unthinkable and untellable quality of the lethal state." This "modesty" is eventually transformed into a taboo: "Is not the taboo word *death* above all others the unpronounceable, unnameable, unspeakable monosyllable that the average man, conditioned to compromise, is obliged to shroud modestly in proper and respectable circumlocutions?" Ironically, while humans find death "untellable," we yet apparently find it something necessary to tell in whatever indirect ways we do talk about it. Our attempts have taken two forms, according to Ariès: "The first attempt to mask unnameable reality made use of rhetoric; the second has resorted to silence."[9]

Before Ariès and Jankélévitch offered their observations about the relationship between death and discourse, Kenneth Burke had written with his usual acumen about the function of the "unpronounceable, unnameable, unspeakable monosyllable" in the realm of human communicative norms. In defining humans as "symbol-using animals," Burke noted that the one "ingenious addition to the universe [that] is solely a product of human symbol systems" is "the negative." Following Hegel's pronouncement that the "moment of negation, insofar as it is posited as natural, and is a determinate aspect of natural being, is death," Burke proposes that there are "no negatives in nature" except "Death itself [which], as the privation of Life, is the Great Negative." Burke comes to the conclusion that "Death" is the most intimate problem in the issue of representation since it is both the only negative in nature and something incapable of being represented by anyone who has experienced it. Therefore, he concedes, the "imagery of Death" challenges the fundamental principles of representational art: "a poet's imagery is expected to deal with positive experience, yet no poet who has experienced death can return to tell the tale."[10]

The tale does get told, however. Indeed, if there is such a thing as a twice-told tale, surely that tale must be a tale of death. In fact, the very desire to produce and consume narratives — which Jameson calls the "central function or *instance* of the human mind" — is closely linked to the final instant of the human mind. One literary theorist suggests that narrative is always indirectly about death, the very function where we mark our ambivalence toward death. On the one hand, "narrative keeps the idea of death constantly in front of us," while on the other, "narrative communication is a constant denial of death." Perhaps, as Walter Benjamin has suggested, we as human readers like "warming our lives upon a death about which we read." Not only does death prove to be an appealing subject for the consumer of stories, but death is in fact intrinsic to the production of narrative, not only because an individual's "real life — and this is the stuff that stories are made of — first assumes transmissible form at the moment of his death," but also because the dying person's body "imparts to everything that concerned him that authority which even the poorest wretch in dying possesses for the living around him." This "authority is at the very essence of the story," notes Benjamin, and therefore "death is the sanction of everything that the storyteller can tell."[11]

The reason death marks so important a place in issues of representation and narrative is that "death" is essentially an open signifier, and the dead individual, as Hegel puts it, becomes an "empty singular, merely a passive being-for-another." The dead individual is someone whose story gets told by another, someone who becomes an absence sanctioning another's narrative authority. This kind of vulnerability — an exaggerated and permanent manifestation of the vulnerability to daily and lifelong misrepresentations — leaves the deceased open to what Hegel describes as those "forces" that had "sought to unloose themselves against him and to destroy him." The only agency able to prevent or undermine the abuse of the "empty singular," the only means of saving the dead individual from being dishonored by those who would exploit that story, is, according to Hegel, "The Family," which makes the dead individual "a member of a community which prevails over and holds under control" those destructive forces of misrepresentation.[12] The site where this first happens is the graveyard. Burial is the first act the family undertakes in its attempt to make the deceased an addition to the community of the dead and yet a member of the community of the survivors. The family, in other words, controls the representation of the dead individual through a social act which lays to rest the deceased while also articulating the structure of the family, now both actively absent a member and yet expanded by its memory of a temporally extended kin. We see, then, how Western thinkers from Hegel to Ariès draw out the connection among death, representation, family, and burial.

We find this same complex of ideas, with differing accents, in African, African-derived, and African American beliefs about death and burial. Margaret Washington Creel noted that both the BaKongo in Zaire and the Gullahs in South Carolina believed that death was not an end but rather a transitional state that promoted and made possible the restructuring of families. The site where this happened in African societies and in African American slave societies was the graveyard. In his study of African cultural survivals in America, Melville Herskovits concluded that "no belief drives deeper into the traditions of West African thought" than the belief that the "funeral is the true climax of life." Students of traditional African systems note that for most African cultures a proper burial is the *sine qua non* for becoming an ancestor deserving of veneration," while a student of slave society in South Carolina notes that "funerals were the real climax of life, the time when one was reunited with one's ancestors." What made funerals so important for both African and African American slave societies is that burial was an act that created ancestors at the same time as it recreated family. "The ancestral cult revolves itself into a few essentials — the importance of the funeral, the need to assure the benevolence of the dead, and, in order to implement these points, concern with descent and kinship." [13] Burial, then, was both a way of marking the decedent's return "home" and the way of defining "family" as an entity with reconfigured forms involving people living and dead.

Since slaves were defined as "natally alienated" or "socially dead" (to use Orlando Patterson's terms), one of the main ways of resisting the imposed definition of their status was for them to construct a symbolic family based on "fictive kinship" systems. As Patterson points out, slaves "differed from other human beings in that they were not allowed freely to integrate the experience of their ancestors into their lives, [or] to inform their understanding of social reality with the inherited meanings of their natural forebears." Because the slave was deracinated from any sense of "family," the slave was defined as a "socially dead person" alienated from all "'rights' or claims of birth." In the case of American chattel slavery, the "social death" of slavery began with the middle passage. It is worth noting that those Africans who literally died during the middle passage flew "home" to their families, while those who survived were defined as "socially dead" *because* they were alienated from any sense of family. Given the conditions of American slavery, then, family for African slaves became as much a matter of social construction as of biological ties. According to Herbert Gutman, the "conversion of kin relationships into symbolic (or quasi-) kin ties" began during the middle passage and continued in the formation of the slave community. "Community ties based on quasi-kin connections emerged, flowing upward and outward from the adaptive domestic arrangements and kin networks that had developed over time among the slaves." And, as Charles Joyner notes, the American slaves' creative notions of family were "mediated by the cultural grammar of African familial traditions."[14] By defining their own African family structures and by placing themselves within these quasi-kin networks, the African slaves were able to construct symbolic families and therefore subvert their definition as "natally alienated" and "socially dead."

In his slave narrative, Charles Ball recounted the story of a child's funeral that shows the survival of the African belief in the importance of the proper burial to ensure the departed person's journey home. The child's father, who was a "native of a country far in the interior of Africa," believed "that after death they shall return to their own country, and rejoin their former companions and friends." The funeral of the child was meant to be emblematic of this belief. The child's "father buried with [the child], a small bow and several arrows; a little bag of parched meal; a miniature canoe, about a foot long, and a little paddle (with which he said it would cross the ocean to his own country)." More important, the father also included "a piece of white muslin, with several curious and strange figures painted on it in blue and red, by which, he said, his relations and countrymen would know the infant to be his son, and would receive it accordingly, on its arrival amongst them." A proper burial had to mark the deceased person's status as a member of a living family in order to ensure his reception into the proper family and community when she or he arrived home. But burials are also about the reconfiguration of the surviving family members and "the extent to which they allowed the participants to feel themselves a human community unto themselves." A funeral on the plantation figured prominently "as a religious ritual, a social event, and an expression of community." Like the practice in what Robert Hall calls "traditional African societies," funeral rites "were often occasions for celebration, creating an intensely renewed sense of family and communal unity among the survivors." For slaves, one of the places where such a "renewed sense of family" was inaugurated was not at the physical or "partial" burial of the departed, but at the "second" or the "definitive burial." At those second burials, slaves recreated their familial bonds.[15]

Although the idea of death differs significantly between "traditional" and "technological" societies, and likewise between Western and African belief systems, we do find, nonetheless, a somewhat shared complex of ideas about death as the event that causes refraction, family as the community in which that refraction is realized, and graveyards as the domain where that refraction is put to constructive use. Burials become the social acts through which families commemorate their departed in order to give meaning to their deaths and restructure their families in order to change the meaning of death itself.

Representing Death

The Chaneysville Incident is likewise deeply interested in exploring the ways death forces family members to stage burials that stabilize meaning in their lives and genealogies. Bradley adds to this his fascination with the way death also refracts systems of representation. Bradley demonstrates how important it is for the family (or at least for certain family members) to tell the story of their own dead in order to understand the meaning of death — both as a general phenomenon understood in cultural terms and as a specific event in the life of the family. But death itself, he shows, is an idea and event that troubles the very verbal and narrative systems of communication with which to do this. One of the major points of the novel is that John will remain unable to understand the meaning of his father's death so long as he relies on the words written on his cards and the narratives he weaves from the information on the cards, because death is an "incident" beyond and subversive of the communicative protocols John inherits. We can begin our examination of the ways "death" is problematized in *The Chaneysville Incident* by comparing it to a novel that similarly plays with the terms and idea of suicide as a symbolic communion with the ancestors.

At the end of Toni Morrison's *Song of Solomon*, Milkman Dead calls out to his friend and would-be assassin Guitar Bains: "You want my life? . . . You need it? Here." "Without wiping away the tears, taking a deep breath, or even bending his knees — he leaped. As fleet and bright as a lodestar he wheeled towards Guitar and it did not matter which one of them would give up his ghost in the killing arms of his brother. For he knew what Shalimar knew: If you surrendered to the air, you could *ride* it." As numerous critics have noted, the conclusion to *Song of Solomon* is irreducibly ambiguous about Milkman's fate, leading at least one reviewer plaintively to ask: "Does Milkman survive to use his new knowledge, or does he die at the hands of a hateful friend?" Some critics, perhaps even most, have maintained that Milkman leaps to his death even as he establishes that his death is relatively unimportant given what he has achieved. Milkman's act of flying for them is "life-affirming even in the moment of death," and his "enlightenment, no matter the cost, is well worth the trip." But perhaps the question we seek to have answered is the wrong question. Given that Morrison is casting her novel's ending in the form of what Gay Wilentz calls an "African dilemma tale" — a narrative generated by a belief that the "many slaves who committed suicide . . . flew back to Africa" — the reader ought to be keenly aware that "death" might not mean what the reader thinks it means or the "dominant culture" ordains it to mean. Maybe the question, then, is "not whether Milkman lives or dies; rather, the question is whether Milkman dies or flies." In other words — in fact, in the words Morrison herself poses in her preface to *The Harlem Book of the Dead* — because the fact of "death" does not occur with the physical demise of the body, but only with the failure of later individuals, families, and communities to remember the ancestors, the idea of "death" does not signify the end or absence of an individual but rather the moment when one flies to or communes with the ancestors. As Morrison says in *Song of Solomon*, when "you know your name, you should hang on to it, for unless it is noted down and remembered, it will die when you do."[16]

The Chaneysville Incident appeared four years after *Song of Solomon*, and critics immediately noticed the numerous connections between the two texts. Both novels have families in which a father names his children by arbitrarily "sticking his finger into the Bible." Both focus on children who seek out stories about their parents, grandparents, and great-grandparents in order to discover how their ancestors' lives determine and direct their own. Both novels take form around an individual who discovers a family secret and comes to understand an ancestral belief at the same moment that the individual dies, either materially or symbolically. Moreover, both make a connection between storytelling as the art of remembering and death as the act of forgetting. Finally, both novels develop and promote a belief system with a set of values about the meaning of death for peoples of African descent in the New World that challenges the beliefs and values of those who abide by what Bradley's narrator calls "the European Cultural Tradition" (208). And toward that end, both novels suggest a change of terms for the material or symbolic act of taking one's own life. What is significant about Morrison's achievement is the way she has recast Milkman's "flight," which would be a suicidal move according to one set of values, into a liberating act according to the set of values the novel endorses, a set of values in which Milkman "symbolically transcends death by embracing flight."[17] Morrison culminates her negotiation of the dialogue concerning the idea of "death" in European and African belief systems by changing terms. So, too, does Bradley.

Consider the scene in which Judith refers unsympathetically to John's possible wish to kill himself as an act in which he might either "take that gun and blow [his] head off" or else use the gun to "blow [his] brains out." Judith here actually echoes the way John himself had talked about his father's suicide once he discovered that his father had not been murdered. After John discovers the reason behind his father's suicide, he changes the terms of reference he uses to describe the event. Rather than saying, as he had done earlier, that "Moses Washington blew his brains out" (322), John starts talking about his father's act as a form of "hunting." For instance, when Judith rephrases what John says — "You're saying that because C. K. Washington died there Moses Washington committed suicide there?" — John corrects her: " 'No,' I said. 'Not suicide. I was wrong about that. We were all wrong. Everybody thought it was an accident. The Judge thought it was a murder. I thought I had discovered it was suicide. But what it really was was a . . . a hunting trip. That's where he said he was going. That's what he told his wife, and that's what he told Old Jack: he was going hunting. And that's what he did' " (388). When Moses Washington set out for the spot where C.K. was buried, he was not "looking for a grave," as John tells Judith. "He was looking for a man. That's what he was looking for all along. He knew when he came here that C. K. Washington was dead; if he wasn't he would have been a hundred years old. So he was looking for his grave or a skeleton or whatever the same way a hunter looks for a hoofprint, or bedding grounds, or signs of feeding or droppings — it was a spoor. And when he found it he did what any good woodsman would do; he put himself into the mind of the game and headed off after it" (388).[18] When Judith responds with bewilderment at the thought of a person's killing himself in order to pursue his dead forefathers — "'That sounds . . . crazy,' she said. 'You're talking about a man chasing after ghosts'" — John again changes the terms with which they can talk about his family's history by changing the terms as they signify for cultural history: "No . . . Ghosts isn't the right word. Ghost is a word that was invented by people who didn't believe, like the names the Spaniards gave the Aztec gods. Ancestors is a better term."

What John does, then, is inform Judith that "death" does not signify equally for all cultures — in either its "literal" or its "figurative" terms. Not all cultures talk about "death" by using that word; not all cultures mean the same thing when they talk about "death" (whatever word is used). In changing terms from "suicide" to "hunting," John transforms the meaning of death, which he now reconceives of as no longer an end of life (and thought) but a process of discovery. Likewise, in changing the terms of the departed from "ghosts" to "ancestors," John alerts Judith to the ways death can be understood as either a final or as a transitional state, which in this book marks the difference between European and African belief systems about death.

The change in terms, the understanding that death is not an event that can be referred to with a stable verbal signifier or one understood to have a stable transcultural meaning, is part of John's growing realization that death causes a rupture in personal and historical narratives, and that narrative itself is a form of coded communication which requires the auditor's attending to the social forces impinging on its telling. This is especially the case when John receives stories about death, particularly the story on which the novel focuses most insistently, the tale about the death of the twelve fugitive slaves. When Old Jack tells John the story of the fugitive slaves "who had begged to be killed rather than be taken back to bondage," he concludes by cautioning against a hasty judgment regarding the facts of the case or the courage of the fugitives. Old Jack pointedly tells John that "you don't want to be judgin' folks too quick, or too hard." Although the most widely believed version of the story about the fugitive slaves reports that they "begged to be killed" because they were "too scared to fight, too scared to run, too scared to face slav'ry, too scared even to kill their own selves," the story an African American ought to generate from the known facts should be one attentive to his or her own social conditions. As Old Jack puts it, while it may be acceptable for "[w]hite folks" to tell the story in this way, an African American historian should generate a more nuanced and informed narrative because a "colored man oughta understand what it coulda been like" for the fugitive slaves, "white folks all around you, an' no place to turn" (63). Old Jack performs such a narrative himself by concluding that he "doubt[s] the killin' part of it" because he believes "they ain't dead" and "they ain't ghosts," but they are rather part of the atmosphere, the very air of South County.

Immediately after he recalls Old Jack telling him this story in his youth, John hears another story from the now-dying Old Jack in the present that reinforces the lesson about the need to decode a narrative produced within conditions of duress. Informing John of the reasons his first haircut occurred in a town forty miles from his own, Old Jack explicates for John the rituals the adults had employed to hide the Town's racist practices from the children. As Old Jack tells John, when the group of elders in the African American community discover that a young boy is ready for a haircut, they devise a system for saving the boy the humiliation of going to the covertly racist Town barber and hearing from him that he did not know how to cut black people's hair. Instead, the elders "worked it out like it was some kinda ceremony" and constructed a ritual narrative explaining why every boy's first haircut had to occur in Altoona, a town forty miles away (65–66). Upon hearing all this explained to him, John feels that "things that [he] had never really understood were suddenly coming clear" (66).[19] His own past starts to make sense now that he has received additional clues as to why some things were done certain ways. By placing John's personal life into a social context, Old Jack shows John how a larger structure transforms the stories a family tells itself or a community of elders tells its initiates. Racist social practices cause a mutation of familial and communal narratives of the past; the only way to decipher those narratives so that they make sense is to reassemble them with an eye toward accounting for the modes of refraction. Like the stories a community tells itself when it is in a state of oppression, history also offers sets of connections that are never obvious and always require retrospective knowledge and imagination; and this is especially so when one deals with the cultural narratives that involve the meaning of life and the afterlife.

Bradley's point is that understanding the past (the task of history), especially when one wishes to see in what ways the past inheres to and helps form the present (the task of the palimpsest narrative), requires a deep appreciation of the crucial role death plays in systems of communication. Because death is unnameable, the exemplification of the Negative, because it is a metaphor for the "deepest structure of narrative discourse as a circuitry of constituent absence and structuring summons," and, primarily, because it causes a rupture in signifying practices and a refraction in narrative performances, death can be said to inhabit systems of communication as the singular moment toward which all signifying tends and in light of which all narrative is transformed.[20] In this novel, tales of the operation of racism can be understood only through other tales more explicitly about death, which, in turn, expose the ways death functions more generally in communication. After all, the story about the fugitive slaves and their death turns out to be a story about how they are *not* dead, which, according to the ideas about death this novel holds, would make sense to someone who believed that death is "a passing on of spirit, a change of shape, and nothing more," but would be nonsensical to someone believing death is "an ending of things." It would communicate effectively to someone who believes in "hunting" and "ancestors," but not to someone using the vocabulary of "suicide" and "ghosts." What Bradley is doing, then, is demonstrating not so much the irreducible indeterminacy of language in the face of death but rather the ways various cultural understandings of death coexist in different ways in verbal and narrative representation. Yet his aim, as I show in the next two sections, is not to argue that certain cultural inheritances prohibit some (say, European Americans) from comprehending the social meanings of others (say, African Americans), but rather to demonstrate the precise ways that death provides meaningful possibilities for cross-cultural communication, because it is, especially in the act of burial, closely aligned to ideas of family.

Symbolics of Burial
As we saw above, historians of Western and African traditions of death have shown how burial provides a moment not only for mourn-

ing but also for coherence, a time not only to remember the departed but to gather the remaining members and reconstitute them as family. Lucille Clifton, for instance, gives us a superb example of the process through which a contemporary subject uses the burial site to create and recreate her family connections. In her *generations: a memoir*, she shows us how the occasion of her father's death and burial causes her to return to the earliest-known member of her family, the slave Caroline Sayles, who was born in Africa in 1822 and passed on in Virginia in 1910. Clifton, then, rehearses the genealogy of the family from Caroline to Clifton's grandchildren, tracing the ways that restructuring family history after the departure of one of its members allows for the making of fictive, symbolic kin, what Clifton describes as the modes by which different families *"began to be related* in thin ways that last and last"* (my italics). What we have in Clifton's work is the need to use the occasion of a burial to create and recreate the genealogy of a biological and a symbolic family. That is what returning "home" means for Clifton. The "homeplace," as Marilyn Nelson Waniek adds, is indeed comparable to a "visit / to the grave of a known ancestor." There, at the burial site, she contemplates "generations, lost to be found, / to be found." The only other "homeplace" she has, like Clifton, is in her symbolic "second family."[21]

By structuring his novel through a series of informative representations of burial and graveyard scenes where families gather and are gathered, and by arguing for the deep and abiding complexity of linguistic and narrative systems when it comes to understanding death, Bradley clearly hints at the relationship between systems of communication and systems of kinship. What links the two is what I have been calling *symbolic relations* — that is, narrative acts (relations of stories) that produce acceptance of familial bonds (kin relations). Burial is the site where symbolic relations are most pointedly enacted, as the family deals with loss by generating a narrative that redefines the new boundaries of the familial structure. At Old Jack's funeral, for instance, John's mother, Yvette Stanton Washington, steps forward and tells a narrative of Old Jack's relationship to her family which produces a symbolic familial network, in which Old Jack becomes related to her as she declares him a "brother to my husband" and a "father to my boy" (217). For Bradley, the act of burial is even more meaningful, though, because it provides the characters in his novel with an opportunity not only to reconstruct families, but to do so while reflecting on their family secrets which play a crucial role for the characters in dividing or consolidating what is signified by "family."

As with the other writers producing palimpsest narratives, Bradley argues that seeking out the meaning of the past requires dealing with not only the meaning of the lives and deaths of departed ancestors but also the family secrets those ancestors consciously or unconsciously passed on to their progeny. In *Corregidora*, we saw how Ursa was haunted by an event in the life of her great-grandmother that could be solved only when she undertook a sexual adventure that replicated her ancestor's actions. As Nicolas Abraham and Maria Torok note, the living descendant is oppressed by the silences and gaps created by ancestral actions which continue to haunt the later generations of a family line. We can gauge the gravity of this oppression by the fact that Abraham and Torok chose to describe it by employing the language of death. Their psychoanalytic project is called "cryptonomy." Its premise is that when psychoanalysis converts silence into speech it conjures up "the concealed lives of the dead whose undetected machinations unhinge the minds of the living," and the terms and concepts they use ("crypt," "phantom," "intrapsychic tomb") are drawn from the language of death, afterlife, and burial. Indeed, psychic illness represents the "existence of the dead buried within the other," while psychoanalysis is a laying to rest of the dead who "continue to lead a devastating psychic half-life in us."[22] And in their reading of literary texts, they seek a work, like *Hamlet*, which presents not only "the effects of a transgenerational haunting," but is also set as "a vast graveyard scene in which the context for a hypothetical secret has remained buried."[23] What makes Abraham and Torok's theories especially useful for a reading of *The Chaneysville Incident* is that Bradley, as much as the other novelists in this study, deals with family secrets that imprint themselves in behavioral patterns of later generations. Even more important, though, he, more than any other novelist in this study, represents a contemporary subject who has to deal with and act on the discovery of a death and a burial in order to create a space for the reader to understand the transgenerational aftereffects which reveal themselves in John's symptomatic and cryptic silences.[24] For John, like Hamlet, the buried speech of the family secret gets unearthed in a graveyard.

At the end of the novel, having discovered the thirteen graves of the fugitive slaves and John's great-grandfather next to the "Tiames family plot," Judith asks John: "Who buried them?" (430). It turns out that Richard Iiames, a white miller, on whose land they died, buried the thirteen fugitives next to his "family graveyard" and "with the same spacing as family stones" (431). This graveyard scene — which Bradley elsewhere calls "the funeral chapter"— provides John with a final opportunity to reach some kind of resolution about both the racial dynamics that divide him and Judith and the family secrets that connect his family to Judith's. In his various comments on burial scenes, Bradley makes three especially pertinent points. First, as we saw in the anecdote he tells of his mother's conversation with his father, graveyards are sites of truth telling. Second, one of the main points in the novel as a whole, which he sees resolved in this "funeral chapter," has to do with the relationship between history and imagination, between what facts exist and to what pragmatic purposes those facts can be put by the historical imagination. Third, Bradley notes that Iiames's act of burying the fugitives serves as an analog for John's historical imagination, since the "pattern" of the gravestones "allows him to reconstruct the family structure and everything else."[25] In this final graveyard scene, then, John comes to understand the deep meanings behind the fact that Iiames buried his great-grandfather, and what significance that fact holds for his relationship with Judith.

The problems of the relationship between Judith and John are social, in the specific ways interracial romantic relations are in this society, historical, in that John insists on telling stories about the difficulties and travails attendant on interracial romances in the American past, and familial, since there is a connecting set of family secrets in the Powell and Washington families that threaten to disrupt this relationship entirely. The Powell family secret has to do with familial connections of which the family is not certain. The Powells trace their ancestry to John Powell, a captain on the *Seafoam*, which, her father insisted, came into the James River in 1620, the same year as the *Mayflower* reached New England; they do not seek to verify the ancestral connection, beyond the fact of a shared name, because Judith's father fears learning that Joseph was "no relation at all," and Judith fears learning that the *Seafoam* might have been a slave ship (241–42). Meanwhile, John has information about the Powell family exploits that he feels radically undermine their relationship, and which he holds in store as a weapon he feels at times impelled to use against her (242). He feels the greatest desire to hurt Judith with this information about her family — "to tell it all to her" — when he is most insecure about his own family secret, which involves the conditions and the meaning of his father's death (380).

Here is where the figure of Iiames becomes important to the relationship between John and Judith, because of the connection between the Iiames and Powell families. Critics have noted that the historical figure of Iiames allows John to escape his habit of lumping "all whites other than Judith into one pile," and also creates the possibility for a form of "racial cooperation" that has a historical precedent. It is also worth noting that John makes the connection between the Powells and the Iiames on the basis of historical "facts" (such as they are). In fact, it is this very connection between the two families on which he had based his previous desire to use historical facts to destroy his relationship with Judith. When he had held her family's past as a weapon he could use against her, he thought how it would pain her to hear "all about how Richard Iiames had come with Joseph Powell, grandson of Thomas, brother of John, captain of the *Seafoam*" (380). Judith's relationship with the Powell family line, of course, is the family secret Judith had mentioned to John. Now, John is using the connection between the Powells and the Iiameses as a way of historically connecting his family with the Powell family. In other words, John's attempt to achieve a reconciliation with Judith and her past by imagining a historical narrative emphasizing connections between past and present is not altogether as fanciful as almost all the critics suggest. It is not just a product of "imagination." There is at least some warrant for thinking of the two families as being involved in some ambiguous way.[26]

Iiames's act of burying the dead is an apt conclusion to Bradley's symbolic representation of the African idea of deathlessness — both of spirit and of history. Moreover, John learns that a burial site is the place where narratives are also constructed and transmitted. Iiames does not simply bury the bodies of the fugitive slaves. He takes the time to distinguish which bodies belong together — who are spouses, who parents — because he believes it matters "to figure out who loved who" and for relatives to be buried together (431). All this John figures out by noting that the fugitive slaves are "buried with the same spacing as family stones." By reading burial sites, John shows us the connection between discourse and burial grounds, and how, in this novel, graveyards are places where discourses are shared. When John concludes the story of the fugitive slaves' suicide, he notes that they sang a song: "And before I'll be a slave I'll be buried in my grave, and go home to my God and be free" (430). It is the very same song Moses Washington had requested to be sung at his funeral in a "letter giving strict instructions about his burial" (21). John recalls that although this was a song "Moses Washington had hummed . . . for as long as I could remember," it was a song whose words he "had never heard before" until his father's funeral (21). By incorporating a song he first heard at his father's burial into a story about his great-grandfather's death, John makes the connection Moses Washington was teaching him to make. Graveyards in this novel are places where shared discourses produce shared relations, where the song sung at one funeral becomes the song imagined in another, where the story of one man's death becomes a paradigm for understanding another's life.

Moreover, Iiames's act of burying the slaves in an order that shows the familial relationships amongst them is a symbol of his own attempt to resuscitate their stories. His act can be seen as a form of narrative enactment of the significance of the fugitive slaves' lives. In a novel in which suicide is liberating, burial, it appears, is reanimating. That, too, is a logical corollary in a cultural pattern in which we have a basic belief that death is not final. In an interview with Gloria Naylor, Toni Morrison noted that her desire to write a narrative about slavery was truly a desire to invoke all those people who were "unburied, or at least unceremoniously buried," and to go about "properly, artistically, burying them." The purpose of burying them, though, is to bring them back into "living life."[27] Narrative, according to Morrison, is both burial and revival. Like Iiames, John makes an effort to discover the stories, the connections, behind the suicides of the fugitive slaves and his father. In addition, to take further what Bradley implies in saying that discovering the "pattern" of the gravestones allows John "to reconstruct the family structure and everything else," I would add that from Iiames John also learns that family structures are capable of being "reconstructed."

Iiames's act not only signifies his faith that death is not the end of things and demonstrates his belief that burial is a site of narrative reconstruction — both of which things John learns — but it also substantiates his basic conviction that familial connections are fluid and capable of being reformed. Iiames had earlier signified for John the irreparable breach between the Powell family and his own; after discovering Iiames's role in the story of the fugitive slaves — a story his father and his surrogate father had told him — John makes Iiames symbolize the connection between the Powells and the Washingtons. Iiames, after all, not only buries the fugitive slaves with the same spacing as family stones; he also buries them right next to his own "family graveyard." The figure of Iiames's burying the fugitives in an order that closely resembles their familial patterns is a figure highly similar to what John is doing in his narrative version of these events. He is artistically burying the unburied and also reformulating familial ties. Just as Iiames constructs familial ties that might or might not be biologically provable, so does John assert that familial ties are social connections based on historical and symbolic acts. One is not simply a member of a familial community or tradition by blood, but by emotional investment.

That, in a word, is the most basic idea behind what I have been calling *symbolic relations*. John realizes that the only way he can proceed in his research and discover the connections between disparate pieces of evidence relating to the deaths of his father, his great-grandfather, and the fugitive slaves is by telling the story orally to Judith. What he has to do is relate the story of his past and his family's past to the person who represents his future and his future family; and the narrative relation is somehow involved in the familial relationship. Bradley's novel offers us an exemplary study of how "relations" are social constructs based on shared narratives, particularly narratives about death. What Bradley does in *The Chaneysville Incident* is offer a meditation on how narrative relations of death form kin relations in three distinct ways. First, only by telling a story about his father's and great-grandfather's deaths can John discover how people whom he has either not known well or not known at all are part of his family; here narrative relation clarifies biological kin relation. Second, by telling this story about his family members' deaths to his fiancée he invites her to become part of his family; here, narrative relation produces a fictive kin relation. Finally, by telling this story in the context in which he tells it, by attending to the role Iiames is playing in his own and in Judith's family narratives, John refigures the past in such a way as to reconstruct his sense of family; here narrative relation reconstitutes both biological and fictive kin relation. What all three forms of "relation" have in common is that they are all about death. A tale about a family member's death is a way of communing with that family member as well as a way of restructuring the very sense of "family."

Race and Mortality

We have seen so far the various ways Bradley represents death as a rupture in linguistic and narrative patterns and a refraction in familial histories. The rupture in systems of communication required a change of terms — from "suicide" to "hunting," from "ghosts" to "ancestors" — which indicated different cultural traditions divided along racial lines. The refraction in systems of kinship required the creation of symbolic forms for incorporating people of different races into one familial network. What, then, is Bradley saying about race itself, and, to be more specific, what is he saying about the relationship between race and death? Bradley, I suggest, acts on the palimpsest imperative by showing us the ways death originally came to and continues to inhabit American racial categories since the Atlantic slave trade. As Gayl Jones had done in *Corregidora*, in tracing the ideas of thwarted and racialized desire back to New World plantation culture, Bradley shows us the origins and trajectory of American racial thinking and demonstrates the foundational role death has played in the creation of and resistance to what can only be called a New World racial epistemology.

Like the other writers in this study, Bradley is contributing to an ongoing dialogue about race in the post–civil rights era; moreover, he largely articulates his position against a vision of race that found favor in the nationalist moment in the Black Power era. In the last chapter we saw how Gayl Jones challenges what she calls the "strictures of exclusion" imposed by the cultural nationalists she knew, and we will see in the next chapter how Octavia Butler radically critiques the ideas about race she encountered in her college years at the height of the Black Power movement. Like Jones and Butler, Bradley, too, came of age during the late sixties, attending the University of Pennsylvania in the early seventies, where he found himself disenchanted with theorists of the Black Aesthetic and displeased with the black nationalists. In an epiphany he had in 1971, he found himself troubled by the fact that "in the sixties the worst thing to say about somebody was that they forgot they were black." Instead, he came to believe that the society and world "we were all supposedly working for was precisely one in which that could happen sometimes." Nonetheless, it was clear to him that, in the present social order, forgetting one was black was impossible (fatal even, he suggests) because American society was still too much pervaded with institutional racism for race not to matter.[28]

Since that realization, he has meditated on the problematic of race and racism, first in the ten years he spent writing *The Chaneysville Incident* and then in the ten years he has since spent writing a non-fiction book, "trying to get at the question of why we have racism." In that nonfiction work-in-progress, Bradley is seeking to examine the ways the "tropes of racism" can be traced back to American colonial writings, especially those of Jefferson and Franklin, and the ways that racism spread "like an epidemic" through the subsequent course of American history. His ultimate hope, he says, is to discover the origins of racism in order to disrupt its foundational place in American intellectual discourse and social life, and ultimately to work toward its demise and therefore enable the vision of the world he had glimpsed in his 1971 epiphany. In *The Chaneysville Incident*, I think, we find the same intellectual presuppositions and engagement, namely Bradley's interest in origins, to "find out who victim zero was," and his hopes for a dramatic social transformation, to "isolate the disease vectors and do something about treating it."[29] The metaphor in the novel, though, was not of disease but of death; and the origins not colonial American intellectual production, but rather the Atlantic slave trade which made possible that intellectual work. In the novel, as he hopes to do in the nonfictional study, Bradley demonstrates how racism is coupled with and infects American economic and political structures by showing the ways it originates in an initial religious conflict between African and Western world systems concerning the idea of death and then the ways it developed in later interracial "incidents." Moreover, and most important, Bradley there is also seeking to substantiate the ways that the rise of American racialist thought (or, to put it another way, the creation and recreation of a discourse of white supremacy) has been resisted, especially by African American trickster figures who expose the premises and flaws in that discourse.

In *The Chaneysville Incident*, Bradley traces the origins of that discourse to the Atlantic slave trade, a historical event not only and not primarily a matter of economics and of shifting balances of power in the emergence of industrial capitalism, but also foundational to the development of the "European Cultural Tradition" and its two premises and outcomes: death and race. The slave trade "was all about . . . death itself," John notes, because "black people did not die" before "the white men came to Guinea to strip-mine field hands" (208). Prior to the slave trade, because African decedents "took up residence in an afterworld that was in many ways indistinguishable from [their] former estate" they "cannot really be said to be, in the Christian sense of the term, dead" (208–9). At the same time the slave trade imposed Christianity on its victims, and introduced death to people of African descent in the Americas, it also created the rudiments of race. As John notes, European notions of class ("master were masters because they were members of a master class") gave way in the face of an egalitarian idea of a classless society to notions of race ("masters were masters because they were racially European") (211).

Death and race, then, were introduced through the same global process, and have since dramatically affected linguistic preferences, epistemological processes, and social behavior. As John notes, the idea of African immortality continues to exist in African American language, since "no matter how light-skinned and Episcopalian a black person is, he or she will never tell you that a person has died. 'Passed away,' perhaps. Or 'gone home.' But never died." At the same time, the introduction of death to people of African descent in the New World creates an irresolvable tension between practices of faith and intellection, between what John calls his "European knowledge" that "death is cold and final" and his "African belief" that the suffering wrought out of the slave trade and slavery—"*all* of it—is still going on" (213). Finally, in such a society where modes of speaking and understanding are racially bifurcated, modes of behavior, particularly modes of resistance, were likewise affected by the prevalence of racism. In a slave society, where domination was structured along racial lines, and in a postemancipation but nonetheless oppressive society where race remained the major form of social demarcation, attempts to resist enslavement or oppression took on one of two forms. In the first, those of the disfavored race attempted to assimilate themselves into the norms and, when possible, appearances of the favored. As John puts it, an African wishing to resist enslavement "could aspire to change his lot by becoming like" the white enslavers, while an African American escaping oppression in the twentieth century could "pursue the physical and cultural appearance of the Europeans at every opportunity" (211–12). In the second form, resistance took and continues to take on the form of exaggerated renunciation of so-called European values, norms, and appearances, culminating in the kind of cultural nationalism Bradley found confused because of its insistence on construing a social and aesthetic system that dramatically distinguished "black models" from "European form[s]," and failed to see the social interconnections and cultural interbreedings that made those terms too facile to describe a complex social reality.[30]

John, in many ways, exemplifies those very features of cultural nationalism that Bradley wishes most to challenge. He believes, for instance, that racial positioning is an inviolable prohibition regarding issues of comprehension; he claims that "certainly" a historian cannot "understand the African Slave Trade . . . if he is white" (207). He thinks of whiteness as a "horrible skin disease" and rapes a woman because he "looked at her and saw white" (73, 75). For him, history is a set of atrocities for which he "hates" and "blame[s] white people . . . because they're white" (75). I do not think Bradley is simply condemning out of hand what John represents, nor do I think he is suggesting that black people must stop hating for and thinking of a past that is atrocious. Instead, Bradley seems to be arguing that John's resistance to American racism takes on many of the characteristics of exaggerated renunciation of things European and makes too easy a division of experience between black and white, a practice that is itself derived from the discourse of white supremacy. So, when he believes that a person is incapacitated from understanding a social phenomenon because of genetic basis, or that a person is the sum of his or her skin color and therefore deserving of punishment for that, John is essentially resisting American racialist thought on its own terrain. This is a primary tension in John's thinking. He desires an easy system of marking race as an impermeable property with historical continuity while simultaneously recognizing that there is a long history of cultural, genetic, and social intermingling that has irreducibly complicated any such system. He begins to achieve a *rapprochement* between his contradictory desires when he starts to forego that primal one dividing his "belief" and his "knowledge" along continental lines, when toward the end of the novel he begins to "know and believe" and therefore be able to "imagine" the past (402).

Part of what allows him to accomplish this integrity is his understanding of the ways that race has been recreated through the nation-state's activities and simultaneously been resisted by black trickster figures who challenged those social structures without succumbing to their dictates. The several narratives John remembers, hears, and generates have to do with the ways race gets formed through historically sequential but essentially interrelated events like slavery, Klan activity, and national imperialism. There is, after all, a deep connection between C.K.'s dying in an effort to escape enslavement in the 1850s, Josh White's and Jack Crawley's near-death experiences at the hands of the Klan in the 1920s, and Bill Washington's failure to get an educational deferral and his subsequent death in Vietnam in the late 1960s (279–81). In each case, the state used legal apparatuses, social vigilante groups, and the educational and military structures to define what it tried to show as the immediate and permanent division between races. John had rebelled against his brother's death by raping a white woman; in essence, he, like Eldridge Cleaver, on whose experiences this episode is based, had already too deeply imbibed the racialist thought of the nation and could respond only in kind to America's racialist discourse. What John learns from other narratives of the past is that there are ways to resist white supremacy without accepting its premises.

After saving Josh White from a Klan lynching because of his attempt to marry a white woman, Moses Washington rejects Old Jack's simple explanation of why the Klan operates ("white folks ain't noted for feelin' kindly towards colored folks") and his likewise facile suggestion for potential responses ("go in there an' start beatin' on everybody white"). Instead of responding in kind — that is, by injuring any white person because white people in general weren't "too particular about which nigger they started in on"— Moses Washington chooses to explore what he calls the "politics" of racial violence. He wants to punish the specific individuals who committed the crime and understand the role of the crime in maintaining racial equilibrium in the society (110). Likewise, C. K. Washington thinks about the politics and economics of slavery in order to transform what are otherwise individual and isolated acts of resistance into a collective enterprise that structurally undermines the entire social order. Neither C.K. nor Moses Washington succeeds in dismantling American racism, obviously, but both succeed to the extent that they do not replicate its practices but do trouble its primary premise of a strict division between black and white. Moses Washington is reputed to be white because of his ruthless resistance to the law (53), while C.K. passes for white as he organizes political campaigns in the North and steals octoroon prostitutes from the South (331, 347, 350, 358–63). Both, in other words, flaunt the primary division in the social order by showing that the boundaries are neither natural nor altogether effective in regulating social movement. The stories of transgressing race lines, of thwarting racial projects like slavery and lynching, and, especially, of choosing death over submission, are tales of trickster figures who playfully expose the ineptitude of the imperialism of American racial thought. In other words, what Bradley chooses to emphasize in the history he tells in *The Chaneysville Incident* is the uneven terrain of white supremacy, showing not a seamless set of conquests and acts of domination giving power to one side of the racial divide, but rather the ways that trickster figures, like his father and his great-grandfather, challenge the premises and practices of the enterprise of defining the force whiteness would wield, the power it would carry, in the changing social order from slavery to Vietnam.

From these stories, John must learn to reconsider his desire for an essentialist system of racial classification, where those who are black look, speak, and think in a particular way and those who are white in another. It is neither necessary nor altogether efficacious to challenge the "possessive investment in whiteness" by investing in its most problematic presuppositions. What John learns at the end of the seventies is what Bradley learned in his epiphany at the beginning of the decade — that being black in America does not depend on defining white incapacities, or in creating a hierarchy among blacks where color and religion are regulated and indicators of authenticity ("no matter how light-skinned and Episcopalian a black person is"). He has to confront the fact that his great-grandfather was light enough to pass because he had genetically more white blood than black, and to accept that he himself had "underestimated" Judith because she was white and therefore "cheated" both of them of a meaningful relationship (331, 411). Again at the end of the novel, and again largely mediated through the figure of Iiames, John expresses his renunciation of that essentialist system and begins to respect the possibilities of a world, both in the past and in the future, where a person could forget his or her race through performing a set of actions indicating either belief in or rejection of a set of cultural imperatives.

In the history John imagined from the slave trade to the present, white people did not understand the deeper meanings of the past, were responsible for the atrocities of history, and remained culpable to the extent that they remained white. Black people, meanwhile, inherited a preferred linguistic usage to talk about death, were largely victims of historical atrocities, and were marked in segregated places, ultimately even in death. By the end of the novel, though, John has to face the fact that black people in his family defy these imperatives while white people like Iiames and Judith act on what he defines as African cultural principles. John's grandfather, the "fairly prominent black mortician" Lamen Washington, rejected a knowledge of his familial past by burning his own father's book in order to prevent Moses Washington from knowing anything about C. K. Washington (368– 69). Such an act, with its implied denial of history and familial connections and its violent treatment of African American documents, shows how invested Lamen was in his Europeanist beliefs about life and death; just as Iiames's act of burying the fugitives in an order resembling their familial connections shows how invested he was in an Africanist belief about the significance of burial and afterlife.[31] The capacity to know something and the willed preference to speak in a certain idiom are not essentialist inheritances but rather cultural developments. Not all black people, even in his own family, respect ancestors; not all white people are disabled from recognizing and acting on the Africanist principles respecting the immortality of the decedent. Having shown how white supremacy was created at the same time as death was introduced in the slave trade, John learns from the narratives and actions of his father and great-grandfather that it is possible to contest the premises, the categories, and the stability of American racialist discourse by resisting its impulses to think of "race" as unalterable difference, and "family" as a site of reproduction of that difference.

Symbolic Suicide

So far, I have been arguing that *The Chaneysville Incident* represents the ways death impacts and affects three interrelated systems — language, family, and race — showing how each of these systems is symbolic and capable of sustaining "relations" that are equally symbolic. By changing the terms one can use to talk about death, from the literal "suicide" to the symbolic "hunting," John is altering Judith's vocabulary and alerting her to the ways symbols operate. Likewise, when he accepts Iiames's symbolic act of burial as a historically meaningful moment of reconciliation of sorts, John signals to Judith in another symbolic gesture that families are open and fluid structures capable of being reconstructed on new grounds. Finally, when he recognizes the functional means by which his father and great-grandfather deviously challenged American racial practices, John learns to forego a model of race that is inflexibly essentialist and accept a model based on symbolic actions of cultural affiliation. The novel, then, is as immersed in ideas of symbolic communication as it is in ideas about death; and that connection between death and symbols, I suggest, should alert us to the deeper meanings behind the ending of the novel. In the final scene, John gathers up all the "tools of his trade, the pens and inks and pencils, the pads and the cards," and makes a pile of them in the snow, pours kerosene over the pyre, "making sure to soak the cards thoroughly," and sets fire to his written records of historical facts relating to his family's past (431–32).

Bradley has suggested that his book is "really a detective novel" with an enigmatic ending which he claims to have "encode[d]" so that the reader has to "make of it what [he or she] will."[32] What most published readers have made of the ending is that John's act represents his successful resolution to three major tensions: 1) in his career, between imagination and history;[33] 2) in his family, between embracing or fleeing his ancestral legacy; and 3) in his political sensibility and his personal life, between indiscriminately hating white people for the atrocities of the past or more carefully distinguishing the blameworthy from the relatively blameless.[34] Recently, critics have begun to suspect that a novel so fully engaged with the exploration of death, especially self-inflicted death, might actually end with John's own suicide attempt. Albert Stone and Cathy Brigham argue that the "novel's enigmatic conclusion" could be read to say that John is "contemplating suicide" and that he will "immolate himself" along with his research records, although both Stone and Brigham add that Bradley "does not explicitly endorse this suicidal response to American life."[35]

John, I would argue, is not about to kill himself; instead, he is enigmatically signaling to Judith that she is both right and wrong in her earlier speculations about his desire to "go hunting with the old men, and sit around the campfire drinking whiskey and telling lies" (389). She is right in noting that he will commune with his ancestors in his own fashion. She is right to see that John wishes to become part of the ancestral line in which his father and his great-grandfather both left this world by acts of their own hands when they came to understand the African belief that "the Stillness That Comes To All, that they called Death, was not an ending of things" (428). She is wrong in thinking that he has to "blow [his] brains out" to do it. Instead, John performs a *symbolic suicide*—or what Shoshana Felman and Dori

Laub call a "substitute for suicide"—by which is meant the performance of an act that indirectly or metaphorically signifies the taking of one's own life.[36] For John, and for many an academic I would imagine, his suicide is symbolically represented by his act of burning his research tools.

Felman and Laub describe "suicide as the recognition that what has been done is absolutely irrevocable, which requires one in turn to do something irreversible about it." In describing acts that symbolically represent such an "irreversible" act, they speak about what they call "substitutes for suicide," that is, ways of encountering and negating an unforgivable past by acting on one's symbolic selfhood with some form of radical will. "What appears to be an erasure of the past is in fact this quasi-suicidal, mute acknowledgment of a radical loss — or death — of truth, and therefore the acknowledgment of a radical loss — or death — of self: the realization that there can be no way back from what has happened, no possible recuperation." *Pace* what Boris Pasternak once suggested about actual suicide, that "a man who decides to commit suicide puts a full stop to his being, he turns his back on his past," this symbolic suicide is meant to provide the subject with a means of *reexamining* the past from the position of one who has indeed acknowledged "a radical loss — or death — of self." After his own attempted suicide, A. Alvarez came to recognize that "the youth who swallowed the sleeping pills and the man who survived are so utterly different that someone or something must have died." And he wonders "if that piece of knowledge isn't in itself a form of death." Antonin Artaud gives us a useful term for describing a symbolic suicide which produces this vista and provides a means for gaining that knowledge, calling it "an *anterior suicide*, a suicide which made us retrace our steps, but to the other side of existence, not to the side of death." Even while treading among the living, then, some who perform a symbolic annihilation of self can claim, with Artaud, that "it is certain that I have been dead for a long time, I have already committed suicide."[37]

At the end of *The Chaneysville Incident*, John's symbolic suicide signals precisely this animating message to Judith — that he has gone "hunting with the old men" and that he has returned — in answer to the question she had earlier asked and he refused to answer four times (389).[38] Bradley offers us a representation of a symbolic suicide as a way of working into his novel issues regarding the indirection that symbolic relations employ in resolving family secrets and in reconstructing families. Moreover, he is also saying something about how narrative form itself provides surviving family members with an opportunity to render meaningful the symbolic relations obtaining between the subject of the narrative (the decedent) and the subject of narrativity (the person to whom the narrative is told and who is "imbricated" into the narrative as subject).[39] For a narrative that explicitly and implicitly demonstrates how historical information is full of "gaps," how communal stories require decoding because they are transmitted in oppressive conditions, and all represented within a text endorsing the idea that death is not the end of life but an event that refracts the symbolic systems of language, family, and race, there is probably no more fit conclusion than a historian's symbolic suicide that alters the terms for death and a burial that augurs a reconstituted sense of family.

The fact that John is a historian allows Bradley easily to raise the primary question that motivates the palimpsest narratives, that is, the role the past plays in forming contemporary subjects and societies. Bradley has some ambivalence himself about this question. On one occasion, he has stated that history to him is "raw material, the past is raw material. We can't be governed by it." On another, though, he stated that "[h]istory certainly recurs," and that sometimes "people are constantly playing out the same sorts of tensions until they get them resolved," and, as in the case of his novel about the "Chaneysville" incident, sometimes the same kinds of things do tend "to happen at the same place," almost, he muses, "as if good or evil is located at particular places."[40] I think we can locate in *The Chaneysville Incident* that tension between not wanting to be governed by the past and realizing that history mercilessly haunts people and places. It is the same tension Bradley feels between his desire to have a world where racial identity is not such a singularly oppressive force and the profound recognition of just how pervasively this is the case now. For this is Bradley's point, I believe; it is never good or evil that is the resident genius of a place but the racial ideologies that are historically formed there out of catastrophic events (the Slave Trade) and daily recreated in the state apparatuses, in the economy, in schools, in cemeteries, and in families. Because of those racial ideologies, which inhere to and are played out in the systems of language and family, history does recur, the past does get revived in noxious ways.

The subject of death in *The Chaneysville Incident* becomes part of the strategy, arguably the most significant part, of Bradley's exposing and not completely resolving that tension, as it serves his project of showing the multiply complex ways the past operates in the production of the present. Bradley takes a Western idea of death as a rupture signifying the unalterability of the past and accents it with an African belief system in which death is part of a continuum from being born to becoming an ancestor. In that model, dying and death itself are part of a process of gaining knowledge about the past, just as Moses Washington seeks out death in order to search for his own ancestor. But that African belief also holds that the dying is never done, never completely and wholly in the past. It's still all going on, all still too much with us, all still the effects of an original, terrible event that introduced death to Africans and race to Americans and all the effects of both to African Americans.

4

Orphans
of the
One-Way
Voyage
The Subject
of Family

We have seen so far that there is a family secret at the heart of each of the palimpsest narratives that reveals the precise need for the narrator to return to a slave past and determines the paths taken in that return. In *Corregidora* and *The Chaneysville Incident*, the "return" is symbolic and takes narrative form. Ursa goes back to a primal scene in the life of her Great Gram and Corregidora to understand the ways desire and hatred coexist in a master-slave dialectic. She tells the story to herself while innovatively reenacting a version of it in her final sexual encounter with Mutt. In *The Chaneysville Incident*, John Washington constructs a narrative, using facts, records, and, finally, imagination, to tell Judith Powell the story of his ancestor's attempted and successful flights to freedom, while allowing him to understand the interracial dimensions of the American past. In both novels, the contemporary subjects (Ursa and John) either tell or act out the story while casting themselves and their lovers into nineteenth-century ancestral roles. At times, Ursa cannot distinguish between her relationship with Mutt and Great Gram's with Corregidora. There are moments in his narration when John picks up cues from Judith's affection in the present to describe Harriette Brewer's actions in the past, even as he uses his own contemporary motives to explain C. K. Washington's work as an activist historian. Octavia Butler's *Kindred*, too, has a family secret, and that family secret is also crucially related to Dana Franklin's "return" to a slave past. The difference, of course, is that in *Kindred* Dana does not return only symbolically to a slave past, but also physically, as she is transported six times from her Los Angeles home in 1976 to the Maryland home of her nineteenth-century great-grandfather.

The family secret at the heart of *Kindred* is that Dana's great-grandfather is a white slaveholder. Having sensed that there is a "blood relationship" between herself and the young boy able to call her back in time to save his life, Dana finds that this young boy would grow up to be the white man, Rufus Weylin, who fathers her grandmother, Hagar Weylin Blake. She recognizes the name of her great-grandfather because Hagar had written that information (the "family records") in "a large Bible in an ornately carved, wooden chest" (28).[1] What Dana finds out is that while the name had been "kept alive in the memory of [her] family," other pertinent information about the ancestry of the Weylin-Blake line had "died" with her grandmother, or, as Dana says, "at least it had died before it filtered down to me." This, then, is the family secret Dana must confront. Her most poignant question is: "why hadn't someone in my family mentioned that Rufus Weylin was white" (28)? Butler uses the occasion of Dana's family secret to generate a series of meditations on issues of purity and impurity, in families, in history, and in racial affiliations.

Butler's exploration of purity, the desire for it and the dangers of pursuing it, is very much a response to the sixties, and indeed she says that she was "really dealing with some 1960s feelings" when she wrote *Kindred*. Those feelings were primarily about the growing desire for purity marking the declining days of the New Left. The anarchist and Progressive Labor factions of the white New Left and the ultra-black nationalist factions of the Black Power movement created a mood where activists were judged by the purity of their motives, the purity of their actions, even the purity of their descent. The boundaries marking off raced, class-based, and gendered identities became firmer and less permeable. It was a time when activists in the Students for a Democratic Society (SDS) couldn't trust anyone over thirty because they believed them to have lost the purity of youthful idealism; those in the Student Nonviolent Coordinating Committee (SNCC) couldn't trust anyone who was a "bourgeois Negro" because they believed them to have lost the purity of racial authenticity. Those factions devoted to violent revolutionary ideals took over the leadership of SDS and rendered impotent anyone whom they found or cast as ideologically suspect. The same thing happened in the Black Power movement. So strongly marked was the desire of some in the leadership of SNCC for purity, which was understood as seamless ideological unity, that Stokely Carmichael would be applauded for saying that "we gonna off" those black people who "don't come home," at the same time as the Chicago Office of SNCC claimed that the way to deal with Uncle Toms was to "ostracize them and if necessary exterminate them" because those black people "do not represent us or even belong to the same black race." Those not so quickly excluded from being "black" or threatened with death for being insufficiently so needed to distance themselves from materialist Western culture by following the cultural and ethical imperatives of Maulana Karenga's *Kawaida* value system, which Amiri Baraka believed to be the only way of serving the "purest Black need."[2]

In examining this desire for "purity," Octavia Butler found herself deeply troubled by the ways certain Black Power militant intellectuals recreated pernicious racial schemas that were self-serving for the sixties activists themselves while misserving generations of black communities. When she attended Pasadena City College, she became concerned about the black nationalist movement because she was surrounded by "people who had gone off the deep end with the generation gap," people who felt "ashamed of, or more strongly, angry with their parents for not having improved things faster." She herself had felt that shame and anger as the child of a domestic worker who "blamed" her mother for taking the abuse her employers heaped on her. It was only later, when she recognized that her mother began her life in the 1920s as a worker on a sugar plantation in Louisiana barely "removed from slavery" and realized that the domestic work her mother performed in California kept them fed and housed, that she began to come to terms with her earlier shame and anger, and started paying attention to "what [her] mother and even more [her] grandmother and [her] poor great-grandmother . . . all went through." In the sixties, however, the dominant intellectual trends in black nationalism did not allow for the historicizing and contextualizing of the past behaviors of earlier generations of African Americans. Whereas Butler was drawing on her knowledge of her family's generational struggle for dignity and freedom, her black nationalist peers at Pasadena City College were seeing a rather more dismal connection between history and family. One fellow student told her: "I'd like to kill all these old people who have been holding us back for so long. But I can't because I'd have to start with my own parents." That moment, Butler claims, gave her the "germ of the idea for *Kindred*," and the novel itself is a result of those feelings and a response to that particular intellectual moment — an attempt for Butler to "resolve [her] feelings" about the shame she felt for her mother's apparent docility in the face of humiliating treatment, and an effort to deal with "some 1960s feelings" about the "generation gap." [3]

Her original idea for the novel was to take a character from the present "back in time to some of the things that our ancestors had to go through, and see if that character survived so very well with the knowledge of the present in her head." As she continued writing, however, the novel came to assume a rather different shape. What she ended up doing in *Kindred* is producing less a morality tale in which a contemporary black nationalist learns to respect the struggles and travails of past generations and more an exploration of the tensions, contradictions, and anxieties attendant on those who attempt to understand and try to accept the genuine impurities in American politics and life: impurity of desires, impurity of family, impurity of racial identity. Butler questions what Itabari Njeri calls a "vulgar, compensatory nationalism" that promises an anxiety-free quietude and is premised on undeviating loyalty to simple, ahistorical racial designations that suppress the complexity of any contemporary subject's genetic and racial makeup. She takes the opportunity of Dana's family secret to explore in what ways family and history are sites for racial formation and provide spaces for the recovery of a more complex and politically useful social subjectivity.[4] We can best begin an examination of Butler's take on these issues of purity and family by looking at how other African American writers have dealt with the historical fact of antebellum miscegenation in their families.

Studies in Whiteness

In her chronicle of an "American family," Pauli Murray wrote about what she called "the unremitting search for whiteness" in families of mixed descent. Researched and written in the early 1950s, and first published in 1956, *Proud Shoes* contains Murray's representation of the effects of social conditioning on people of African descent in the period from just before the Civil War to just before the civil rights movement. She emphasized the ways continuous oppression, generation after generation, led to the inevitable belief that "*whiteness* — the ability to pass unnoticed in the crowd, the power to avoid humiliation and abuse — was one's most immediate and effective protection" in a country where neither law nor social custom gave justice or relief to people of African descent. Given those pervasive social conditions, people in her family chose to pass when they could, boasted of the advantages of their light skin to their darker kin, and lived lives of deep anxiety at the fear of being exposed by family or atavistic genes. The person who stands out in *Proud Shoes* as the most curious example of anxiety and bewildering ambivalence is Murray's maternal grandmother, who exhibits a strange mixture of commitment to her African American family and an abiding nostalgia for the glory of her slaveholding ancestors. Her grandmother, Murray noted, "sailed back and forth like a shuttlecock between the extremes of her own dual legacy as half slave and half slave-owning Smith," between that half of her enslaved because of one color and the other half empowered because of another. Whether it was motivated by a "search for safety," a "quest for acceptance," or a desire to be part of the glorious and mythical American past, Murray's family more often claimed than denied the whiteness in their mixed heritage. "It did not matter how far back the mixture took place or whether the proportion of white blood was great or small. There needed only to be evidence of the mixture." "To deny that it is a part of one's heritage," she concludes, "would be like saying one had no parents."[5]

Later family histories, generated out of the civil rights and Black Power movements, tend to represent an entirely different set of desires in African American families. Dorothy Spruill Redford, for instance, wrote about how the Black Power generation utterly repudiated that "search for whiteness." Redford did not seek evidence for connections to white ancestors. Instead, she claimed that she had no desire to "know anymore" because she "could not bear the idea that [she] might have white blood inside [her]." She rationalized to herself that whatever phenotypical features she possessed that didn't seem transparently and genuinely African—"my high cheekbones, my almond eyes"—were products of an imagined Native American ancestry. Like Redford, Jan Willis also sought to disaffiliate herself from her white ancestors, and not to acknowledge her light skin as the product of a history of miscegenation. There is no ambivalence here, only thoroughgoing expression of "embarrassment and shame" at discovering "white ancestry" in her family line, feelings of "dirt" and "pollution" at having to acknowledge that her maternal great-grandfather was white. For Willis, the specter of "white blood so generationally close" was almost unbearable, making her feel sick ("The whole thing *turned my stomach*") and cancerous ("There were, literally, 'white' blood cells living inside of me that were out of the closet and out of control").[6]

Both Redford and Willis work through these feelings of alienation and illness and achieve some kind of personal coherence by situating themselves in a historical enterprise made possible by their own excavation of their family narratives. Redford quickly discovered that "recovering a lost heritage" required her to "find the white connections" since they were the sole means of tracing the lives of African American slaves. Once she set out on this project, she found herself transformed, no longer feeling "hatred" toward white slaveholders but rather a profound and "uplifting surge of a need for our black family to come together" and "move forward in love." In the end, she organizes a homecoming for the progeny of both the slaves and the slaveholders of Somerset because she had realized that "we can live with the past without being dragged down by it." Willis, too, recognized that the formidable task she set for herself of tracing back her family line through all eight lineages of great-great-grandparents required her to take a "cold, hard look at [her] direct white kin." Finding solace in her Buddhist beliefs, consoling herself with memories of the black kin she had found and located in her lineage, and aware of the need for considerable "healing," Willis sought a homecoming like Redford's, although hers had less to do with a physical space like Somerset and more to do with what she describes as the need to "find a way to accept my self, and to love, *me*."[7]

One of the key issues raised in these family narratives is purity. Redford decides to trace her lineage back through her mother's rather than her father's line because, while her father's "line led to a white man," her mother's line was "pure." "Her people were all very tall, very dark. They could take me all the way home." It is only later that she recognizes the interconnectedness that makes purity a notion both false and futile. It is a hard lesson to accept, however. Even though she knows very well that this "sort of *purity* cannot be found — not amidst any living race of people" — Willis nonetheless feels polluted, shamed, dirtied, and victimized by the impurity of origins she finds in herself. To know that we are, all of us, as humans, genetically impure, mixed in deep and complex ways, does not calm the uneasiness we feel about racial impurity as a stigma, nor remove the desire we have for stable and singular origins. One commentator on Alex Haley's *Roots* noted that 88 of Haley's 256 six times great-grandparents were of European or Native American descent. So, even as Haley was attempting to trace his familial origins back to a very specific and local place in Gambia — and even as "*Roots* tells its readers of the ultimate origin in general, the source, the root, the *terminus ante quem*: who you really are" — Haley himself had to deal with the fact that more than one-third of his ancestors do not have African origins. Purity, as this commentator notes, "can only ever be tentative," the product, in fact, of highly selective acts of memory, questionable processes of retroactive affiliation, and circumscribed family narratives.[8]

In 1978, while recollecting the feelings she had when forced to confront the "ghosts of the past" in her family narrative twenty-two years earlier, Pauli Murray felt a sense of relief at no longer being "constrained by suppressed memories." She began to see herself as the "product of a slowly evolving process of biological and cultural integration," a "New World experiment, fragile yet tenacious, a possible hint of a stronger and freer America of the future, no longer stunted in its growth by an insidious ethnocentrism." Looking back at her mid-1950s book from the other side of the Black Power movement, Murray found prophetic her 1956 resolutions to live with and celebrate the multiracial origins of her own family. After what she calls the "intervening stages of pluralism and ethnic consciousness" of the 1960s and early 1970s, America, she sensed, was preparing to accept a complex past and to dispense with a desire for racial purity. Two centuries of "criss-crossing of racial lines and recirculation of genes within designated races" makes highly questionable the very "notion of racial purity." To accept "the possibility of relatedness," she felt, would "defuse the highly charged discussions on race" and possibly help "ease the transition to a more humane society."[9]

In reality, of course, the twenty years since Murray last wrote about her family have not witnessed a widespread acceptance of the multiracial origins of most Americans, have not produced any less tension in national dialogues on race, and have certainly not led to a more humane society with a less invidious ethnocentrism. On every side, there is suppression, denial, and evasion. The eighties and nineties saw tremendous growth in informal groups and formal societies devoted to maintaining white purity, a resurgence in the Ku Klux Klan, and rising enrollment in fascist groups like the Aryan Nation. Given this rightward neofascist turn in the nation, and globally, the most honest reaction to the historical fact of racial mixing, and perhaps the most desirable one in these political conditions, is still ambivalence. If purity is always tentative, based on partial memories, false constructions, and incomplete narratives, the discovery and acceptance of impurity does not produce certainty, liberate the memory, and give a sense of fullness to family narratives. Rather, the recognition of impurity produces a difficult and wearying set of contradictions.

Jan Willis knew that there was no such thing as "purity" in any living race of people, yet she had difficulty confronting the complexity of her own makeup. She knew the long history of racial mixing in America but did not easily accept the fact of that mixing in her own family. As a theoretical proposition, based on the visible fact that the lightness of her complexion attested to a history of racial amalgamation, Willis was not pained by the idea that her "'fair' skin came from someplace." But when she discovered that it came from a "specific some*one*," that abstract idea became "living flesh" and led to "emotional turmoil." These are the contradictions involved in the act of familial excavation. On the one hand, one may feel the joy of knowing precisely who one's ancestors were, while, on the other, one can feel what Willis describes as "absolute bereftness" at having to accept white ancestors.[10] The truth may set us free, but it comes with a cost — the cost of feeling ambivalence.

Like these family narratives, *Kindred* also probes and explores the difficulties and tensions in a contemporary African American's having to recognize the "living flesh" of a white ancestor. Butler uses the occasion of Dana's family secret to ask questions about the desire for and impossibility of purity, while also demonstrating the costs incurred in confronting the past. Unlike these family narratives, though, and unlike the earlier palimpsest novels, *Kindred* is about the physical return to the antebellum South. Butler's point, here, I think, is to make literal what earlier and other writers have thought about metaphorically. For this reason, Butler has spent a great deal of time in several interviews downplaying the significance of the "time travel" in her novel, and even contesting the idea that the novel is a work of "science fiction." She refers to the novel as "fantasy," and argues that her use of time travel is closer in spirit to magical realism than it is to science fiction. "Time travel," she concludes, "is just a device for getting the character back to confront where she came from."[11] It is origins, then, returning to where one comes from, that interest Butler, and, in *Kindred*, her focus is on the losses that come with having to confront and coming to know one's origins. In the first words of the novel, Dana tells us that she has "lost an arm," "lost about a year" of her life, and lost "much of the comfort and security" she had "not valued until it was gone" (9). The physical, temporal, and psychic losses signify the cost of "return." The past, especially the slave past, is not a terrain without treacherous dangers, grave and perilous conditions, even for a contemporary sojourner. As Butler herself noted, Dana loses so much to the past because it is impossible to visit the past and "come back whole." Antebellum slavery "didn't leave people quite whole."[12] The significance, then, of Butler's having Dana return literally to the slave past is to allow her to feel that loss of wholeness physically.

What Gayl Jones does by having Ursa claim to feel the "old man still howl[ing] inside" her, what Willis does by describing the feeling of nausea and the symptoms of cancer attendant on her discovering her white ancestor, Butler does by having Dana's body become the site of familial and historical markings. When, at the end of the novel, Dana touches "the scar Tom Weylin's boot had left on [her] face" and the "empty left sleeve" where her arm used to be, she is literally and symbolically touching the places where her body has been scarred and dismembered by her ancestors (264). Tom Weylin, who kicked her face, and Rufus Weylin, who grasped and tore off her arm, are her great-great-grandfather and her great-grandfather, respectively. Dana's scarred face and lost arm are less signs of how the peculiar institution brutalized her body — although her body certainly suffers from its exposure to slavery — than symptoms of how recovering the past involves losing a grip on the present. The task of "genealogy," notes Foucault, is "to expose a body totally imprinted by history and the process of history's destruction of the body."[13] Butler, who is writing a kind of genealogy in *Kindred*, literally represents history (or remembrance of the past) in the process of destroying a body. What Dana's physical losses signify is that fleshing out the past means leaving part of one's being there.

By having Dana return literally to the past, and suffer bodily harm from that transition, Butler is also giving a new twist to the idea of family secrets. We've seen so far that Nicolas Abraham and Maria Torok argue that the family secret affects the subject because that subject's ancestors left something unspoken, which continues to haunt later members of that family line. Butler is showing how that psychic trauma is acted out in and on the body. As a character remarks in another of Butler's novels, "people's bodies remember their ancestors."[14] In the case of *Kindred*, so strong is the hold of the ancestor on the body of its progeny and their progeny that people's bodies can apparently be dismembered by the ancestors they remember.[15] By showing the pain involved in recovering the past, Butler attests to a deep contradiction between seeking to recall and understand the past as a means of "possible political self-recovery," a way to become "whole," and the destructive potential historical excavation harbors for the contemporary African American subject.[16]

Yet, quite clearly, Butler is also commenting on the necessity of that excavation, both for individual subjects and for national histories. The first time Dana is called back to her ancestors' past, and forced to acknowledge that part of her family is enslaved and part white, is on her twenty-sixth birthday, suggesting that confronting her past is part of the maturing process at this transitional date (marking a new year in her life, a new quarter century in her existence). She is called back the last time on July 4, 1976, suggesting that the nation also has to recognize its mixed, impure history at this transitional date (its 200th birthday). Drawing for us the connection between personal and national history, between the genealogy of a family and the makeup of a state, Butler is using Dana's family secret to raise questions about the desire for purity in family and in nationhood. For Dana, the act of return and the discovery of the family secret force her to reconstitute her sense of family, to inquire about what it means to belong to a family having a particular set of lineages. The novel asks: what does "family" mean as a biological or social category, and as a metaphor for racial unity and identity, given the national history of forced and voluntary miscegenation? What and who constitute family? The answers to the family secret involve querying the basis and potential of "family" itself. In addition, Butler asks about the hidden but key term in the discourse of American nationhood — "whiteness." That, after all, is the singular answer to the family secret in this novel (Dana has white kindred). The novel inquires: who can be "white" and what sort of thing can "whiteness" be in a country having a history of miscegenation and racial domination? In asking these questions, in aggressively challenging the idea of family as a term for racial belonging and whiteness as a term for national identity, Butler complicates and resists the delusive comforts of easy racial or national subjectivities.

From Family to Kindred

The concept of "family" has long maintained a privileged place in the discourses of nationalism, the nation being most commonly figured in space as a conglomeration of nuclear and in time as a line of extended family units. Drawing on European discourses about the family as the source and strength of nationhood, African American intellectuals espousing black nationalism have long argued that the black family represents the site for the development of the black nation. Alexander Crummell, for instance, argued that "family" is "the root idea of all civility, of all the humanities, of all organized society." The "formation of states and commonwealth," the "beginning of all organized society is in the family." Turning around, then, and arguing from the other side, Crummell maintains that family is also the concept best able to explain "race." "Races, like families," he writes, "are the organisms and the ordinance of God; and race feeling, like the family feeling, is of divine origin." In fact, he concludes, "a race *is* a family." In the end, then, family represents the origins of both racial and national identity. As Crummell puts it, the "principle of continuity is as masterful in races as it is in families — as it is in nations."[17]

The terms of debate have not altered much since Crummell wrote in the late nineteenth century. Moments of resurgence in black nationalism in the twentieth century have been marked by the replaying of this same discourse of family. Since the rediscovery of black nationalism in the sixties, activists and intellectuals have been either deploying or challenging this discourse. In dramatic, literary, and filmic representations, one school of African American artists has produced what Wahneema Lubiano calls the "black nationalist patriarchal family romance," premised on the emergence of strong African American males and the often simultaneous marginalization or denunciation of African American women. In the late sixties, for example, Jimmy Garrett's "We Own the Night: A Play of Blackness" ends with the African American hero acting on his philosophy — "motherfuck Daddy and Mama and them house niggers. . . . Death to the house niggers" — by shooting his mother in her back while proclaiming: "We're . . . new men, Mama . . . Not niggers. Black men." In the eighties and nineties, films like John Singleton's *Boyz N the Hood* and Bill Duke's *Deep Cover* continued to produce images of strong black men who have to escape from or compensate for inept black mothers. *Deep Cover*, as Lubiano has convincingly shown, is very much a movie suffused with the subject of family and about the "patriarchal fitness" of the male hero who at the end adopts the orphaned boy of the unfit drug addict mother. Lubiano notes that there are "no 'fit' black mothers (or any mothers of color) left alive or visible" in the film until the black woman at the end of the movie is "rehabilitated" by giving up her white boyfriend and assuming maternal authority over the orphaned boy.[18] The mothers in *Boyz N the Hood* are even less successful, as they are either sincerely well intentioned but simply unable to control their sons or emotionally distant from the boys they have no interest in raising. These representations are premised on the connections among family, race, and nation. Those families representing the race can form a nation only when the patriarchal power is evident. In *Boyz N the Hood*, for instance, the two sons of the single black mother are murdered in the streets, while the son of the black patriarch goes off to college with his fiancée (he to Morehouse, she to Spellman) to become a well-educated and productive worker for the black nation his father theorizes and represents.

The discourse of family in these black nationalist productions operates in several different ways. Primarily, it controls the options for African American women who are seen as betraying the race when they seek options other than raising families. In addition, black nationalists use the language and concept of family to police the potentials for inclusion and identification. Family tropes "function in part to circulate specific notions of racial authenticity," by counting as "within the family" those whose behaviors and choices conform to the sexual and gendered expectations and "outside of the family" those who don't. In this way, family becomes a means of excluding some from the race — "not really black," "not really a brother," "not really a sister"— in the name of establishing a race-based nationalism. Such a gesture, of course, places both the individual and the family on perilous terrain — the individual because she or he has to have a stake in familial reputation, and the family because families become "*the* sanctioned site for the reproduction of authentic racial ethnic culture."[19]

Several black intellectuals have challenged the black nationalist discourse of family, by showing how it limits and polices African American women's experiences, by arguing that it rejects the complexity of historical black families and instead produces a "terrifyingly rigid and tyrannical notion of 'family' — one that collaborates with and consents to normative and demonizing notions of race, community, and culture."[20] Lubiano, for instance, has shown how the "black nationalist patriarchal family romance" even goes so far as to support or at least share a discourse with the state in policing African American agency. Both the state (with its "family values" rhetoric as a way of establishing its "right to influence and even direct the private sphere") and the "black nationalist family project" (with its belief in "responsible black male fathering and subordinate black female mothering") share a motive and system for containing the desires and life options for African American women and others whose life choices or sexuality place them beyond the "parameters of the black nationalist 'family.'" When it deals with family, then, which is after all a central tenet of its vision of the kind of social order it would see established, black nationalism unwittingly supports and furthers the state's forms of policing African American people.[21]

Probably no contemporary critic has written as much on the subject of black nationalist discourse on the family as has Paul Gilroy, who is largely critical of most deployments of black nationalist family rhetoric but somewhat sympathetic to the sensibilities underlying that search for a metaphor to describe a united people. He considers Afrocentricity, for instance, a parochial and provincial enterprise whose use of "the trope of family" he demeans as a "characteristically American means for comprehending the limits and dynamics of racial community." He is likewise critical of Spike Lee's use of this discourse, in whose films he sees consistently "the politics of race played as the politics of family." Indeed, Gilroy finds it disturbing that the class divisions in African American society are "dissolved in a dewy-eyed representation of kin, blood and communal harmony in which presenting race as family is the key to making" conflict within races appear unnatural and "conflict between races and ethnic groups appear to be a natural, spontaneous and inevitable feature of social life." For Gilroy, it is not necessarily the family metaphor at issue, though, since what both Afrocentricity and Lee lack are a broader, more international vision of the social and cultural life of people of African descent.[22]

Indeed, Gilroy finds some promise in the "family trope" as it is used in certain black political discourses. For one thing, in a global context defined by the "profane realities of black life amidst the debris of deindustrialisation," there are few tropes having the discursive power to counter the denigration of black political life and to assert the "connectedness and experiential continuity" of people of African descent as the "idea of the racial community as a family." Moreover, this family trope might signal the "emergence of a distinctive and emphatically post-national variety of racial essentialism" that perhaps doesn't have the same problems as the racial essentialism of black nationalism. Such appeals to the race as family might, instead, be seen as "both the symptom and the signature of a neo-nationalist outlook that is best understood as a flexible essentialism." In the end, though, Gilroy remains suspicious of "even the best of this discourse of the familialization of politics" because he believes it will likely rely on and promote representations of black masculinity and black heterosexual familial ideals. He concludes that the best way to "think black sociality" outside the discourse of family is to draw on the profane aspects of the black vernacular, which for him come together in the "traditions of musical performance that culminate in hip-hop" in which he finds an "ethics of antiphony — a kind of ideal communicative moment in the relationship between the performer and the crowd which surpasses anything the structure of the family can provide."[23]

As we saw in the introduction to this chapter, Butler first began to imagine the story for *Kindred* when she encountered at college a black nationalist idea about family similar to the one in Jimmy Garrett's "We Own the Night," in which matricide becomes an act of political liberation and inaugurates a new world of "Black men." She, like the later cultural commentators critical of black nationalist family discourse, saw the multiple dangers in the trope of family when it was wielded by those intent on misunderstanding the past and not questioning the revolutionary rhetoric of the present. On the other hand, though, for Butler, family in the present and generations of family in the past offered connections to history, and any renunciation of that family was a denial of history itself. Her exploration of family, then, including her examination of the efficacy of family as a trope for racial community, follows neither the dictates of cultural nationalists who celebrate a rigidly constraining model of patriarchal family life nor the cultural commentators who seek to repudiate family as a social structure or political metaphor. Instead, Butler seeks to rehabilitate the discourse of family by expanding and infusing it with more political significance. Whereas Gilroy would replace family-based discourses of race with a communicative mode drawn from black vernacular culture, Butler chooses to refurbish the discourse of family by incorporating into it a larger ethics, making it of greater social moment, and imagining it as an inclusive instead of exclusive structure.[24] In doing so, though, she is not involved in a utopian exercise; indeed, she concludes her interrogation by showing the deep problems as well as the immediate benefits of salvaging the discourse of family.

First, it is important to note that Butler does not offer any representations of patriarchal black families. Indeed, the only black family we see at all is one slave family, Nigel and Carrie and their children, who exemplify what Angela Davis described as the "egalitarian tendencies" between African American men and women in slavery.[25] Other than that, the main familial dynamic in the novel involves black women and white men: in particular, Dana's tense relationship between her white great-grandfather, her "kindred," and her white husband, Kevin Franklin, described as her "kindred spirit" (57). By setting up her novel in this way, Butler is surely saying something about the meaning of "kindred," about the potentials for familial discourse to describe and transform racial and interracial relations. When noting that she writes about reproduction in virtually all her novels — the Patternist series is about a god trying to create a master race through reproduction, the Xenogenesis series about the struggle of humans to resist the reproductive colonization of the Oankali — Butler makes two especially important points. The first is that she is not writing about family ties as a way of commenting on the deep power of genetics. While we do need "to accept that our behavior *is* controlled to some extent by biological forces," she insists that "[s]ometimes we can work around our programming if we understand it." The second is that she is not writing about family as a genetically related set of people. "Family," she insists, "does not have to mean purely biological relationships either."[26] Both points attest to Butler's strong statement about the need to repudiate the desire for purity that genetics and the family seem most to promise and ultimately least fulfill. In addition, Butler insists that family is socially constructed and, understood as such, can be a useful way of imagining healthier relationships in a broader social order.

In *Kindred*, Butler presents this idea by showing us how Dana reconceptualizes her sense of "family" so that "family" encompasses not merely, not only, and not necessarily those with whom we share biological or common genetic stock, but rather those whose ethics and politics agree with our own. From the start, Dana questions the nature of her relationship to Rufus. When she realizes that they share a "blood relationship," her first thought is that her return in time is to save Rufus from his various accidents and therefore to keep alive her "mother's family." "Was that why I was here?" she asks herself. "Not only to insure the survival of one accident-prone small boy, but to insure my family's survival, my own birth" (29). Dana is not certain, however, that her life depends on her saving Rufus's. She finds it odd to think that his "life could depend on the actions of his unconceived descendant" and equally odd, therefore, to think that her life depends on the survival of a preconceived ancestor. "Somehow," she says, "it didn't make enough sense to give me any comfort." She concludes that her relationship with Rufus is unique: "We had something new, something that didn't even have a name. Some matching strangeness in us that may or may not have come from our being related" (29). It is highly significant that she discounts the importance of their blood relationship; there are, she intimates, more significant ways of being connected to and of becoming disconnected from our putative ancestors.

Eventually Dana will move toward what we might call *disrelating* herself from Rufus and the Weylin clan. It all begins because Rufus is intensely possessive of Dana; when he tells her that she is "home," he means that she is safe in his possession (143). After he discovers one of his field slaves, Sam, talking to Dana, Rufus sells him to an itinerant coffle driver. Dana sees Sam "being chained into line" and "people a few feet away from him crying loudly. Two women, a boy and a girl. His family" (238). She pleads with Rufus not to sell Sam: "I caught Rufus by the hand and spoke low to him. 'Please, Rufe. If you do this, you'll destroy what you mean to preserve. Please don't . . .'" As Dana tapers off, Rufus hits her. As Dana notes, "It was a mistake. It was the breaking of an unspoken agreement between us — a very basic agreement — and he knew it" (239). She goes into the house, warms some water, washes her knife in antiseptic, and slits her wrists. She wakes up in Los Angeles, but the act symbolizes more than her desire to return home. By spilling her own blood, Dana manages to escape her "blood relationship" with Rufus.

Having symbolically disrelated herself from her biological kin, she now makes it understood on what presuppositions she establishes relations with those she now thinks of as her family. The only time Rufus and Dana talk about this incident, which they had always "talked around" before, Dana establishes the importance of that event to her sense of family. "'I'm black,' I said. 'And when you sell a black man away from his family just because he talked to me, you can't expect me to have any good feelings toward you'" (256). At the beginning of her adventures, Dana says that her connection to Rufus "may or may not have come from [their] being related" (29). Now, though, she has realigned her connections. Her sympathies do not follow the contours of blood relations; they flow toward the community to which she feels she belongs. Her "family" is in the quarters and not in the big house; her sense of family is wrought from a common experience, and is not simply a matter of blood. And this is true in the present as well as in the past. When Dana's uncle disapproves of her marriage to a white man, she feels she has "to get away from him"; when Kevin's sister likewise disapproves, the couple "pretend [they] haven't got relatives" (111–12). She has, effectively, rewritten the family Bible so that her relations are with a different set of ancestors, just as ultimately she would rather salvage her relationship with Kevin, her "kindred spirit," than her "blood relationship" with Rufus or her uncle, her "kindred."

Those who are "kindred spirits," those with whom one shares deep ethical values and a common vision of an acceptable social order, become family by showing themselves deserving of that designation. Consider, for instance, the case of Margaret Weylin. When at the end of the novel Kevin and Dana go to modern Maryland in order to search out the records of what happened to the Weylin plantation slaves, they discover no mention of Hagar or Joe (Alice and Rufus's other child).[27] What Dana has to do, then, is consider their potential histories and, in the same gesture, reconstruct their familial ties. "Margaret might have taken both children. Perhaps with Alice dead she had accepted them. They were her grandchildren, after all, the son and daughter of her only child. She might have cared for them. She might also have held them as slaves" (263). Margaret, who is Dana's great-great grandmother (Rufus's mother), *might* be claimed as kindred if she did raise and care for Hagar and Joe, or she, like Rufus, *might* be disrelated if she chose to enslave them. It is another story, but equally a story about how to reconstruct a family according to the history she relives. It is significant, of course, that Hagar is the one who wrote the family records in the family Bible — and yet her own story requires her granddaughter's reconstructive touch, which is entirely fit for a novel about how history is a contingent entity.

Likewise, Dana's relationship with Kevin depends on knowing his response to the historical forces that grant him a certain kind of power. Telling Kevin that she needs to know "[o]ne more thing . . . [j]ust one," she asks him if he had been "helping slaves to escape" while he lived in the past (193). Upon finding out that he had been, Dana smiles and says nothing. What is important for her is to know that Kevin had acted upon his beliefs and tried to alter the past. His ethics, his actions, and his motives are what give them the "shared experiences" that makes family a meaningful concept. What finally provides Kevin and Dana with a shared communion is the experience of altering the past so that their sympathies can be recognized as historical agencies. Each returns to the time of American chattel slavery and gambles against its history. They both lose something, and they both gain something. Ironically, what they most lose — a sense of "home" — is also what they most stand to regain in a newer, stronger form. When Dana returns to the past, she reconstructs her family ties so that her blood ancestors become less important to her sense of home and family than those people who are spiritual kindred — the slave community on the Weylin plantation, people like Sam and his family, and, ultimately, Kevin. "Natal alienation" is Orlando Patterson's term to describe the deracinated slave. Barbara Chase-Riboud also provides us with an interesting metaphor for African Americans looking at their slave past: "We are orphans, standing on the blank page of America, waiting to be acknowledged." In *Kindred*, both Kevin and Dana, we learn, are orphans (55), and both return to history to claim and reclaim a reconstructed family which is based not on biological but on social ties.[28]

Butler's story does not propose that those who would alter their familial alignments can simply transcend them, because those alignments belong to a past which must be confronted if it is to be altered. Rather than pretend to lose their relatives, Kevin and Dana must remember the past and reconstruct from its debris a new sense of kindred. Some kindred come to you by blood, but others come to you by love and common experience. After recounting the utter importance of his biological family to his sense of identity, Ralph Ellison concludes: "even while I affirm our common bloodline, I recognize that we are bound less by blood than by our cultural and political circumstances."[29] At the end of *Kindred*, after she has lived in history and seen the dislocations slave families suffered and the adaptions they made, Dana recalls the loss of her "father who had died before [she] was old enough to know him" (252) and "remember[s] the pain of [her] own mother's death" (258). As she does at the beginning of the novel, Dana remembers the loss in order to reform its ramifications. Her recollection of becoming an orphan is part of her act of remembering and defining new kinship ties. Butler's heroine shows us how an excavation of history can provide the orphan with a family — partially by relation and partially by disrelation.

In the end, then, Butler challenges both the politics of the cultural nationalists and the premises of their critics by arguing that the discourse of family can prove politically useful without necessarily requiring patriarchal structures or establishing exclusionary boundaries or manifesting otherwise reactionary political imperatives. Writers like Richard Sennett, Stephanie Coontz, and Robert Bellah make the point that in and since the 1970s the idea of family as a political metaphor has been a conservative one because the "language of private relations and family values" leads to a contraction and a deformation of the public realm. When family relations become "our only model for defining what emotionally 'real' relationships are like," we find ourselves able to "empathize and interact only with people whom we can imagine as potential lovers or family members." What happens, then, is that potentially social relationships get constructed on such "personal activities as leisure and consumption." Even worse, the discourse of family leads to "suspicion of people who are different and attempts to exclude them from 'the family circle.'"[30] Butler challenges these ideas by presenting us with a sense of family that is about establishing kinship connections on meaningful political grounds and insistently challenging the exclusionary gambit of more provincial concepts of family. For her, there is nothing wrong with interacting only with people we can imagine as potential family members, if and only if the sense of who can be family is capacious and not restricted along existing social lines of demarcation and domination. That is why it is important that Dana is able to claim and deny kin, to relate and disrelate herself, across racial lines. Butler's point is that we should not allow our constricted sense of family to delimit our social connections but that we should allow a generous social and political will to enlarge our understanding of family.

The Pale Within

Family, then, for Butler does not conform to and help recreate the preordained patterns of the divided and fault-ridden social order we inherit and inhabit, but rather allows us to challenge and change that order. Two points are worth making here. First, in arguing that a sense of family can and should transgress racial lines, Butler is offering us a more historically accurate portrait of the racial makeup of most American families. What, after all, should best form our sensibilities of who can be a "potential family member" than a full rendering of all the types of people who have in fact been real family members, especially those hidden or denied in a given family's genealogy? This is as true of the black families described by Pauli Murray, Dorothy Redford, Jan Willis, and Alex Haley as it would be of those so-called white families attempting honestly to claim pure lines of descent from European forebears. Just as David Chioni Moore reminds us that more than one-third of Alex Haley's family can be traced back to European or Native American ancestry, so does George Schuyler challenge "all Caucasians in the great republic [to] . . . trace their ancestry back ten generations and confidently assert that there are no Black leaves, twigs, limbs, or branches on their family trees."[31] Families, then, like individuals and civilizations, are not pure; and that fact should help undermine those schemes of "difference" premised on its denial.

Second, Butler's choice to represent Dana's relationship to two white men, one of whom is biologically kin and the other emotionally kin, raises the question of what "whiteness" means. Given the biological difficulties in trying to establish racial identity, and taking seriously Butler's point that genetics is not determinative in any case, we have to see that Butler is interrogating the social construction of whiteness, just as she had asserted the social basis of family. By showing us two white men in the process of defining themselves and their relationship to Dana, Butler explores the social forces at work in creating and recreating whiteness. Published the year after the reissue of Murray's *Proud Shoes*, *Kindred* follows Murray's advice and example by also dispensing with the "notion of racial purity" and accepting the "possibility of relatedness" between whites and blacks in the same family. The Redfords and Willises follow suit. As Itabara Njeri advised many years later, "every Black person with White ancestry should, no matter how they came by it, own it." For Njeri, owning up to white ancestry is "not a rejection of African American identity, but an affirmation of the complex ancestry that defines us as an ethnic group." It can also serve as a political strategy for normalizing "what is erroneously treated as an exotic and, consequently, divisive characteristic among African Americans" and thereby ending "the official silence on America's historically miscegenated identity."[32] Njeri here primarily emphasizes the need for African Americans to own up to the whiteness in their families and veins. Approaching the issue from the other side, Butler casts a suspicious look at the idea of "whiteness" itself.

Most contemporary studies of the origins, the discovery, the invention, and the production of "whiteness" tend to focus on the ways the administrative and legal apparatuses of the state created "whiteness" from the early colonial court cases and statutes to the most recent congressional bills and Supreme Court decisions on affirmative action and other "racial" issues.[33] A minority of such studies also focus on the operation of race in the formation and history of American nineteenth-century labor movements.[34] Finally, a few studies take up the issue of how "whiteness" has assumed a certain political valence through institutional and social means, so that in a racialized democratic state, whiteness is something that is "property" or something in which one has a "possessive investment."[35] The texts we have been looking at in this study have also explored the phenomenon of "whiteness." In *Corregidora*, for instance, we saw how the courts played a role in defining who was property while the plantation proved a site for the distribution of privilege based on race; we saw how Corregidora became white by defining those he owned as not white. In *The Chaneysville Incident*, we saw how whiteness inflects and is maintained in institutions otherwise as divergent in purpose as barbershops, the military, schools, and cemeteries.

Butler, too, takes up and investigates the sources of whiteness in *Kindred*. Her argument is that whiteness, like family, is a social construction that depends more on a politics of intent than a politics of descent, more on affiliations based on who one can become socially than those based on who one is genetically. In other words, we can say that Butler's point is that whiteness is primarily an ethical issue, a matter of response to a given environment. Kevin and Rufus are both not simply white, as if whiteness were a monolithic and historically continuous entity. Kevin and Rufus are both formed and reform themselves as racial beings by the actions they perform, the ethics they exhibit. Butler, of course, is not saying that race is something one makes by one's own decisions, but she is equally not saying that race is a permanent, immutable, and stable set of genetic factors. To be more precise, Butler is making the case that the kinds of power and powerlessness that circulate in a given society (antebellum Maryland or bicentennial Los Angeles) are clear determinants of the social meaning of a racial identity. Access to and volitional use of the kinds of power granted on the basis of race help define the meaning of what "race" a given individual may be said to possess.

Consider the case of Dana herself. Because she is perceived by the slaves on the Weylin plantation to have some access to Rufus, the master, and therefore access to the kind of power he wields, they consider her white. Sometimes this is because of behavioral quirks and the way she talks (74), but it is most often because they associate her with things deemed white, like learning — Alice calls her "Reading-nigger. *White-nigger*" — or think that she "always tr[ies] to act so white" when she is a mediator for the master's power (160, 165). Indeed, so closely associated are whiteness and power that it is said of one particularly resistant slave that "he thought he was white" (138). When Dana asserts her power over him, Rufus proclaims: "You think you're white" (164). Whiteness, then, becomes the source of power, even when the power is exercised by people who are not white, because the society of antebellum Maryland is structured in such a way that white people are presumed to and do hold that kind of dominating power over black people.

Conversely, the society of bicentennial Los Angeles, in the wake of the Black Power movement, is structured in a way that black people who are presumed to have access to white power are condemned as desiring whiteness and therefore being insufficiently wedded to African American cultural or political imperatives. As we saw in the introduction, Butler is keenly aware and highly critical of the ways certain cultural nationalists in the Black Power movement deployed the language of slavery to deny that certain African American people even "belonged" to the "same black race" the nationalists proudly inhabited. When Dana discovers that the slave Sarah was afraid of books and the concept of freedom in the North, she feels a sense of "[m]oral superiority" because she can use the terms of racial inauthenticity circulating during the Black Power movement to define and delimit the "blackness" of this woman. Sarah, Dana says, "was the kind of woman who might have been called 'mammy' in some other household," the "kind of woman who would be held in contempt during the militant nineteen-sixties. The house-nigger, the handkerchief-head, the female Uncle Tom" (145). Later, ironically, Dana herself will be called all these names, including "mammy" (167), and will find relief only when she is assured of her racial authenticity by being told that the "black" doesn't "come off" (224).

By establishing this bi-temporal racial formation — what whiteness means in early nineteenth- and late twentieth-century America — Butler is able to explore the contingency at the heart of social meanings of racial identities. First of all, Butler establishes that the social systems that create racial difference and maintain racial privilege are not inconsiderable, both in their pervasiveness and their sheer potency. In one particularly poignant scene, Butler has Dana and Kevin witness the slave children playing a game of slave auction. When she overhears the children fighting about their relative values — "'I'm worth more than two hundred dollars, Sammy!' she protested. 'You sold Martha for five hundred dollars!'" (99) — Dana feels disgusted and begins thinking that "this place is diseased." Even the games children play, Dana remarks to Kevin when he suggests that the children are merely playing at something they do not understand, "are preparing them for their future — and that future will come whether they understand it or not" (99). This game represents one of those everyday acts by which racial schemas get repeated, reinforced, and reinstated. Eugene Genovese reports that white children would often grow jealous at being unable to play this game with their slaves — one slave child replied to his young master's inquiry about his own value, "Lord, Marse Frank, you'se white. . . . You ain't worth nothing!!"[36] But those same white children would of course grow up to realize that part of what makes them white is that they cannot be commodified, just as the slave children would grow up to realize that part of what made them black was that they could. The children's game "broke through" Dana's act because she now learns how easily and fluidly ideology works: "The ease. Us, the children . . . I never realized how easily people could be trained to accept slavery" (101; Butler's ellipsis). Systems of racialization, Butler shows us, operate in both dramatic and invidious ways; and this is equally so for those institutions and practices that create whiteness.

Butler structures her novel so that Dana visits Rufus at several different ages, letting us see in what ways the innocent young child becomes the menacing slave master to the same extent that he is interpellated into the systems that give whiteness its meaning in domination. Dana attempts to make her ancestors' future more tolerable by educating the young Rufus to treat slaves with more respect: "I would try to keep friendship with him, maybe plant a few ideas in his mind that would help both me and the people who would be his slaves in the years to come" (68). Dana attempts to educate Rufus into being a more benign master, but must ultimately confront the fact that having access to property ownership in other people sanctioned by various institutional apparatuses in the larger society is too powerful a socializing force to counter with formal or informal counseling. Kevin's remark when he discovers her plan — "you're gambling against history" (83) — applies as much to the history of whiteness as it does to the history of her family. Rufus in the end is too immersed in the powers available to him, and is unable to remain satisfied with any human relationship he can't control through ownership. For him, indeed, whiteness is property, the very property that prevents him from considering the black mother of his children and the black woman who has saved his life as people with whom he could have a familial instead of a property relation.

Butler also structures the novel so that Kevin returns to antebellum Maryland in order to see how he responds to the ethos of unlimited white privilege, to demonstrate in what ways he is able to resist the allure of power available to him, and to show in what ways he as a liberal white man of the mid-1970s is still residually and unreflectingly the heir of the system of American patriarchy. From early on in their relationship in Los Angeles, Kevin takes certain things for granted — that a woman wouldn't mind typing (109) or writing his correspondence for him (136), or think her property is as valuable as his (108). When he is in the antebellum South, Kevin quickly adapts to that society because it is organized in such a way that he does not have to consider his racialized power.[37] When Kevin negotiates with Thomas Weylin about assuming the duties of Rufus's tutor, he forgets to mention anything about Dana (79). He is hardly troubled by the accommodations they have to make to live in the house of a slaveholder, she pretending to be his slave and mistress (97). Dana, it appears, has good reason to fear exposing Kevin to this slave society since it is clear that "some part of this place would rub off on him," because he already inhabits easily the white male privileges of his own century (77). In the end, though, Dana's fears about Kevin's five years in the nineteenth century — "What might he be willing to do now that he would not have done before?" (184) — are allayed when she discovers that he was unwilling to accede to the white privileges the system of slavery permitted. On the plantation itself, the white master describes Kevin as someone who got into trouble because he "couldn't tell the difference 'tween black and white," treating each equally (150). The slaves respond positively to this egalitarian sensibility, some, like Alice, behaving in front of him "as she would not have" in front of the other white men on the plantation (184). Both whites and blacks, then, see, with either disfavor or admiration, that Kevin does not subscribe to the primary racial divisions and therefore give them social significance. For Dana, the fact that he helped liberate slaves, "gambling against history" in his own right, shows her that he employed his energies and resources in resisting white power.

The cases of Rufus and Kevin, then, reveal different responses to the institutionalized and informal means by which a given racialized society recruits those who would accept the customary rights and thereby extend the life of white supremacy. Butler's point is that the social order, with its racially based access to power, is hegemonic, but not inexorable. The systems by which race is negotiated and governed do not determine behavior despite anything humans can do as acculturated beings; but those systems do exert an enormous inducement to behave in a particular way and do possess the apparatus to coerce, ensure, coordinate, and reinforce that behavior. Kevin, for instance, despite his brave work on behalf of fugitive slaves, and his insistently democratic attitude toward all, nonetheless remains bound to thinking of Dana in a way that differs from Rufus only in degree. On the first day in the antebellum South, he jocularly thinks of Dana as "belong[ing]" to him "[i]n a way" because she is his "wife" (60). After his sojourn, he is unable to comprehend why Dana is frustrated with him in their discussion about rape. When he says that he "could understand" if "anything did happen" to her, she has to remind him that she does not need him to "forgive [her] for having been raped" (245). It is a sign of how hegemonic those systems of recruitment and thought are that even those who otherwise resist white privilege are still sometimes unreflectingly caught in thinking of others as their property.

Butler's point about whiteness, like her point about family, is that these are socially and historically recreated processes that aren't immutably negative. The problem is not family, nor is it whiteness; the problem is the politically malign ways to which these structures can be and have been put. As George Lipsitz notes, the problem with whiteness is "not because of our race, but because of our possessive investment in it."[38] Butler shows how that possessive investment, at the personal level, can be challenged if not offset. But she also reminds us that the institutions operative in ensuring continued investment in whiteness are massive and highly potent. Like family, then, another social structure whose strength comes from its apparent naturalness, whiteness, or indeed the concept of race itself, is situated in a particular national history, having specific local permutations, and can be contested, as family can only be redefined, by a thorough historical excavation.

Remembering Generations

What *Kindred* does, then, is enter into that debate on family and race at the end of the 1970s by demonstrating the possibilities for refiguring the meaning of kinship so that "kindred" can become a substantially more important political category, a relationship presupposing a common set of values not genes, and race can be understood as a historical concept that is less about an already unstable set of biological factors and more about a much more stable, but also nonetheless changing, set of social forces. More than *Corregidora* and *The Chaneysville Incident*, *Kindred* troubles the category of family by more explicitly staging the specific strategies by which family becomes familial, that is, the ways we fabricate kinships with people genetically distant from us and disestablish kinship with people who aren't. I suggested in my reading of *The Chaneysville Incident* that Bradley's choice of having John Washington value Iiames's act of burying the fugitive slaves and devalue Lamen Washington's act of burning his own father's book could be read as a statement about metaphorically replacing a biological ancestor with a symbolic one. In *Kindred*, Butler has her heroine actually kill her ancestor as a sign of the deep significance of acts of disrelation. She also has Dana develop a deeper commitment with her white husband, Kevin, and imagine the possibility of an interracial family of her white great-great-grandmother Margaret Weylin and her own two black grandchildren as a way of showing the processes through which we establish kindred relations, sometimes with people who are family, sometimes with people who become family.

Like the other palimpsest narratives, then, *Kindred* intervenes into the debates about family and race in the late seventies by insisting on a historical exploration of those subjects. Her question, like Jones's and Bradley's, concerns what it means for an African American to come to a sense of historical identity, especially when the period of history from which that identity is drawn is slavery. What place should slavery occupy in the personal imagination and national imaginary? How does one reconcile the sense of freedom in imagining and constructing identities in a late capitalist consumer culture with the sense of constraint on identity formation in an epoch when the African American individual was indeed a primary object of consumption?

In the end, these questions inquire into the curious dialectic in which the past is prologue to the present and yet also a foreign entity, in which the slave experience is both formative of and yet indisputably distant from contemporary society. When she first saw listed as slaves in the census the names of her own ancestors, Dorothy Spruill Redford felt a curious pain in her heart. "This was no discussion group," she realized, "no CORE group debate, no protest slogan. 'Before I'd be a slave, I'd be buried in my grave.' I'd sung that line, marching for my civil rights. Now I felt so arrogant. So smug. It was easy for me to sing about a choice I never had to make. But here were people who had lived the life I chanted about. People with my blood in them."[39] The palimpsest narratives make precisely the same points as Redford does. The thought and fact of slavery humbles; it heightens awareness of what an unfree life means. In *Corregidora*, no matter how much Great Gram represents a willful old woman who insists on making her life the center of attention for three generations, we have to recognize that the horror and suffering she went through are almost beyond belief, and that it took three generations for that concentrated pain to begin to be made manageable enough to be transmuted into art. John's descriptions of the way C. K. Washington struggled to deny his own subjective responses to a race riot that killed his pregnant wife attest to his admiration for his great-grandfather's sensibilities as a historian, but he also recognizes, I would argue, that slavery and the racial system it created stole everything his fugitive ancestor had except his ability to take his own life. And, certainly, there are few narratives about slavery that are more effective than *Kindred* in representing the mundane but bitter reality of savage punishment and daily, grinding tedium in a slave's life on a plantation. What Dana feels most of all is the shelter she has in the present that remains unavailable for the slaves on the Weylin plantation. It may serve as an apt metaphor for present social relation, it is almost certainly the original cause for racial oppression, and it may well be the institution that most accurately reveals the hidden dynamic in American history, but slavery, for the palimpsest narratives, is ultimately an experience that cannot and should not be co-opted for easy comparisons or facile historical analyses because it represents the embodied and collective lives of ancestors who had no choices, for whom slavery was not a symbolic condition but a materially concrete and devastating fact.

All the palimpsest narratives, then, make us deeply aware of what it means to be within a system that attempts to drain meaning and desire out of life, that institutes barbaric regimes of policing physical and mental obedience, that tears the fabric of family life. And they all make us fully conscious of how their narrators' contemporary lives both differ from those ancestral ones and yet are products of the system of indenture that had maligned those earlier lives. In *Kindred*, Dana sees the connection between slavery and present-day street violence, rape, labor exploitation, sexual relations, wife beating, and apartheid (33, 42, 52, 97, 151, 196). She also feels sharply the difference between her two lived experiences, between the luxury for which she feels guilty in the present and the rawness of life in the antebellum

South. For, finally, the palimpsest imperative is not to deny the historical differences in order to argue for a basic analogy or to see a simple causal line of descent from one epoch to another. Rather, it is to trace the ways we can make sense of lives lived in the present through the filter of an earlier narrative, indeed the earliest narrative for people of African descent in this continent. It is to see how the present differs from but still contains profound effects of the past, to discover, as Redford puts it, how in the present "we can live with the past without being dragged down by it."[40] That, finally, as I suggested in the beginning, is the question that haunts each of these haunted narratives: what does one do with the past?

Ernest Gaines once observed that one cannot escape the past. "There is a difference between living in the past and trying to escape it," he noted. "If you do nothing but worship the past you are quite dead . . . [b]ut if you start running and trying to get away from the past . . . [i]t will run you mad, or kill you in some way or the other. So you really don't get away. It's there and you live it." There is a point, Octavio Paz once noted, in "those empty spaces" when "times intersect and our relation with things is reversed: rather than remembering the past, we feel the past remembers us." At such times, he concludes, "the past becomes present, an impalpable yet real presence."[41] The palimpsest narratives define that dynamic of living with a past that is living through us, asking in what measure one needs to celebrate or condemn that history, revel in the discovery of ancestors or be traumatized by the sufferings their lives often represented. Each of the palimpsest narratives meditates on that question — what to do with the past — and answers it by exposing the personal and national family secret that had been shrouded in silence and covered with shame. That audacious act, it needs to be noted, challenged the reticence of generations that came before and helped produce the intellectual and cultural conditions for the remembering generation that came next.

5

A Legacy
of History,
An Enchantment
of History
The Subject
of the Present

In the 1950s, E. Franklin Frazier used to ask his students at Howard University to raise their hands if they were the descendants of slaves. He reported that no hand was ever raised. In the late 1960s, of the more than seventy people interviewed in Studs Terkel's *Division Street: America*, only one talked about slavery, a white male advertising agent who felt that Americans need to "quit calling up this old baggage of the past" and pointed out that he, after all, "had nothing whatever to do with bringing slaves over here." When Terkel returned to interview many of these same people in the late 1980s and early 1990s for his oral history *Race*, he found several African Americans who recalled hearing stories about slavery from their families. One recalled the stories her 101-year-old aunt told her about slavery, while another remembered the stories his grandmother would tell him. Terkel also found individuals who learned from their families to "make up for four hundred years of slavery" by making the next generation better, others who commented that it would take "ten generations to get rid of a slave mentality," and at least one who changed his name to identify himself with a slave who was part of his family history. I am not trying to suggest that the subjects of slavery and slave ancestry went through a simple evolution from 1950s shame and reticence to 1990s pride and visibility. For one thing, there are still deep reservoirs of shame attached to slavery. In the 1996 journal he kept during the filming of *Africans in America*, Orlando Bagwell recorded his reluctance to film the scenes in the slave factories in Ghana because of the "shame that [he] knew would well up again." For another, there are still many who in the 1990s agree with the white advertising agent of the sixties that the "memory of oppression" is detrimental because it "pulls the oppression forward, out of history and into the present."[1]

It is clear, nonetheless, that in the 1970s something happened in the social and cultural conditions of this country that challenged the dearth of discussion about slavery in the 1950s and anticipated the plenitude of it in the 1990s, that made slavery a subject of considerable importance, worthy representation in not only different forms of writing but also in diverse media. In the 1970s, many came to realize that the oppression of slavery was not that far back in history, that the people who lived through that institution were not that long gone. In the 1970s, Dorothy Spruill Redford began research on her family history, while Haile Gerima began working on his 1993 film *Sankofa* — she inspired by *Roots*, he drafting scripts while listening to media reports of the Attica prison revolt that sounded like they were covering the Nat Turner rebellion. In 1975, while conducting fieldwork in Nicodemus, the last surviving black town settled by the exodusters in Kansas, Stephen Steinberg found Mrs. Ola Scruggs Wilson an impressive source of historical information about the town, about her family, and about the surrounding communities. When she told him a story about the joy her mother felt when she learned of her freedom, Steinberg "was struck by the ease with which Mrs. Wilson invoked the word 'master.'" A word that had a "cold abstract" meaning for him had deep personal significance for her. He was startled to realize that she was "only a generation removed from slavery," that he was, in fact, "conversing with someone whose *mother* had been a slave." It was for him a "chilling reminder of how proximate slavery is to the present." But his startled reactions equally attest to how distant slavery is in the American imagination. It is with something like an epiphany that we suddenly see how near in time, how close in generations, is this historical episode from the Old South. When she first read the names of her ancestors as "slaves" in a census, Redford realized not only that these were "[p]eople with my blood in them," but also "how close [she] really was to their lives." Suddenly, she writes, "the past seemed so near, so immediate." In a "very real, very personal sense, time was squeezed, the generations were pushed together." It was also in the mid-1970s that James Baldwin recognized his earlier inability to see that proximity, to trace his familial identity to that institution, as he puts it, to "make the connection between *slave* and *grandmother*."[2]

It is rather curious that the seventies should have seen this development, for it was a period in which mainstream discourses about the pertinence of the past were characterized by a solemn reluctance to probe too deeply. In the early seventies, what Christopher Lasch called a "preoccupation with survival" became a prominent feature of American culture. The era's survivalist mentality, in which the sheer fact of continued existence becomes more important than the quality of dignified or heroic life lived, is largely a product of two historical developments: first, the historical examples of totalitarian regimes and the atrocities they committed, and, second, the rising threat of nuclear war. The response to these conditions led to the creation of a survivalist mentality or a sense of "minimalist self" which in turn led to a decline in the perception and production of narratives about the past. The past itself becomes an object of horror, and approaches to it marked by what Lasch aptly terms a "prevailing fear of nostalgia," because modern subjects proved unwilling to explore a past that would yield even greater and more compelling proof of the brute nature of a species able to carry out the inhumanities committed in recent memory. Instead, those who would survive choose not to enlarge their understanding of the past but instead achieve a compact but fragmented self, which leads to a "decline of the narrative mode both in fiction and in historical writing." Since people prove unable to see themselves as subjects (of narratives or of their lives), but rather see themselves as "victims of circumstance . . . being acted on by uncontrollable external forces," they become detached observers who have and hold "the passive, spectatorial, and voyeuristic attitude toward history so character-istic of survivors."[3]

The other possible attitude toward the past, the one taken by the people who focused on slavery as a subject of importance to under-standing the present, is to remember it in a new way, to recover his-tory through a "counter-memory" that "forces revision of existing his-tories by supplying new perspectives about the past." This strategy requires focusing on "localized experiences with oppression" and find-ing those "hidden histories excluded from dominant narratives."[4] This form of representation was especially useful to those communi-ties and groups of people who felt that the "dominant narratives" failed both to show the past achievements and griefs of those groups and also to articulate the connection between that past and this pres-ent. The palimpsest narratives, products of and reflections on the sev-enties, are in many ways an antidote to the survivalist mentality Lasch describes. Their protagonists do not fear an understanding of the past, although they are also neither nostalgic in the usual sense of the term nor altogether eager to face a past that so delicately impinges on the present. They enter into narratives that are necessary for their com-prehending their ancestors' lives and they dwell on the heroic aspects of those lives. They also challenge the passive and spectatorial atti-tude toward history by showing us characters whose attempts to work through the effects of the past are directly related to their con-temporary subjectivity. This is true as much of *Kindred*, the extreme case of materially intervening into the past, as it is of *Corregidora* and *The Chaneysville Incident*, where the interventions are narrative and symbolic.

This kind of historical sensibility exhibited by the authors of the palimpsest narratives became even more pronounced in the 1990s, largely, I think, as a result of those efforts in the seventies to make slav-ery a subject of inquiry instead of a family secret. The 1990s witnessed a virtually unprecedented amount of attention to slavery. Even with-out listing the scores of novels and historical studies that appeared just in the past decade, we see the ways slavery assumed unusual promi-nence in American popular and political culture. A series of indepen-dent and Hollywood films on slavery appeared — *Sankofa, Amistad*, and *Beloved*. In 1994, Wynton Marsalis premiered his three-hour or-atorio about slavery, *Blood on the Fields*, at the Lincoln Center for the

Performing Arts, which toured the country in 1997, was released in the same year as a three-CD boxed set, and, in April 1997, became the first jazz composition ever to win a Pulitzer Prize.[5] In the summer of 1997, Tony Hall, the Democratic congressman from Ohio, sparked a considerable public debate when he sponsored a bill in Congress to have that body apologize to contemporary African American citizens for the enslavement of their ancestors. This bill, which died aborning, followed not only on the heels of President Clinton's apology for the Tuskegee syphilis experiment but also Pope John Paul II's public apology for Catholic involvement in the slave trade and the Southern Baptist admission of complicity in and apology for American slavery and segregation. In the summer of 1998, President Clinton's expressions of regret for American involvement in the slave trade during his visits to Uganda and Senegal set off another uproar.[6] While one can and many did wonder about what an "apology" for a historical institution of four hundred years' duration might mean, it was clear that slavery explosively emerged as a matter of social, cultural, and political significance in the 1990s.

Not since those eight days in January 1977, when *Roots* aired and captured the country's attention, had the nation seen so intense an interest in African American slavery. In a period of just two weeks in October 1998, Oprah Winfrey's film version of *Beloved* opened to favorable reviews, and the highly acclaimed WGBH documentary on the African American slave experience aired for four nights on PBS. Mainstream trade presses supported this visual renaissance of slavery studies by publishing and releasing in September and October companion volumes to each event. Steven Weisenburger's *Modern Medea* is a historical study of Margaret Garner, whose story Morrison retold in *Beloved*; and Charles Johnson, Patricia Smith, and the WGBH Series Research Team arranged the companion volume to the PBS series, *Africans in America: America's Journey through Slavery*. There is even an audio component to this renaissance, as the editors of *Remembering Slavery* provide the readers of that volume with audiotapes of original recordings of former slaves and celebrity readings of other slaves' life stories.[7] Slavery was being read about, slaves' actual voices were heard on cassette tape, their stories were subjects of films, television documentaries, and even an oratorio. In such a moment of widespread reflection on American slavery, it is difficult to remember the historical amnesia that motivated the palimpsest writers to recall slavery as a cause and analogue for the present political situation in America.

Amidst this new level of awareness of how slavery is not so distant from our generation, of how much the institution remains residually present in the current social order, emerges something distinctively new. In earlier decades, and still for the most part, many of the artistic and political communications that make the statement of the past's relevance to the present came from what George Lipsitz calls "aggrieved communities." Like the "counter-memory" he also brilliantly theorized, this form of cultural production is based on a dynamic in which "the past becomes part of the present through genealogical practices that construct a chain of association between different historical moments to bring to the surface the sedimented hurts of history that hold enduring meaning for the present."[8] The cultural productions assuming this genealogical form and making this powerful statement about the continuing significance of the past are important because they counter the amnesia of those who hold that present-day social problems have no historical roots and expose the fact that we live in a society conditioned to respond to victimage more than injustice. What is new in the recent productions about slavery is that many of these statements are being made by those who don't belong to "aggrieved communities." Indeed, several authors of European descent wrote about slavery in the past two decades with a sensitivity and awareness that was applauded by scholars and critics of African descent. What, finally, is most surprising is that some of those cultural workers are using those "genealogical practices" to trace their family secrets not to the slaves but to the slaveholders from whom they are descended. And they are doing so in order to assume some kind of responsibility for the history from which their families profited.

I would like to conclude this study by examining a few of those productions of the 1990s that came after the palimpsest narratives, to see in what ways some contemporary texts address the same questions as did the narratives of the seventies, to examine in a variety of different disciplines and media how this discourse about slavery is now playing itself out, and, finally, to see how intellectuals who are not of African descent are commenting on these issues. I will end by looking first at some of the issues raised when we talk about historical responsibility, and then look at two texts that raise the question of how a slaveholder's great-grandchild may approach the same past that the great-grandchildren of slaves broached delicately in the palimpsest narratives.

Historical Responsibility: Lyrical and Narrative Models

In the last chapter of her autobiography, *Dust Tracks on a Road*, Zora Neale Hurston imagines having a conversation with the grandson of the slaveholder who owned her family. The slaveholder's grandson defends himself by making two pertinent points: first, he cannot be held accountable for the actions of his ancestors since he was not yet born, and, second, that the Civil War did not end the "principle of slavery" which continues to manifest itself in exploitative economic relationships and international colonialism. Sensing that this is the best she could expect from the slaveholder's grandson, Hurston claims to have "no intention of wasting [her] time beating on old graves with a club" or trying to "pry loose the clutching hand of Time." With her usual optimism and her long-held disdain for what she calls the "uselessness of gloominess," Hurston concludes that she would turn all her "thoughts and energies on the present" rather than holding "a handkerchief over [her] eyes crying over the landing of the first slaves in 1619" or "trying to fix the blame for the dark days of slavery and the Reconstruction." Some of us might take issue with Hurston on the question of history or responsibility — believing the slave past more of a determinant on the present than Hurston suggests, arguing for a more collective sense of responsibility, perhaps — but none of us, I am certain, could disagree that Hurston was most decidedly right in noting that in 1942 she was not expecting any slaveholder's grandson to be "falling out on the sidewalk before [her], and throwing an acre of fits in remorse because his old folks held slaves."[9]

A little more than fifty years later, though, it appears that some great-grandsons of slaves, while not quite "throwing an acre of fits in remorse," are taking upon themselves a different sense of responsibility for their ancestors' deeds and assuming a newly apologetic stance in relation to the descendants of their ancestors' slaves. Macky Alston's documentary "Family Name," which won the 1997 Freedom of Expression Award at the Sundance Film Festival and the Gotham Open Palm Award, before airing on PBS on September 15, 1998, is the story of a white filmmaker's search for the connections between his family line and the families of those his ancestors held in bondage. Edward Ball's family history, *Slaves in the Family*, winner of the 1998 Southern

Book Award and the National Book Award for nonfiction, records the history of the Ball slave plantations and the biological and social connections between the white and the black families who lived on and emerged from those plantations.[10] The publication of Ball's *Slaves in the Family* and the airing of Alston's "Family Name" represent the beginnings of a public testimonial from the great-grandchildren of slaveholders. This moment of anti-nostalgic reflection also constitutes an important development in the ongoing conversation about the meaning of race in contemporary America.

It is interesting to see how these stories about personal confessions of complicity written by the progeny of slaveholders ask somewhat the same questions about the meaning of the past in the production of contemporary familial and racial relations as those raised by the palimpsest narratives. Like the works I have focused on, written by the progeny of slaves, these texts attest to the relevance of the slave past for the post–civil rights present. They dwell on the nuanced and complicated operations of race in large and small ways, in institutional structures and domestic spaces. And they ask questions about responsibility. In these texts, though, the author attempts to take responsibility for ancestral deeds. Before turning to the works of Ball and Alston, we need first to explore some of the philosophical issues pertaining to questions of historical responsibility. What does it mean for someone to be responsible for events performed by her ancestor? What does it mean for an epigone to share in the guilt of or to atone for the actions of her forebear? What sense of personal autonomy must one renounce or does one exhibit when he considers himself somehow implicated in a larger corporate identity that exceeds the individual and transcends a single lifetime?

I will look at two different philosophical sets of answers to these questions. One set of answers — which I will call the *lyrical model* — proposes that since a stable and singular collective identity is impossible to ascribe, individuals cannot be held responsible for either the actions of communal groups in the present or for crimes of ancestors in the past. The other — which I will call the *narrative model* — holds that it is possible to argue for a present-day collective sense of responsibility for actions performed by past corporate bodies. These two models are incommensurable and differ in several of their presuppositions about the terms for identity, the question of responsibility, and the power historical forces either have or have not exerted in creating present conditions. As their names suggest, the lyrical tends to deny while the narrative emphasizes the importance of continuity. A lyrical moment often reads as a spontaneous expression of feeling; the lyricist does not attempt to describe the social context within which those feelings emerged or the story behind them. A narrative, though, is a mode that dwells on causal relationships (this led to that), and provides an exemplary way of exploring the play of historical forces in the making of an individual or a group. The lyrical model values autonomous and somewhat disembodied individuals, while the narrative espouses connectedness, to others and to the past. We can begin our exploration of the idea of historical responsibility by first looking at what in a liberal democracy constitutes guilt.

For most Americans, it would be a singular act of injustice for someone to be held responsible for something he or she didn't do. The person who caused an event to happen is responsible for it, and whoever did not cause cannot be held responsible. Direct and causal agency is the most important factor in determining responsibility in the commission of a crime. We cannot be guilty of something that we ourselves did not commit. At the heart of such a belief system is the idea that we as morally autonomous beings are capable of *choice*. If we choose to commit crimes, we can then be held culpable. If others make that choice and we do not, then it is grossly unfair for us to be punished for something we did not choose. Given that mindset, which is a fair representation of a basic tenet of liberal jurisprudence, the idea of holding an individual or a group responsible for something that happened in an earlier historical period becomes ridiculous because those later individuals have clearly not chosen to perform those acts. Such an idea offends our sensibilities of what is just and what it means for someone to be guilty of something.

The kind of individual presupposed in this philosophy of justice is what political philosopher Michael Sandel calls an "unencumbered self." An unencumbered self is not bound to moral positions that are not freely chosen by that particular self. There are of course simple liberal principles necessary to make social life possible, and naturally the unencumbered self is governed by those. So an unencumbered self must respect the dignity of all persons and abide by the "universal, natural duty not to commit injustice." But the unencumbered self is otherwise "without any special obligations to his or her fellow citizens."[11] The only things owed by the unencumbered self is what that self agrees to owe, and the only duties or obligations are those the unencumbered self voluntarily incurs.

Taken to its extreme, the unencumbered self is not even encumbered by its own historical actions. Steven Knapp, for instance, suggests that it is possible to argue against punishing an individual for committing a given crime since the person punished can be said to exist in a different relationship to the previous act for which the person is now being punished. Punishment in this sense is a social practice meant to have criminals "identify with the act [they committed earlier] in a way that will *constitute* their taking responsibility for it." What this means existentially, however, is that society insists on a notion of responsibility in which it is not the historical act that is important but the present sense of implication in the act. Being responsible in this sense "precisely *means* having a disposition to identify with one's own actual past, to think of oneself as inseparably bound to it, even as if one were presently performing one's past acts and therefore appropriately liable, in the present, to the experience of aversion that should have accompanied" the original act.[12]

The unencumbered self is marked, then, by its insistence on *choice*. It chooses its obligations, and even chooses when to be implicated in the actions performed by a previous incarnation of that self. This is the self we find in the lyrical model, a self unencumbered by what it considers contingent features of identity, since these are things that can be shed or assumed voluntarily.

The narrative model proposes a quite different self with a dramatically more restricted sensibility about what it means to choose, a more rigorous feeling of responsibility, and a vastly greater appreciation for continuity. This self of the narrative model is encumbered by a sense of its own evolution (what I did earlier is in part why I am this person now) and by a sense of its social and historical placement. What Sandel approvingly calls "thickly constituted, encumbered selves" have obligations of membership that clearly "presuppose that we are capable of moral ties *antecedent to choice*" (italics added). It is not by contractual agreement or by willful choice that the encumbered self becomes obligated to others. By virtue of inhabiting a certain community, the encumbered self owes obligations of solidarity to fellow members of that community. To belong to a nation is not a matter of choice but a matter of having civic responsibilities beyond the minimalist liberal ones of respecting others' dignity and not committing injustice. In a larger sense, the encumbered self also owes obligations to those in other communities with which one's own community has a "morally relevant history."[13] To belong to a nation is also to assume responsibility for the relations that nation has with other groups, within and without its borders, that it may have engaged in unjust war or colonized or discriminated against.

The encumbered self, in sum, is defined by those communal obligations that flow from the self's historical and political and moral situatedness. In the narrative model, the self is neither freed of responsibilities it does not choose to assume nor unburdened by a history it does not choose to accept. That does not mean that the self is bound by those constraints; it means, rather, that the self is rendered more meaningfully capable of acting within its social and historical placement. In Sandel's words, the encumbered self is marked by its "disposition to see and bear one's life circumstance as a reflectively situated being — claimed by the history that implicates [that self] in a particular life, but self-conscious of its particularity, and so alive to other ways, wider horizons."[14]

Alasdair MacIntyre provides us with another formulation of the kind of self presupposed in the narrative model. Like Sandel, MacIntyre also inquires into those intellectual forces at work that deny the historical sources of personal identity. In his critique of what he calls the "culture of bureaucratic individualism," MacIntyre challenges a theory of selfhood that he refers to as "emotivist" and traces to the philosophies of G. E. Moore, and sees filiations of in the existentialism of Jean-Paul Sartre and the sociology of Erving Goffman. Emotivism is the doctrine that all evaluative and moral judgments "are nothing but expressions of preference, expressions of attitude or feeling, insofar as they are moral or evaluative in character." In its insistence on indeterminacy and arbitrariness, emotivism is to ethics what poststructuralism is to linguistics, what deconstruction is to ontology; that is, they are theories that challenge the foundationalism of prior systems accounting for action, speech, or being. Without foundations for making meaningful and rational distinctions, the "self" in these theories, what MacIntyre sometimes calls a "democratized self," has "no necessary social content and no necessary social identity." It can therefore "assume any role or take any point of view, because it *is* in and for itself nothing." MacIntyre sets for himself the task of taking on this emotivist philosophy and demonstrating the flaws in the culture of bureaucratic individualism, while not resorting to a simple or conservative nostalgia for a time before modernity, for a philosophy before the Enlightenment, for a set of fixed and universal ethics cast into Aristotelian terms. Toward that end, he generates a theory of "practices," gives an account of what he terms "the narrative concept of selfhood," and develops a framework for a "vibrant tradition."[15]

A practice for MacIntyre is "any coherent and complex form of socially established cooperative human activity through which goods internal to that form of activity are realized in the course of trying to achieve those standards of excellence which are appropriate to, and partially definitive of, that form of activity." What is important about a practice is that it counters the antifoundationalism of postmodernity because it "involves standards of excellence and obedience to rules as well as the achievement of goods." Entering into a practice requires accepting "the authority of those standards" and subjecting one's own "attitudes, choices, preferences and tastes to the standards which currently and partially define the practice." A practice, then, is an arena for the enactment of activities that have histories and social consequences. The kind of self able to enter into that arena has to have a sense of its own historical and social contexts. Unlike the free-floating emotivist or lyrical self, which believes that those material conditions in which it lives and has its being are "merely contingent social features" of its existence, the encumbered self involved in practices possesses "the unity of a narrative" that is simultaneously "embodied in a single life" and "embedded in the story of those communities" from which the self derives its identity.[16]

So far, then, we have seen how the lyrical and narrative models differ in the kind of self they assume, and the kind of responsibility that each model's self can or will assume. The lyrical self operates by choice, the narrative by obligation determined by belonging to a specific place and time. The lyrical self denies communal obligations, the narrative accepts them as part of the debt of being a member of a community. With these differences between the two models clarified, we can now turn to the question of historical responsibility.

Sandel had mentioned that there were obligations members of one community owed to those in another community because of a "morally relevant history" between the two communities. What he is saying, in other words, is that contemporary individuals in the present are somehow implicated in the actions of people who came before them.

He uses as his examples the "morally burdened relations of Germans to Jews, of American whites to American blacks, [and] of England and France to their former colonies."[17] Contemporary German people owe a debt to contemporary Jewish people because of what earlier Germans did to earlier Jews. This idea, as I mentioned earlier, is a difficult one for citizens in a liberal democracy to accept since the basic principle of justice is that one is guilty of one's own actions but not of others' and certainly not of the crimes committed by historical actors with whom one has no obligatory relationship. And since the lyrical model holds that relationships with the past are products of choice, one need never choose to be accountable for historical events.

Again, Knapp takes this point to its extreme when he considers the question of historical responsibility, asking whether it makes sense to get individuals "to take responsibility for the acts of groups to which they belong." Because he has already argued that individuals punished for individual crimes are actually punished for being earlier "organisms" of themselves with whom they don't necessarily have to keep identifying, Knapp is not troubled by the conventional argument against collective responsibility. As we saw above, the usual argument is that it is wrong to punish individuals for crimes they did not commit themselves. Knapp quickly dispenses with that argument. The problem with proposing that we can punish "someone for an act committed by an ancestor," he writes, is *not* that the contemporary person "stands in a different *metaphysical* relation" to the acts of those ancestors than one does to one's own acts. Since in both cases, he argues, the act and the "state of the organism as it existed in the moment of action" are no longer present, in both cases the "justification for punishment cannot be metaphysical but can only be normative." The problem with punishing individuals for the acts of ancestors, rather, is that the rationale for normative punishment is not compelling. Punishing individuals for the acts committed by their ancestors turns out to inhibit that crucial sense of proleptic guilt which should and ideally would prevent them from future criminal behavior.[18]

At the soul of the lyrical model's critique of historical responsibility is the value that its proponents place on *choice*. To be held responsible for historical events requires that one invest in a collective identity. To be a contemporary German citizen who feels and acts on that "morally burdened relation" with Jewish people, it is necessary for that citizen to assume the collective identity of "German." An unencumbered self can choose to shed that identity as contingent, as an identity the self doesn't choose to accept, as one of many possible individual identities that offset that particular collective identity. Since "collective identities, unlike individual ones, frequently overlap"— one can be Bavarian as well as German, a Catholic and a woman — the unencumbered self cannot be bound by any one collective identity that forces on it a particular responsibility the self chooses not to shoulder. The lyrical model, then, is deeply opposed to ascriptions of collective identities. Since identity is a matter of choice in the lyrical model, the unencumbered self is able to deny what it considers contingent identities that don't benefit that self. Indeed, proponents of the lyrical model suggest that advocates for the narrative model might be accused of attempting "to restore a preliberal mode of identity, so that membership in some privileged collectivity will once again override the plurality of identifications that tends, in our present context, to defeat ascriptions of collective responsibility."[19] In essence, the lyrical model holds that present individuals cannot be held responsible for actions done by others in the past because the present individuals have not chosen to accept that responsibility. Moreover, they cannot be forced to choose that responsibility based on some perceived shared identity with those past agents because the unencumbered self can simply deny that shared identity as a contingent and not essential feature of its being.

It is clear that these two models — the lyrical and the narrative — differ in their beliefs about identity and about responsibility, about choice and about communal belonging. At the heart of their disagreements, and the basis for the assumptions they each make about identity and responsibility, is arguably the question that had motivated the palimpsest narratives: what is the relationship of the past to the present?

The lyrical model takes a skeptical approach to this question. At first, lyrical model advocates concede that the past is related to the present in one of two ways, either "the relation of *analogy*" or "sheer historical continuity." Continuity connects the past and present "via historical sequence," while analogy connects them "via a property common to both." The past is either the cause of the present or a mirror held up to it. It is clear, however, that the idea of "historical continuity" has to be jettisoned in the lyrical model, since the idea that the past has in some way residual force in the present would implicitly constrain the freedom of choice so crucial to the lyricists. What they do, then, is argue that the past cannot be understood *as past* because we understand it in the present. The startling point proponents of the lyrical model make is that the search for historical information is essentially unnecessary. To go back to history to find models of conduct is a futile act since, as Knapp puts it, "we use, for promoting and reinforcing ethical and political dispositions, only those elements of the past that correspond to our sense of what presently compels us."[20] In exploring the past, the lyricist emphatically proclaims, *"the locus of authority is always in the present"* (italics added). Given that what present-day historians look for in the past is determined by what they hold important in the present, why not instead construct models of ethical conduct out of present-day materials? The lyrical model in essence renders the past a structure that changes according to what we in the present find compelling.

The narrative model, on the other hand, proposes that the past is not contingent in this whimsical way. It is not something that serves as an analogy for the present because we in the present have some set of concerns for which we can find parallels in the past. The past is something that has formed the present in deeply meaningful ways. Here is a crucial point worth dwelling on. To argue that the "locus of authority is always in the present" is to argue that somehow or other that "present" exists as if it had no relation to the past, as if what "presently compels us" is not affected by or formed through a set of historical forces that created the "us" and the society of which we are a part. Quite simply, the past in the lyrical model assumes the relation of analogy so that lyricists need not be troubled about historical continuity. For the narrative model, though, the continuity from the past to the present is precisely what makes the present what it is. The past is not something one chooses to see in a particular relationship to the present we occupy; the past is what formed the present and the people who occupy it in the particular way we do.

Let me conclude this comparison of the lyrical and narrative models by turning to an exemplary dialogue between the lyrical and the narrative models to show how differently they approach the question of historical responsibility. The case, appropriately enough, concerns American slavery. Alasdair MacIntyre argues that "modern Americans" either "deny any responsibility for the effects of slavery upon black Americans" by claiming individual innocence ("I never owned any slaves") or they "accept a nicely calculated responsibility for such effects measured precisely by the benefits they themselves as individuals have indirectly received from slavery." So, for instance, in 1999 a great-great-grandchild of a slaveholder who in 1865 owned, say, sixty-seven slaves would calculate what his or her great-great-grandfather earned from owning slaves and then trace how those profits were willed from generation to generation until he or she is able to calculate approximately what one has inherited as a beneficiary of slavery. In either case, whether responsibility is denied or nicely calculated, MacIntyre concludes, the idea of "'being an American' is not in itself taken to be part of the moral identity of the individual."[21] For the narrative model, then, the past is something for which particular groups are responsible because the individuals making up that group participate in that collective identity. That identity is not a matter of individual ancestry (whether one's ancestors owned or didn't own slaves) but a matter of belonging to a communal group that confers benefits and incurs obligations.

Steven Knapp challenges MacIntyre's argument by returning to the issue of how it is that collective identities can overlap. Claiming that MacIntyre is arguing that modern Americans should accept responsibility for the effects of slavery "simply insofar as they belong to the American collectivity and thus partake of an American identity," Knapp proposes that this means all modern Americans — regardless of race — should be held accountable for slavery. He claims that, if we rely on those slippery collective identities, there is no reason not to believe "why modern black Americans are any less responsible for the effects of slavery than Americans generally." The kind of argument that stated that the "disadvantages of belonging to the collectivity 'black America' cancel out the guilt that one would otherwise inherit as a member of the collectivity 'America'" does not work, Knapp maintains, because saying that "disadvantages can outweigh collective guilt is presumably to exhibit the same sort of 'nice calculation' that MacIntyre perceives in Americans who measure their guilt for slavery by the benefits they have received from it."[22] For Knapp, then, the options that come with ascribing collective identities is that either everyone is responsible (all are Americans) or no one is responsible (all are individuals). The only other option, which he feels MacIntyre has discredited, is to ascribe responsibility by calculating individuals' direct or indirect gain.

Knapp commits two errors in his reading that allow him to caricature MacIntyre and to shift the grounds of the argument to where he wants them to be. First, he presents MacIntyre's argument as if it were about collective identity when it isn't; it's about individual responsibility within collective practices. Second, he treats history as if it were a matter of choice about identity. The first error allows Knapp to turn the discussion from the issues of responsibility for a past that has ongoing significance into a discussion of collective identity in a present that has apparently no relation to the past. Whereas MacIntyre is trying to show that slavery has enduring material effects that significantly determine life chances in contemporary society, Knapp is trying to show that ascriptions of collective identity are flawed because one can belong to more than one collectivity. The second error allows Knapp to reinforce this argument by making the counterintuitive argument that modern black Americans can be held responsible for the effects of slavery because they are "American" and therefore benefit from that collective identity. The only way Knapp can do this, of course, is by effacing history, treating the past as if it were a contingent and willed feature of one's identity and not a constituent set of experiences that are formative and not volitional. The modern black Americans in his example are clearly detached from the history of slavery; they exist in a present society that apparently has minimal relationship with its slave past. In sum, then, Knapp manages to make the point about collective identity by wholly misreading MacIntyre's point about the importance of history in the formation of present social subjects.

Here we see clearly the different positions adopted by advocates of the lyrical and narrative models on the question of historical responsibility. The modern American who denies any personal involvement in slavery or who accepts a "nicely calculated responsibility" based on benefits gotten from slavery are examples of the emotivist or unencumbered self at its most defiant, since any kind of responsibility is assumed through choice. This a self that says: "I may biologically be my father's son; but I cannot be held responsible for what he did unless I choose implicitly or explicitly to assume such responsibility. I may be legally a citizen of a certain country; but I cannot be held responsible for what my country does or has done unless I choose implicitly or explicitly to assume such responsibility." The kind of encumbered selfhood that the narrative model promotes, though, cannot deny responsibility by claiming individual innocence or assume responsibility whimsically in relation to individual gain. That self says: "What I am . . . is in key part what I inherit, a specific past that is present to some degree in my present. I find myself part of a history and that is generally to say, whether I like it or not, whether I recognize it or not, one of the bearers of a tradition."[23] Slavery, then, is not something best hidden or denied because knowledge of it endangers contemporary ethical behaviors; slavery is one of the unfortunate practices in the formation of contemporary America. The encumbered self who must own up responsibly for slavery and its contemporary effects does so because it is a part of the history that formed the society that both together (history and society) constitute that self.

In the lyrical and narrative models, then, we have two rival and incommensurable versions of personality and activity. In one, a lyrical self freed from history and social constraints behaves in a particular way based on individual choices, preferences, and values; its locus of authority is the present. In the other, a narrative self is involved in practices offering specific resources and demanding particular standards which are simultaneously derived from and help redefine the traditions of that society. There are two especially significant points to be made here. First, what can be said about the differing conceptions of history each model of selfhood presumes; and, second, what is the significance of the ideas of identity each model holds? The lyrical self exists in a present largely unaffected by the past while the narrative self inherits from its familial, civic, tribal, and national pasts a "variety of debts, inheritances, rightful expectations and obligations." Likewise, we can say the lyrical self denies identities that presuppose continuity or collectivity, while the narrative self depends on both. Unmoored from society and history, a lyrical self feels no obligation to identify with either past incarnations of itself or larger entities like communities or nations. A narrative self, on the other hand, finds coherence in the unity of a life in which previous actions hold meaning for present and future ones, and discovers meaning in the particularities of civic, tribal, and national identities.

There are good personal and political reasons for vying interest groups and corporate bodies to believe in either a lyrical or narrative model. As a general rule, we can say that those who find the group with which they identify has suffered in recent historical experience tend to value the narrative model since it holds accountable those at whose hands the group has suffered. Likewise, those who have little to gain from a collective identity rooted in the past, and would indeed find it unpleasant to discover certain historical facts pointing to less than noble means of their ancestors' acquisition of the wealth and power they inherited and currently inhabit, tend to favor the lyrical model since it holds accountable each individual for his or her present status and accomplishments. These ideas, these models of ethical conduct and political identity, are neither new nor capable of easy resolution. It is important to have them before us, to acknowledge their incommensurability and the tensions within each model, as we turn now to less abstract reflections on precisely this same problematic.

Palimpsests in White

In 1705, the Virginia General Assembly ratified the racial basis of slavery in the colony by passing a statute declaring all non-Christians, all Native Americans, and all African slaves "to be held as real estate." Once enslaved, these populations lost all rights, especially the right to be considered human. The next sentence in the statute declares that any master who accidentally kills a slave in the course of correction "shall be free of all punishment . . . as if such accident never happened."[24] I would like to point to two of the many paradoxes in this statute. First, an individual is "free of all punishment" if that individual commits murder in the course of punishing someone who is not free. Second, it is a curious law that can change something that happened (an event) into something that "never happened" (a nonevent). This dialectic between freedom and unfreedom, between event and nonevent, is, I would suggest (stealing a phrase from Patricia Williams), precisely the alchemy of race and rights. In declaring an event an accident that did not happen, this particular statute, and the American legal and moral discourses on which it is based and to which it is progenitor, create race in the process of distributing rights. What Henry Louis Gates describes as the "natural 'absence'" of blackness in Enlightenment philosophy, what Hazel Carby calls the "'absent' presence" of the slave subject, is a product of this alchemy; blackness is what you are possessed by and what you have to own up to when your death can be an accident that never happened. What George Lipsitz calls a "possessive investment in whiteness," what Cheryl Harris calls "whiteness as property," is equally and necessarily the product of this alchemy; whiteness is what you possess and what you own when your death can never be a nonevent.[25]

to the African American descendants and share the information about their common families; and both conclude by raising questions about the responsibility of familial descent. The two texts differ, I think, in their resolutions to their family secrets. Where Ball's major impetus is to apologize for the past, to perform an act of public penance and argue for the importance of other public institutions in the creation of future shared family histories, Alston's is to find a model of connectedness that will serve to promote racial harmony both personally and for the society at large. I'll begin by looking briefly at the scenes of secrecy, resistance, and search for black family, before turning to a more extended exploration of the scenes of awkwardness around race and the statements of resolution.

Both *Slaves in the Family* and "Family Name" begin with a "family secret." Edward Ball's father used to make a joke about the family's slaveholding legacy. "'There are five things we don't talk about in the Ball family,' he would say. 'Religion, sex, death, money, and the Negroes.'" When Ball's mother would ask, "What does that leave to talk about?," his father responds: "That's another of the family secrets." Macky Alston begins his documentary by announcing that he is a gay man who found his sexuality something difficult to address with his family; as a child he went to elementary school in a predominantly black school where he found many African American children also named Alston. Both these things, he tells us, were "something I couldn't talk about." As children, then, both Ball and Alston found that certain subjects of conversation were proscribed, and both had some connection with race. The Ball family could not talk about black people, while young Macky recognized the impropriety of inquiring into the connectedness of black and white Alstons. The reasons for this silence and its connections begin to make sense when both Ball and Alston are given published family histories of their slaveholding ancestors. When his father gave the eleven-year-old Edward a book called *Recollections of the Ball Family of South Carolina and the Comingtee Plantation*, he told his son that one day he would want to know about his ancestors. Edward noted that the "tone of the old joke was replaced by some nervousness." The "story of his slave-owning family" became a "mystery he could only partly decipher." Macky's father also gives him a book — *The Alstons and Allstons of North and South Carolina Taken from English, Colonial, and Family Records* — which reveals the Alstons to be one of the largest slaveholding families in

That phrase — "as if such accident never happened" — also tells u
much about the willed silences in American history. A statute able t
produce a nonevent can be the law only in a country that can efface
historical institution. For most of the period after 1865, slavery h
been an "accident" that "never happened" in America. It remained t
family secret that psychotically haunted the national imaginatic
One of the most important discoveries of those who theorize abo
the health and development of the psyches of individuals and coll
tive groups has been the damaging effects of repressed memories
suppressed histories. In her recent accounting of what she calls "
murder and slavery," Nell Irvin Painter states the importance of
suing the "hidden truths of slavery," which she deems essential
our mental health as a society," and which "depends on the abili
see our interrelatedness across lines of class and race, in the past,
the present." What most needs exposing and resolving, Painter
cludes, are "the family secrets of slave-owning households."[2
cently, that project has gotten started. The publication of E
Ball's *Slaves in the Family* and the airing of Macky Alston's "
Name" constitute the beginnings of a public testimonial fro
great-grandchildren of slaveholders. These texts are to the pali
narratives what in general "whiteness studies" is to Ethnic an
can American Studies, the addressing of the same set of issu
the other side of the racial divide. *Slaves in the Family* and
Name" should be viewed as part of that remarkable amount o
arship showing the social constructedness of white identity.
also, as the titles indicate, about "family." In other words, they
same issues as did the palimpsest narratives: what is race, wha
ily, what is the relationship?

   Slaves in the Family and "Family Name" share a common
discovery and revelation, what might be a paradigm of sla
family histories. Both texts reveal the presence of a family se
describe a moment of receiving gifts of published books of f
tories that partially reveal that secret; both meet family re
the project when they set out on a process of supplementing
lished record with reference to historical manuscripts ar
American oral accounts; both show an initial awkwardness
seekers find themselves confronting African Americans v
scended from people their ancestors owned; both express
find black family members who share common ancestors;

North Carolina. Reflecting on his sexuality, his childhood silences, and his family's slaveholding history, Alston asks: "Is something a secret if everybody knows it, but nobody talks about it?" Both then set out to discover what Alston refers to as "the whole story behind my family name," and what Ball calls "a piece of unfinished business."[27]

When they set out to expose the family secret, both meet deep resistance from white family members. Ball's cousin, Bennett, snapped at Edward that his project was demeaning and would destroy the good family name. "To do this is to condemn your ancestors!" he exclaimed. "You're going to dig up my grandfather and hang him!" In a poignant scene in which his daughter says that she feels betrayed at not having been told more about her family history, Macky's father makes some ambivalent remarks about his confused desire to take pride in and to have shame about certain parts of that past. In addition, Macky's grandmother proves a very reluctant informant, who mutters to herself under her breath about the silliness of her grandson's project. Meeting resistance from their own family members and recognizing the deep flaws in a family history in which on one side stood "ancestors, vivid, serene, proud" and on the other "slaves, anonymous, taboo, half human," Ball and Alston then turn to African American subjects in order to give substance to their family stories. The plantation heritage, as Ball puts it, "was not 'ours,' like a piece of family property, and not 'theirs,' belonging to black families, but a shared history. The progeny of slaves and the progeny of slave owners are forever linked. We have been in each other's lives. We have been in each other's dreams. We have been in each other's beds." To recover the story of such a curious mix of intimacy and desolation, Ball and Alston set out to find the contemporary African Americans descended from their great-grandparents' slaves to "meet, share our recollections, feelings, and dreams, and make the story whole."[28]

Making the story whole requires or at least takes on two interrelated strategies. First, the family historians must seek out the fullest possible "family" they can find, which requires them to delve into the distinct possibilities that their ancestors fathered children with slave women. Ball contemplates this likelihood when he discovers possible grounds for a sexual liaison between his first American ancestor Elias Ball and Dolly, the "Molattoe Wench" referred to in Elias's will. He is provoked to wonder about the state of the relationship, whether it was coerced or consensual, whether Elias raped Dolly or Dolly manipulated Elias into more lenient treatment, whether desire was possible in a state of such unequal power relations, whether either could possibly have felt love for the other? These are also the kinds of question Barbara Chase-Riboud asks in her remarkable novel about Thomas Jefferson and his slave lover, *Sally Hemings*, as she describes the tension between desire and dominance in her meditation on "the blood of race, polluted, displaced, and disappearing in rape and miscegenation, and cross-ties of kin — that fine lace of bastardy that stretched across the two races like the web of a spider filled with love and hate — claiming cousins and nephews, daughters and sons, half sisters and half brothers." Ball spends a lot of his time trying to discover those lost relatives, what one elderly African American woman called the "step-aside" children, the children a white slaveholder fathers and then "steps aside." After discovering a long series of sexual connections between white Ball slaveholders and their female slaves, he sets out to find his modern-day relatives. As he puts it in describing his first such encounter, "I had reason to believe that I was related to a black family."[29]

Although Ball expends a lot of energy in describing the possible interracial sexual unions in the past, defining the historical forms of evidence employed to "establish family relations," and delineating his search for what are now his black relatives, he is not as consumed by the idea of finding black relatives as is Alston.[30] While this partly defines the difference in their projects, Ball's to write a full family history, Alston's to discover the meaning of a "family name," there is yet something desperately willful in Alston's deep-seated need to discover the possibility that each African American Alston he meets might be related to him. Whereas Ball sets out to recover a family history he expects to yield information about black relatives, Alston sets out primarily to discover them. Early in the documentary he states his desire: "I want to find someone who through slavery somehow might actually be my cousin." After spending time talking to Rousmaniere Alston, an elderly black woman who was the sister of Spinky Alston, a Harlem Renaissance artist, he goes out to try and prove that the artist and his sister are his relatives. "If I could find out that we are in fact related," he says, "I wonder what kind of conversation then we would have with that knowledge?" At times, this zealousness reveals itself in the most ironic ways. Trying to get information about the father of Spinky and Rousmaniere Alston, Macky produces and publishes a flier with the picture of Primus Priss Alston on it that looks haunt-ingly like a fugitive slave poster. Whereas Ball's inclination is to apol-ogize to the black people whose ancestors his family owned, Alston's is less to "make amends for what [his] family did," which is but a small part of the project, and more to discover, as he tells himself about some African American Alstons, whether and in what ways "we really could be kin."

The second strategy in making the story whole is to take back to the now-extended family the information that the researchers un-cover. The scenes of Alston's and Ball's sharing their discoveries with the African American families provide some of the most beautiful and moving moments in both the narrative and the documentary. The scenes with Fred Alston Jr. and his son Jeff, who both travel to North Carolina with Macky Alston, are powerful in showing us how deep and stirring is the search for family and history on plantations and in graveyards. Alston is unable to deliver to Rousmaniere Alston the information about her father that he would have liked to have given her because she passed away, but he does make good on his promise when he gives one of Reverend Primus Alston's sermons to Reverend Dolores Alston Perry who then delivers it to her own congregation. Likewise, in *Slaves in the Family* perhaps the most vivid and touching scenes occur when Ball gives the Martins a family tree tracing their lineage to their first American forebear, the ten-year-old Priscilla from Sierra Leone, or when he tells Sonya Fordham about her rela-tive, the Angolan slave rebel Tom White. The Martins study each other, the family tree, smile, talk excitedly, and take immense joy in their new-found family history. Sonya Fordham recalls that during her days as a student activist in the sixties she sometimes felt like she "was speaking in tongues." "I would give a speech, and it was as though someone was speaking through me, like I was possessed." "Maybe in a family," she thinks, "the dead are able to communicate through the living."[31] The scenes of sharing show us how the living give to each other the gift of the past.

So far, I have been showing how the two texts share a common structure; each narrator discovers a family secret that stimulates him to seek out fuller information, is momentarily stymied by familial re-sistance, and eventually finds a set of distant black cousins who help him uncover their common history, which he then returns to them in an act of goodwill in either domestic or congregational settings. The story, then, to use the term both Alston and Ball employ, is "whole." I'll conclude my examination of these two texts by focusing on how they offer differing resolutions to their family secrets, on the ways they make it "whole" not only for themselves, not only for their immediate and newly discovered families, but for the larger national public. Here we are best served by looking at two sets of scenes where the researchers demonstrate their awkwardness in confronting the African American people who are descended from their ancestors' slaves, and then seeing how they resolve the family secrets that are at the root of that interracial awkwardness.

Both Ball and Alston, two extremely well-bred members of a particular class of the South, find themselves baffled by the etiquette of interracial communication and downright frustrated at the huge divide between great-grandsons of slaveowners and great-granddaughters of slaves. Ball is clearly more at ease with people of African descent than is Alston, although even Ball, as many reviewers noted, tends unaccountably and clumsily to dwell on the physicality and the variety of colors of the black people he meets and his "otherwise facile writing turns wooden" when he describes the encounters with the slaves' descendants. One reviewer found that Ball's descriptions of black people "almost revert to formula," another that he was "often strained, one-dimensional, saccharine and unintentionally patronizing" in these parts of the book.[32] That perhaps overstates the case, but it is clear that Ball exposes the difficulties of assuming comfort in particular social occasions when so much history is in evidence, when, in fact, the very fact of slave history is the reason he is spending time with people he might otherwise have never met in the daily life of a severely segregated society. Even more than Ball, Alston shows an almost disquieting social ineptitude in his encounters with African Americans. After a few meetings that tested the patience of both interviewer and interviewee, Alston himself recognized that he too zealously sought confirmation of his own beliefs rather than trying to understand the feelings and sentiments of the people whose stories he was after all trying to discover. Eventually, he becomes more comfortable, especially around the black Alstons he meets in New York and Philadelphia. But even then he exhibits an inability to make people around him comfortable. There is a wonderful scene in which one of the African American Alstons he meets in New York, Fred Alston Jr. stares with obvious but charming weariness into the camera Macky is holding in the back seat as they drive toward North Carolina. It's the kind of weariness that comes from having to respond to what one reviewer called the "beguiling sincerity" of an over-eager zealot or facing the prospect of a long drive with an overactive, too inquisitive child in the back seat.[33]

In Alston's case, the failure of his early interviews becomes part of the documentary's self-conscious sensibility, its daring effort to make the seams show, to appear unfinished, under-edited, amateurish almost. His use of the Hi-8 camera on the steering wheel of the car he is driving, filming himself in a soliloquy that is hard to pay attention to as we peer up his nostrils, like his highly and self-consciously staged moments of revelations that prove nothing (having two people open a book again and again in front of a courthouse) appear to be strategic acts of giving his documentary the feel of a work-in-progress. I suppose there are less charitable ways of reading these scenes and moments of apparent technical unimaginativeness, but I think "Family Name" in many ways is clear-eyed in representing itself as a process, and its director, I suspect, aware of the artistic and editorial choices he makes and doesn't make. For him, I would argue, the moments of technical heavy-handedness, the moments of staged failures, and the awkward moment when he asks a black minister whether she is "angry" at him for her ancestors' enslavement, only to have her respond angrily that she had never thought anger the appropriate response until he mentioned it, are all of a piece. The difficulties of healthy and natural interracial communication are the result of the socialization Alston describes to an interviewer: "I was raised thinking in terms of otherness — we are white, they are black, we are not connected."[34]

In Ball's case, the moments where he becomes excruciatingly careful about his presentation of self and other, moments of painful self-consciousness at his inability to fit into these lives he is somehow invading, attest to his awareness of the difficulty of his own task, of what kind of effrontery he might be exhibiting as he offers painful information about the past to people who were so misserved by his ancestors. His own earlier experiences gave him good reason to be wary. Some listeners on radio call-in shows angrily challenged him: "your people raped my people, and now you are telling me about my history?" One African American New York newspaper where he ran an advertisement seeking information about Ball slave descendants ran an editorial, under the headline "OF THE GALL, Massa Ball!," accusing him of "looking for 'mammy' stories to sell books and claimed he was only perpetuating the exploitation of blacks by his forebears."[35] It is partly to prevent such judgments that Ball is highly self-conscious, but, mostly, I think, it is because Ball seems to be aware of his own distance from the kind of understanding the African Americans he talks to acquire about the meaning of this shared past. In one of the key scenes in *Slaves in the Family*, Ball describes a conversation he has with Charlotte Smalls Goodson, the black person with whom he develops the closest and warmest relationship. On their way to lunch, Goodson tells him about a friend of hers who makes her laugh when he comments: "I don't understand these white people! They forced us to come here . . . then they hate us!" Both Goodson and Ball laugh, although Ball recognizes that her "laughter was a little sharper" than his. She continues by asking Ball: "I mean, the plantations, who thought this thing up? Who said, 'Okay, we're going to go to this continent, take a bunch of people, chain them up, bring them over to this place, and make them work.' Who was standing around and said, 'Hey! That's a great idea!'" Ball laughed and shook his head, "but Carolyn," he notices, "was no longer laughing."[36] Moments like this, and certainly this particular moment in its representativeness, show how disparate are the understandings about the meanings of the past.

For Goodson, moments of recognizing the brutality and inanity of the slave trade and slavery are perpetually there as the other side to the happy discovery of previously unknown ancestors. When she first saw a document that her enslaved ancestor had marked with an X, Goodson felt as if she had "brushed up against something," as if she had "hit the past." She was surprised that it wasn't a "chilling feeling," but rather one of "awe, a kind of presence." But finding kin in slavery means having to come to terms with the institution itself, which she tries to do by sharing a joke she can sustain for only so long. For Ball, though, Goodson's laughter is a crucially important factor he requires as confirmation of his own acceptance. There is another moment in the book that sheds light on this need. One of the most interesting relationships Ball develops is with Thomas Martin, a retired assistant school principal, with whom he travels to a Ball plantation and discusses black people's anger. Ball is clearly intimidated by Mr. Martin's demeanor and moral seriousness. The final scene between them occurs after Ball brings the Martin family a gift of slave lists that document their lineage back to their earliest American ancestor, a ten-

year-old girl transported from Sierra Leone in 1756. As the family realizes the magnitude of this genealogical discovery, they begin to talk,
smile, and laugh. "It was the first time I had heard Thomas Martin
laugh since we met," Ball notes as he concludes the chapter. It is the
counterpoint to and correction of his earlier *méconnaissance* with
Goodson, where he had laughed at what he thought was a joke; now,
he provokes laughter in and brings joy to the most serious of the black
people he met in his family history. I suspect the reason Ball spends
a great deal of time describing Goodson's "radiating smile and lim-
pid eyes," focusing on how she "peeled back her lips and showed her
teeth" when she laughed, is, as Toni Morrison remarked about Sena-
tor Danforth's comments regarding Justice Clarence Thomas's boom-
ing laugh, that he needs that "most clearly understood metonym for
racial accommodation." He needs to know they can joke together, that
he is able, if only momentarily and only to a limited extent, to enter
into that shared communion that white Americans construct and envy
as African American humor.[37]

Like Alston, Ball also noted that he grew up in a segregated community where he did not know any African Americans and therefore
developed a "fear of black people" that "created a neurosis in [him]
that lasted into [his] adult years." Both Ball and Alston state that their
desire was to contest the effects (and indeed affects) of their segregated childhoods — in Alston's words, to discover "that relationships
are very possible on the side of honesty and they are not so great when
we are not honest," and, in Ball's, "to release that fear" that African
Americans would "hate" him when he revealed his slaveholding family history.[38] The moments where they exhibit awkwardness in their
communications and interactions with people of African descent are
moments when the honesty becomes difficult and the fear returns,
moments when we can see the depths of the family secrets they are
trying to reveal and the personal shame they are trying to resolve.
Ball's solitary and self-conscious laughter at a joke that had ended and
Alston's inept conversations with people whose emotions he assumes
he can prescribe are nervous symptoms of a more pervasive social illness, what I described in the beginning of this study as the failure to
acknowledge the large family secret of slavery. I suggested that the fact
that American intellectuals from the colonial era to the present failed
to find a way of speaking about slavery was a sign of the deep-seated
anxiety that the history of slavery held and still holds in this country's

imagination. Alston and Ball take quite different strategies in trying to relieve that anxiety, expose the secret, and reach some kind of resolution about the possibilities for the future in light of such a past.

At the end of his documentary, Alston leaves the viewer with a paradoxical set of statements. The search for his "family name" concludes with a discovery he made about the legitimacy of the Alston line. At the conclusion of the film, we read a final statement: "In his research, Macky Alston discovered that his great-great grandfather was illegitimate. He was not an Alston by blood. So Macky Alston is not really an Alston after all." It is both an odd statement in itself and a highly curious moment in this documentary. For one thing, we are not told what sort of illegitimacy this might be. Is the great-great-grandfather a bastard who is either adopted into the Alston clan or made a pariah because of his illegitimacy? And what does not being "an Alston by blood" mean in this instance? A child born out of wedlock does not possess a different set of biological family members, and someone adopted into the name and familial traditions possesses a deep social connection to those family members. So the "blood" here is a curious notion that in many ways challenges the premises the documentary had set earlier. The statement the film had been making up until that point was that biological kinship was clearly important; Alston did not just seek out the descendants of people his ancestors owned, but those who were his "cousins," who were "related to him," who turned out to be his "kin." He had doggedly tried to establish familial links, blood ties, genetic connections; he was seeking "family" more than "name," and family meant "blood." Now, at the end of the film, all this is turned on its head as Alston discovers that he is not "really an Alston after all." The irony, as reviewers noted, is that in seeking his "family name" Alston discovers that "family" is either a flawed concept or an entirely promising model for interracial relationships. Some reviewers thought that "the secrets of a family" the film "discovers cause us to question the very definition of a family," while others went even further and argued that the point was to see a liberatory model, a "powerful image of the unity of the human family."[39]

An optimist would agree with this, I guess, and argue that Alston's film does state the importance of social instead of genetic relationships. In an interview, he himself noted as much: "The truth is, you make of it what you will. How much stock do you put in the bloodline and purity of your historical descent? What does family mean to you in contrast to the relationships forged in the process of one's life?"[40] A skeptic, though, would probably sense that there is also something suspicious in this new-found belief in sociological rather than biological connectedness. After all, it was not familial blood but racial identity and wealth that made Alston's great-great-grandfather a slaveholder; so whether he was an Alston or not is a moot point in a film that clearly established that slaveholding was a family secret and a source of shame. Dissipating the sense of family does not negate the facts of history, and it instead appears to be an attempt to evade the responsibility that earlier Alston had seemed ready to shoulder. It is also curious that the reviewers should read the end of the film as an easy statement about the beauty of "the human family." After all, one of the most memorable scenes in the documentary involved a humorless Eugene Alston Vivra, Jr., who stood in front of the camera at the white Alston family reunion and traced the Alston family line back to Charlemagne, Alfred the Great, and Adam and Eve. This figure, clearly an object of humor in this scene, is essentially saying the same thing as Alston does at the end: that we are all members of a human family, traceable in this instance back to an original pair of parents.

It seems to me that Alston is saying something like that, but in a rather different way that finally has quite different implications. There are two scenes with his father, Wallace MacPherson Alston Jr., that speak to these issues in what I believe to be both the most intelligent way and, I would argue, the way this film ultimately endorses. In one scene, Macky asks his father whether he would have been a slaveholder if he lived back in that time. His father says that it would be "historically arrogant" to assume that he would have been able to claim a higher moral authority, to distinguish himself from his peers and family, and seen the impropriety of slavery and renounced it. In the other scene, Wallace Alston tells a story about his tenure in the Navy. After passing a check point manned by an African American soldier, Wallace Alston made disparaging remarks to his other white mates about the intelligence of the African American. One of those mates turned to him and asked him how he could mock another "human being." From that moment on, Wallace Alston became a different person, renouncing that heritage of hatred and embracing a religious calling that entailed working for civil rights in the sixties and gay rights in the nineties. The moment is significant in that it revealed to Macky Alston for the first time that his father had not always been progressively working toward a more just and fairer society (as if he were born good) but that he had a history of his own growth from a benighted to a more egalitarian vision of the world.

The two scenes with his father are even more important to the statement the film seems to be making. The first scene tells us that societal pressures are as determinative as familial ones in governing an individual's choices of how to behave (and they are equally forceful in maintaining the status quo), while the second tells us that there are larger models than "family" for patterning moral behavior toward others. Let me put it this way. The film poses three different structures for racial harmony. The biological model is that we should all treat each other with justice and fairness because we are all connected by "blood." The familial one argues that we should do this because we are all "family." The humanitarian model, implicitly described by Wallace Alston, is that we should seek to create a better world by treating each individual as a human being regardless of biological or familial connection. The difference, I suppose, is that the humanitarian model has no investment in seeking out "blood" ties as a basis of ethical conduct or purchasing into familial patterns, which, as we saw in the first chapter, often entail a patriarchal structure of authority. The humanitarian model eschews "blood" as irrelevant since we are all impure and illegitimate in some way or other and rearticulates "family" as "kinship," where every person deserves to be treated well as a fellow human being who is symbolically a member of a larger and more significant corporate body than the family, the community, the nation. This might ultimately be the same thing as saying "we are all family," but "family" in this documentary has been viewed primarily as a matter of blood (as Macky Alston seeks cousins and then discovers his alienation by illegitimacy) or exclusion (for the point Eugene Alston Vivra makes at the family reunion is *not* that we are all derived from the same original parents but that certain people of European descent have done more than others). The humanitarian model, then, seems more promising, and strikes me as more clearly an echo of the point the palimpsest narratives of the seventies were making. There are blood connections that make us relatives, there are social connections that make us family, and there are humanitarian imperatives that should make us better.

Ball's *Slaves in the Family* reaches a rather different resolution and through different means. While Alston gives us three rival versions of moral paradigms, genetic, familial, humanistic, Ball gives us two connected stories ingeniously woven together throughout the family history. First, there is the narrative of symbolic accountability as he apologizes in person to the individuals and families who are descendants of the Ball family slaves. Second, there is the narrative of material decline as he traces the diminishing fortunes of the Ball family from its height during the eighteenth-century slave trade in Charleston to its depths when the former plantations are sold to public corporations for a pittance at the beginning of the twentieth century. These two narratives frame the book as a whole. He begins by claiming that while he is not guilty for "the past" or "culpable for the acts of others, long dead," he nonetheless feels "accountable for what had happened, called on to try and explain it," and ends with his apology to Mrs. Frayer: "I'm sorry for what my family did to your family." He also begins by noting that the "wealth created by the slave system was destroyed, and the latter-day Balls had no inheritance from it," and ends by showing us the rapid decline of the Ball family fortune by the time his grandfather was a contractor, his father an underpaid Episcopal priest, and he a Brown University undergraduate "on a scholarship and loans." "There was no land, no inheritance, no slave money."[41] What Ball is implying through the confluence of these stories is complex. On the one hand, he is genuinely apologetic and feels that there is an integral connection between the past and the present, between his family's pedigree and racial identity and what cultural capital he inherited as a possessor of both; while on the other, he also attempts to divorce accountability from the question of economic gains and therefore the issue of material reparations.

He concludes the book by marrying these two narratives in two distinct moments. In an epilogue to the family history, he describes his trip to Bunce Island in Sierra Leone, his visit to the descendants of the families of the Africans who sold other Africans into slavery, and their collective ceremony of commemoration on the banks of Port Loko Creek in Sierra Leone. In this moment, he widens the circle of those "accountable," thus buttressing his point about accountability for the past and also his point about economic reparations. In that final scene, on the banks of a river in a poor, war-torn African country, the reparations will assume symbolic proportions as a splash of rum and the rolling of kola nuts on the ground constitute the commemoration of those "sixty million" to whom *Beloved* is dedicated. In the other moment, Ball ends the book by "making a plea to the families of former slave owners" who kept records of their plantations to donate their "private letters and papers" to "public hands — archives, historical societies, museums, universities." These papers, he comments, "contain the family histories of millions" because they tell the stories of the slaves these families owned. What is important is the generating of stories of a shared past, of common ancestors; the papers donated to these public institutions will allow the wider distribution of the one gift he was able to give to the black families descended from Ball plantation slaves — genealogies, family trees, and knowledge of ancestors. The reparations for accountability, then, are spiritual and symbolic, assuming the forms of apologies and narratives of shared lives. In one interview he called his own book "a form of restitution."[42]

Perhaps it is cynical to say so, but part of what made Ball's book a media event, aside from the fact that it is a well-written and powerful account fairly daring in its approach and pretty impressive in its execution, is that he made quite clear that his restitutions would be symbolic, that his apologies would be verbal, that his reparations for the past crimes of his family would be more family history. Mainstream media hastily picked up on the favorable response such symbolism would evoke. In 1994, National Public Radio ran a 35-minute feature on Ball's family called "The Other History." After the publication of *Slaves in the Family*, Ball appeared on the Oprah Winfrey show to apologize on network television to the descendants of the Ball slaves. He now speaks and conducts conversations on race relations around the country. *Slaves in the Family* is starting to assume a privileged place in national cultural dialogues about race and responsibility. We can compare its popularity and the widespread attention it has garnered to a less well-known fact that in 1989 Representative John Conyers introduced a bill to establish a national commission to study reparations for African Americans, a bill voted down in the House that year and each and every year since.[43] The contrast between the receptions accorded these two calls for symbolic restitutions or material reparations is probably unfair, since congressional bills don't receive the media coverage of publishing events, but it is nonetheless telling, I think. In a climate of opinion where there is massive resistance to the idea of even an apology for slavery, claims of symbolic action are much more easily accepted than demands for material restitution. Of course, even symbolic actions, and purely personal ones at that, come under fire in such a climate, and Ball has had his share of detractors who claim that he has neither the responsibility nor the right to apologize to the descendants of Ball slaves.

Let me now take up what are arguably the two most pertinent issues in Ball's family history: the public ceremony of commemoration in Africa and the act of apologizing in America. There is a distinct difference between the book's reception in England and its reception in mainstream American presses. English journalists consistently comment on Ball's trip to Sierra Leone, while white American journalists tend to focus almost obsessively on his apologies on native grounds. I'll start with the issue the English reviewers raise. Almost without fail, the English journalists found problematic the final scene of Ball's visit to the individuals in Sierra Leone descended from slave-trading families. At the least critical, some considered the closing chapter a "coda rather than a climax," while the majority more critically thought it a moment where Ball showed his true colors when he "ridicule[d] the African chiefs . . . in true Ugly American fashion, for not sharing his sense of moral outrage about slavery." Most thought he exhibited precisely the kind of "'obliviousness' he condemns in his own family" by haranguing the Africans "in a way the Ball slave descendants have never harangued him."[44] While the strident tone Ball assumes in his visits with the descendants of slave traders in Sierra Leone is quite a departure from the usually equanimous and sometimes sorrowful ones he uses throughout the rest of the book, it is less his tone than his deeply flawed historical assumptions that are troubling in this scene.

In his discussions, through a mediator, with the venerable Chief Alikali Modu III, Ball states that he thinks the Ball and Modu "families have a shared responsibility" for the slave trade of the eighteenth century. "In part, it's my family's responsibility," he notes. "And in part it's the responsibility of the Africans who sold their own people." The problem with a family history, I suppose, might be that the "family" becomes the unit through which to understand "history." There can be no other way to explain what otherwise seems like Ball's willful obliviousness to the difference between the Modu family's role and his family's. To state the case as he does — two families are guilty of participating in an evil — is to ignore the glaringly obvious fact that there is a huge disparity in the kinds, levels, and degrees of responsibility here. The slave system on the West Coast of Africa was created by the Portuguese and refined by the English. It was dependent on the establishment of the great entrepôts in the delta ports at places like Elimina Castle, La Maison des Esclaves, and Cape Coast Castle. It represented "the first principal manifestations of modern, mercantile capitalism on the west coast of Africa." From those factories were transported the "human stock essential to New World wealth" and capitalist production in this country. Black Africans were marked as marketable objects, beings alienated from their humanity and valued as commercial commodities. White Europeans were marked as free entrepreneurs within a free market. This system, the slave trade, was *not* a result of mutual participation by the Loko and the American people, or the Madu and Ball families.[45] The slave trade was not an equal opportunity enterprise; and representing it as if each family were somehow mutually and equally responsible is to misrepresent it in a truly devious way. It reduces to caricature what was a complicated and coercive project that altered the economies and societies of three continents, that represented the largest forced migration in world history, and that directly created the underdevelopment of Africa and the degradation of those in the African diaspora. This is not a family affair, nor is it, at all, an affair in which these two particular families can claim or have ascribed equal responsibility.

On the whole, mainstream American journalists tended to ignore the description of Ball's trip to Sierra Leone and found themselves instead compelled to remark on the scenes where Ball apologizes to the individuals and families descended from Ball slaves, most likely because the book appeared at a point in American history when there was an extended dialogue about the possibility and meaning of apologizing for slavery. Some argued that the distinction between "culpable" and "accountable" was unclear, "a formula which he never manages to explain." In interviews, Ball has spelled out the difference. He told Dianne Aprile that "[a]ccountability requires exposing the truth, while responsibility requires assuming personal guilt," and clarified to Laura Lippman that one can be either "culpable, like a criminal who is culpable for a crime — or accountable, which is, for example, as a government is accountable for treaties it undertakes."[46] These clarifications are hardly satisfying, though. It can be objected that anyone can "expose" the truth, not only those who are descended from the people who committed the acts in question, and yet it is clearly Ball's privileged position as a direct descendant of slaveholders that makes his public apologies meaningful and worthy of the attention of a national media. And the accountability of national governments for legal treaties and individuals for their forebears' actions is hardly comparable, it seems to me. What is more important than the curious distinction Ball makes between accountability and culpability is the act of apologizing itself.

Ball has stated that "he has apologized only to the black families he became close to during his research because he believes apologies are personal matters between people who know each other well." "A blanket apology to all Ball plantation descendants would be an empty and perhaps arrogant act," Ball said. There are a couple of points raised by this distinction between personal apologies to an individual or family whom one knows and a large-scale apology to unknown individuals. For one thing, it plays out in a small and personal drama what is more meaningfully understood in large and political terms. It reduces what is a huge national issue (how did the country in its legislation and social mores mistreat African Americans for four hundred years in a way that currently affects the economic and social condition of people of African descent) to a personal matter between two people who in an hour's televised appearance can iron out the differences of a complex and horrific past. There is also something insidiously coercive about a person who does have and admits to having the privileges of caste initiating an apology for the historical crimes of his ancestors to people who are, in equal measure, denied those very same privileges of caste. What it effectively does is "shift the moral burden onto the offended party by focusing upon the issue of forgiveness." The scene of Ball apologizing to Mrs. Frayer as they visit the plantation where she was born is highly significant not only because it provides a moving account of two people of quite different backgrounds weeping together with sorrow and joy on the grounds of history, but also because it shows us the tension involved in this exchange, this dialectic of apology and forgiveness. Mrs. Frayer's response to Ball's first faltering effort to apologize is, "Don't think nothing of that, because that is past and gone." Her response to his second and personal statement of sorrow is a bit of a rebuke: "That's out of your jurisdiction altogether." Her final words after his third request for "forgiveness" are beautifully measured, not only in their cadence but also in the degree to which she does not accept all of the apology: "'Yes, we forgive,' she answered. 'It didn't hurt me, now, but the people before me, and they all gone.'" Just as there is no blanket apology, so Mrs. Frayer does not give a blanket forgiveness. What he is doing in bringing black and white people together is good, what he is accomplishing in recovering the past historical record of shared lives is important, but his apologizing for crimes that are too large and done to people who are "all gone" is, as she brilliantly puts it, "out of his jurisdiction."[47]

One final point about Ball's act of apologizing needs to be made. What is it that Ball's act truly accomplishes? A cynical reading would suggest that it is self-congratulatory. One reviewer, for instance, who called the book "self-flagellating," makes this point by quoting Russell Baker's 1997 comment on the idea of apologizing for historical events: "Apologizing for the country's past can only gratify the apologizer's desire to feel good about himself. It invites the audience to compare his moral tone to that of his ancestors, so derelict in their respect for humanity, and come out a winner. It not only enhances the apologizer's self-esteem. It doesn't cost him anything." This is precisely the point Wallace Alston was making by telling his son how "historically arrogant" it would have been to assume his morally pious stand in a historical moment that he can never fully recover and presume his ability to evade the ideological force of an institution he can never wholly comprehend. Yet, I would disagree with this cynical reading, since Ball strikes me as being far too sincere and feels far too implicated in some ways. What his apologizing does instead, I would argue, is unintentionally promote the conditions for undoing instead of redressing the past. In one of the few wise moments in a book otherwise marred by a simpleminded popular psychology of race, Shelby Steele commented that no kind of reparations, from affirmative action to a million dollars for each black family, could answer the "historic suffering of the race" or "obviate the residues of that oppression." Reverting to easy conservative bromides, Steele manages to avoid the obvious implications of that statement and see in what ways there can and should be a concerted national effort to evaluate and redress those past wrongs that have continuing effects. A sociologist of apology has noted that one of the curious characteristics of apologizing is that one of the major tasks of an apology is "to resolve conflicts and somehow restore an antecedent moral order by expunging or eradicating the harmful effects of past actions." I don't think Ball is actually trying to apologize in order to make moot any claims of the social effects slavery has had on African American citizens, but his action can be understood, especially in a national neoconservative ethos that believes in rugged economic individualism and denies the relevance of the collective past, as precisely the kind of symbolic gesture that gets slavery behind us instead of in front of us. Put least charitably, an apology, misunderstood as an insincere means of evasion, one that, in Baker's words, doesn't cost anything, can effectively replicate the alchemy of the 1705 statute. It can again make slavery an "accident [that] never happened."[48] And that would be unforgivable.

I have so far noted the differences between the white American and the English receptions of *Slaves in the Family*. It is worth noting in conclusion the responses of four black journalists who wrote about Ball's book. Caryl Phillips praised it because "the author has understood something that most African-Americans know intuitively: that history and the past are not irrelevant, and they govern the present." Leonard Pitts found it remarkable because "Ball is the first white person [he's] ever heard of — the very 'first' — to acknowledge . . . that white families have black kin." Vivian Martin felt Ball performed solid work, and thought that a "blanket apology" for slavery was "not necessary," but that a "full, contextual acknowledgement of the historical record is." Mae Gentry found that she and Ball were "distant cousins, linked by a common ancestor from the 17th century."[49] While the white American journalists focused on the issue of apology, and the English journalists tended to comment on the scene in Sierra Leone, the African American journalists attended to the curious and complex set of ideas among history, race, and family. They admired Ball's willingness to see the connection between the past and the present, between black and white kin. They admired, in other words, just what the palimpsest narratives written by African American authors in the 1970s raised as the pertinent issues about America's vexed and vexing relationship with its slave past.

Recent American attitudes toward history, as we see in this brief survey, can vary from the lyrical to the narrative, from the genetic to the apologetic. It is certainly not my intent to judge between the lyrical and narrative models of ethical conduct or the humanitarian and apologetic discourses in the family histories, although I don't think I have been coyly hiding that I am largely in agreement with the ideas and principles behind the palimpsest imperative and thus more in sympathy with those models and practices and stories in the present that recognize the relevance of the past, especially the slave past that hitherto received too-scant notice and is now perhaps subject to a too-superficial regard. It is rather my intent to describe some of the discussions, debates, and dialogues that emerge from and attest to the continuing pertinence of the topic of slavery in American culture, especially as those debates and dialogues of the seventies took and gave shape to contemporary manifestations of that discussion. What does "family" mean in a society where some 100,000 people of African descent can trace their lineage back to just the Ball plantations outside Charleston, South Carolina? What does "race" mean when a white man and a black woman share not only what Alston calls a "family name" but also a common ancestor? And what does "apology" mean in light of such a history of biological connection and social division? What is the shame or the crime for which the nation attempted and failed to apologize?

Let me conclude this study by briefly pointing to two representative anecdotes. In November 1998, the *New York Times* reported that scientists at the University of Virginia had conclusively proven through DNA testing that Thomas Jefferson had indeed fathered a child with his slave Sally Hemings, a point of contention among American historians since James T. Callender published an article alleging that Jefferson was indeed having an affair with his slave in the September 1, 1802, issue of the *Richmond Recorder*.[50] This new information proved that the African American testimony was right all along; those black descendants who claimed ancestry from Thomas Jefferson by referring to their own oral traditions and family histories have finally been validated, as Jefferson scholars began to recognize. What is especially interesting is the sense of intimacy and distance this story evokes. It is, after all, about a 210-year-old paternity suit. Yet it speaks to the struggle of not only the particular descendants of this specific line of Jeffersons but all African Americans to get recognized as *kin* in America. It exposes once more just how persistent that family secret of slavery is, just how secret and just how deeply embedded in the idea of family. The second anecdote reveals the reason for the social distance. Slaves transported from Sierra Leone in the eighteenth century were branded with the acronym for the Royal African

Company of England (RACE).[51] I can think of no more eloquent pair of images to expose the deep flaws in American culture's attitude and modes of behavior toward people of African descent: one portrays the familial intermingling of slave and slaveholder, the other the brand of race that has kept that family, that kin, from recognition.

Notes

CHAPTER ONE

The title of this chapter is taken from Michael Harper, *History Is Your Own Heartbeat* (Urbana: University of Illinois Press, 1971).

1. Edmund S. Morgan, *American Slavery, American Freedom: The Ordeal of Colonial Virginia* (New York: Norton, 1975), 3–24, 363–87. Vincent Harding, "Beyond Chaos: Black History and the Search for the New Land," in *Amistad 1*, eds. John A. Williams and Charles F. Harris (New York: Random House, 1970), 283. John Leo, "So Who's Sorry Now?," *U.S. News and World Report* (June 30, 1997): 17. Dierdre Glenn Paul, "America Owes Blacks an Apology—At the Very Least," *The Record*, Review and Outlook Section (July 13, 1997): 4.

2. W. J. T. Mitchell, "Narrative, Memory, and Slavery," in *Cultural Artifacts and the Production of Meaning: The Page, the Image, and the Body*, ed. Margaret J. M. Ezell and Katherine O'Brien O'Keeffee (Ann Arbor: University of Michigan Press, 1994), 200.

3. Toni Morrison, *Beloved* (New York: NAL, 1987). Geoffrey Hartman, "Public Memory and Its Discontents," *Raritan* 13 (1994): 36. Mitchell, "Narrative, Memory, and Slavery," 212.

4. Shoshana Felman and Dori Laub, *Testimony: Crises of Witnessing in Literature, Psychoanalysis, and History* (New York: Routledge, 1992), xix. The comment is about *Shoah*. See Claude Lanzmann, *Shoah: An Oral History of the Holocaust* (New York: Pantheon, 1985); Lanzmann, "Seminar with Claude Lanzmann 11 April 1990," *Yale French Studies* 79 (1991): 82–99; and Lanzmann, "The Obscenity of Understanding: An Evening with Claude Lanzmann," *American Imago* 48 (1991): 473–95.

5. Richard Terdiman, "Deconstructing Memory: On Representing the Past and Theorizing Culture in France since the Revolution," *diacritics* 15 (1985): 14–15.

6. In an interview with Gloria Naylor, Toni Morrison noted that her desire to write a narrative about slavery was truly a desire to invoke all those people who were "unburied, or at least unceremoniously buried," and to go about "properly, artistically, burying them." The purpose of burying them, though, is to bring them back into "living life." Lanzmann refers to wanting to "incarnate" and "resurrect." See Gloria Naylor and Toni Morrison, "A Conversation," *Southern Review* 21 (1985): 584–85. Lanzmann; quoted in Felman and Laub, *Testimony*, 216.

7. Felman and Laub, *Testimony*, 67.

8. Morrison, *Beloved*, 36–37.

9. I adapt these two paragraphs from my "'Rememory': Primal Scenes and Constructions in Toni Morrison's Novels," *Contemporary Literature* 31, no. 3 (Fall 1990): 302.

10. Thomas Carlyle, "On History," in *The Works of Thomas Carlyle*, 30 vols. (London: Chapman and Hall, 1889–1905), 27:90, 88.

11. Gayl Jones, "From *The Machete Woman*: A Novel," *Callaloo* 17 (1994): 399, 402.

12. Deepak Narang Sawhney, "Palimpsest: Towards a Minor Literature in Monstrosity," in *Deleuze and Philosophy: The Difference Engineer*, ed. Keith Ansell Pearson (New York: Routledge, 1997), 130. For another discussion of the dynamics of what she calls a "palimpsest text," see Hortense Spillers, "Introduction: Who Cuts the Border?: Some Readings on 'America,'" in *Comparative American Identities: Race, Sex, and Nationality in the Modern Text*, ed. Spillers (New York: Routledge, 1991), 1–25.

13. Some of the ideas and language in this and the following two paragraphs are adapted from my entry for "Neo-Slave Narratives" in *The Oxford Companion to African American Literature*, eds. William L. Andrews, Trudier Harris, and Frances Smith Foster (New York: Oxford University Press, 1997), 533–35. I am here narrowing the definition of palimpsest narratives from those works in either first or third person to only those works in the first person.

14. Hazel V. Carby, "Ideologies of Black Folk: The Historical Novel of Slavery," in *Slavery and the Literary Imagination*, eds. Deborah E. McDowell and Arnold Rampersad (Baltimore: Johns Hopkins University Press, 1989), 125–43.

15. Rayford Logan, *The Negro in American Life and Thought: The Nadir, 1877–1901* (New York: Dial Press, 1954). Carby, *Reconstructing Womanhood: The Emergence of the Afro-American Woman Novelist* (New York: Oxford University Press, 1987). Eric J. Sundquist, *To Wake the Nations: Race in the Making of American Literature* (Cambridge: Harvard University Press, 1993).

16. See my "Neo-Slave Narratives," *Oxford Companion to African American Literature*, 533–35.

17. Howard Junker, "Who Erased the Seventies?," *Esquire* 88 (Decem-

ber 1977): 152–55. Daniel Bell, *The Coming of Post-Industrial Society: A Venture in Social Forecasting* (New York: Basic Books, 1973). Christopher Lasch, "Toward a Theory of Post-Industrial Society," in *Politics in the PostWelfare State: Responses to the New Individualism*, ed. M. Donald Hancock and Gideon Sjoberg (New York: Columbia University Press, 1972), 36–50. J. David Hoeveler Jr., *The Postmodernist Turn: American Thought and Culture in the 1970s* (New York: Twayne, 1996). Michael Omi and Howard Winant, *Racial Formation in the United States from the 1960s to the 1980s* (New York: Routledge, 1986). Michael Harrington, *Decade of Decision: The Crisis of the American System* (New York: Simon & Schuster, 1980). For a more positive assessment of the politics and social movements of the 1970s, see Peter Clecak, *America's Quest for the Ideal Self: Dissent and Fulfillment in the 60s and 70s* (New York: Oxford University Press, 1983); for a more whimsical look at the popular culture of the decade, see Andrew J. Edelstein and Kevin McDonough, *The Seventies: From Hot Pants to Hot Tubs* (New York: Dutton, 1990).

18. Hoeveler, *The Postmodernist Turn*, 4. Harrington, *Decade of Decision*, 234.

19. Lasch, *The Culture of Narcissism: American Life in an Age of Diminishing Expectations* (New York: Norton, 1979), 4, 6, 30, 237, 238. Stephanie Coontz, *The Way We Never Were: American Families and the Nostalgia Trap* (New York: Basic Books, 1992), 102–6, 176–78. George Gilder, *Naked Nomads* (New York: Times Books, 1974), 10. For another argument about the seventies themselves as a "Hobbesian" decade, see Irving Louis Horowitz, *Ideology and Utopia in the United States, 1956–1976* (New York: Oxford University Press, 1977), 6–7.

20. [Daniel Patrick Moynihan], *The Negro Family: The Case for National Action* (Washington, D.C.: Office of Policy Planning and Research, United States Department of Labor, 1965). For information on the events leading up to the writing of the Moynihan Report, see Nicolas Lemann, *The Promised Land: The Great Black Migration and How It Changed America* (New York: Random House, 1991), 170–81. For information on the reception of the report, see Lee Rainwater and William L. Yancey, *The Moynihan Report and the Politics of Controversy* (Cambridge: MIT Press, 1967); James Farmer, "The Controversial Moynihan Report," *Amsterdam News* (December 18, 1965), reprinted in Rainwater and Yancey, ibid., 409–11; and William Ryan, *Blaming the Victim* (1971; rev. ed.; New York: Random House, 1976), 63–88.

21. Omi and Winant, *Racial Formation*, 120–22. Moynihan, Memo to Nixon, quoted in Peter Carroll, *It Seemed Like Nothing Happened: The Tragedy and Promise of America in the 1970s* (New York: Holt, Rinehart and Winston, 1982), 41. Omi and Winant, ibid., 113.

22. Robin D. G. Kelley, *Yo' Mama's Disfunktional: Fighting the Culture Wars in Urban America* (Boston: Beacon, 1997), 8–10. Wahneema Lubiano, "Black Nationalism and Black Common Sense: Policing Ourselves and Others," in *The House That Race Built: Black Americans, U.S. Terrain*, ed. Lubiano (New York: Pantheon, 1997), 246, 250.

23. George P. Rawick, *From Sundown to Sunup: The Making of a Black Community* (Westport, Conn.: Greenwood Publishing Company, 1972). John W. Blassingame, *The Slave Community: Plantation Life in the Antebellum South* (1972; New York: Oxford University Press, 1979). Eugene D. Genovese, *Roll, Jordan, Roll: The World the Slaves Made* (New York: Random House, 1974). Herbert Gutmann, *The Black Family in Slavery and Freedom, 1750–1925* (New York: Random House, 1976). Moynihan was, of course, drawing on the work of Stanley Elkins, whose *Slavery: A Problem in American Institutional and Intellectual Life* (1959, 3d ed.; Chicago: University of Chicago Press, 1976) inspired or at least provided a point of critical entry for most of the historiography on slavery in the 1970s.

24. "Why 'Roots' Hit Home," *Time* (February 14, 1977): 69–70. David Gerber, "Haley's *Roots* and Our Own: An Inquiry into the Nature of a Popular Phenomenon," *Journal of Ethnic Studies* 5 (1977): 87–111. Willie Lee Rose, *Slavery and Freedom* (New York: Oxford University Press, 1982), 118–21. Seven of the eight episodes of *Roots* ranked among the all-time Top Ten–rated television programs in audience size. For studies on the reception of *Roots*, especially its differential reception between black and white Americans, see Kenneth Hur, "Impact of 'Roots' on Black and White Teenagers," *Journal of Broadcasting* 22 (1978): 289–98; Hur and John Robinson, "The Social Impact of 'Roots,'" *Journalism Quarterly* 55 (1978): 19–21; John Howard, George Rothbart, and Lee Sloan, "The Response to 'Roots': A National Survey," *Journal of Broadcasting* 22 (1978): 279–87; Halford Fairchild, Russell Stockard, and Philip Bowman, "Impact of 'Roots': Evidence from the National Survey of Black Americans," *Journal of Black Studies* 16 (1988): 307–18; and Richard M. Merelman, *Representing Black Culture: Racial Conflict and Cultural Politics in the United States* (New York: Routledge, 1995), 255–81.

25. Edward Ball, *Slaves in the Family* (New York: Farrar, Strauss and Giroux, 1998), 64. James A. Hijiya, "Roots: Family and Ethnicity in the 1970s," *American Quarterly* 30 (Fall 1978): 548. Gerber, "Haley's *Roots*," 87–88. Hijiya, "Roots," 549. Rose, *Slavery and Freedom*, 120. Hijiya, "Roots," 552. Gerald Early, "The American Mysticism of Remembrance," in *Race: An Anthology in the First Person*, ed. Bart Schneider (New York: Crown Trade, 1997), 12.

26. David Chione Moore, "Routes: Alex Haley's *Roots* and the Rhetoric of Genealogy," *Transition* 64 (1994): 7. Cf. Michael Kammen, *Mystic Chords of Memory: The Transformation of Tradition in American Culture* (New York: Random House, 1991), 618–54.

27. Margaret Walker, "Religion, Poetry, and History Foundations for a New Educational System," in *The Black Seventies*, ed. Floyd B. Barbour (Boston: Porter Sargent, 1970), 292. Vincent Harding, in "An Exchange on Nat Turner," *New York Review of Books* (November 7, 1968): 35–37. Ralph Ellison, "Hidden Name and Complex Fate: A Writer's Experience in the United States," in *Shadow and Act* (New York: Random House, 1964), 148. Ellison, William Styron, Robert Penn Warren, and C. Vann Woodward, "The Uses of History in Fiction," *Southern Literary Journal* 1 (Spring 1969): 57–90,

reprinted in *Conversations with William Styron*, ed. James L. W. West III (Jackson: University Press of Mississippi, 1985), 127.

28. Margaret Walker, "How I Wrote *Jubilee*," in *How I Wrote Jubilee and Other Essays on Life and Literature*, ed. Maryemma Graham (New York: Feminist Press, 1990), 56, 64. Ernest J. Gaines, "Miss Jane and I," *Callaloo* 1, no. 3 (May 1978): 37–38. Pauli Murray, *Proud Shoes: The Story of an American Family* (1956; New York: Harper & Row, 1987), viii, 59–60. Alex Haley, "Black History, Oral History, and Genealogy," *Oral History Review* 1 (1973): 1–25, reprinted in *Oral History: An Interdisciplinary Anthology*, eds. David K. Dunaway and Willa K. Baum (Nashville: American Association for State and Local History, 1984), 286. I am not suggesting a radical difference between Gaines's and Walker's attitudes regarding the place of historical documentation in an oral history, however, for Walker, in her own way, was equally determined to use her great-grandmother's oral tale to dismantle the sense of "history" as a set of "literary documents" or a series of "books in the libraries." At the end of her essay, after noting her indebtedness to Georg Lukács for giving her an "understanding of the popular character of the historical novel," Walker points out that she was among the first novelists who represented "characters looking up from the bottom rather than down from the top." What this change in vista provided, she continued, was a change in the magnitude of the players in the Civil War and Reconstruction. She gained an understanding that "Abraham Lincoln as a world historical figure . . . was always a minor character [when] seen through the mind of the major characters" of her grandmother's oral history. As much as Gaines, then, Walker went back from her library research to what her grandmother and others have to say in order to supplement the "old documents."

29. Derrick Bell, *Faces at the Bottom of the Well: The Permanence of Racism* (New York: Basic Books, 1992), 1. "Alice Walker and *The Color Purple*," BBC TV Documentary (1986); quoted in Barbara Christian, "'Somebody Forgot to Tell Somebody Something': African-American Women's Historical Novels," *Wild Women in the Whirlwind: Afra-American Culture and the Contemporary Literary Renaissance*, ed. Joanne Braxton and Andrée Nicola McLaughlin (New Brunswick, N.J.: Rutgers University Press, 1990), 326. Walker, "How I Wrote *Jubilee*," 51. Murray, *Proud Shoes*, 60, 62. Dorothy Spruill Redford with Michael D'Orso, *Somerset Homecoming: Recovering a Lost Heritage* (New York: Doubleday, 1988), 21. Cf. Kathryn L. Morgan, *Children of Strangers: The Stories of a Black Family* (Philadelphia: Temple University Press, 1980), 111, who also describes how her family muted the stories about the family's slave experience. We can get an idea of the prevalence of "shame" in slave ancestry by noting the "pride" in the Madden family's claim not to have any slave ancestors. "We have always been free," T. O. Madden Jr. proclaimed in the biography of his Virginia family. "Though we have sometimes been servants, sometimes laborers, no member of our family has ever been a slave." T. O. Madden Jr., with Ann L. Miller, *We Were Always Free: The Maddens of Culpeper County, Virginia, A 200-Year Family History* (New York: W. W. Norton, 1992), xxiii.

30. Jan Willis, personal communication. Willis, "Orphaned Again" (manuscript), 6–8, 11. Willis carefully records the sequence of her emotions at discovering this fact about her family history. She responded initially with a kind of despair in feeling utterly powerless and helpless. Eventually, she began to "feel orphaned again" as she gradually acknowledged the destruction of a "family that was *my* kin." "[U]nhinged and disturbed," she suffered a bout of "deep soulful crying." Finally, for "days after learning of Adam's sale," Willis writes, "I was *ashamed*, when talking to friends, to 'admit' it." Even when conversing with her sister Sandy, she found herself "ashamed." I would like to thank my friend and colleague Jan Willis for allowing me to quote from her book manuscript.

31. Ralph Ellison, *Invisible Man* (1952; New York: Random House, 1982), 15. Redford, *Somerset Homecoming*, 32–34. Derrick Bell pointed out that the acceptance of a genuine history of slavery produces a deep "pride" in the humanity and courage of slave ancestors. Alice Walker replaced her family's "whispers" with loud and boisterous conversations with her fictional creations when they "would come for a visit." Margaret Walker defied her father's assessment of her grandmother's "old slavery-time stories," and went on to write the story of her great-grandmother's life under slavery and Reconstruction, the path-breaking *Jubilee*. Pauli Murray discovered that "true emancipation lies in the acceptance of the whole past, in deriving strength from my roots, in facing up to the degradation as well as the dignity of my ancestors." Likewise, Jan Willis struggled against the "shame" she had temporarily felt and continued on a search determined to discover for herself an "expanded family" of "new kin" and for her mother a "direct and far-reaching life-line," a "solid ground and strong familial roots." Renouncing the residues of personal shame, dispelling family silences about the past, identifying and celebrating slave ancestors, these African American subjects found themselves ultimately closer to kin and a feeling of freedom. See Bell, *And We Are Not Saved: The Elusive Quest for Racial Justice* (New York: Basic Books, 1987), 215–35. Alice Walker, "The Color Purple Didn't Come Easy," *San Francisco Chronicle Book Review* (October 10, 1982), reprinted as "Writing *The Color Purple*," in *In Search of Our Mother's Gardens: Womanist Prose* (San Diego: Harcourt Brace Jovanovich, 1983), 359, 356. Margaret Walker, "How I Wrote *Jubilee*," 51. Murray, *Proud Shoes*, 61, 62. Jan Willis, "Allen G. Watters" (manuscript), 9, and "Orphaned Again" (manuscript), 6.

32. Carole Ione, *Pride of Family: Four Generations of American Women of Color* (New York: Simon & Schuster, 1991), 12–13, 188, 207. Murray, *Proud Shoes*, 61, 62.

33. Fredric Jameson, *The Political Unconscious: Narrative as a Socially Symbolic Act* (Ithaca, N.Y.: Cornell University Press, 1981), 173, 180.

34. Esther Rashkin, *Family Secrets and the Psychoanalysis of Narrative* (Princeton, N.J.: Princeton University Press, 1992), 47, 44. Nicolas Abraham and Maria Torok, *The Wolf Man's Magic Word: A Cryptonymy*, trans. Nicolas Rand (Minneapolis: University of Minnesota Press, 1986), lxv.

35. Jacques Derrida, "Foreword: *Fors*: The Anglish Words of Nicolas Abraham and Maria Torok," trans. Barbara Johnson, in *The Wolf Man's Magic Word*, xxxvi. Nicolas Abraham and Maria Torok, "Introjection — Incorporation: Mourning or Melancholia," in *Psychoanalysis in France*, eds. Serge Lebovici and Daniel Widlöcher (New York: International Universities Press, Inc., 1980), 9.

36. Nicolas Abraham and Maria Torok, "A Poetics of Psychoanalysis: 'The Lost Object — Me,'" *SubStance* 13, no. 2 (1984): 17 (n. 1). Abraham and Torok, *The Wolf Man's Magic Word*, 76. Nicolas Rand, "Psychoanalysis with Literature: An Abstract of Nicolas Abraham and Maria Torok's *The Shell and the Kernel*," *Oxford Literary Review* 12, no. 1–2 (1990): 60, 61. For more on the "phantom," see Abraham and Torok, "Notes on the Phantom: A Complement to Freud's Metapsychology," *Critical Inquiry* 13 (Winter 1987): 287–92. Also see the essays collected in Abraham and Torok, *The Shell and the Kernel: Renewals of Psychoanalysis*, ed. Nicolas Rand (Chicago: University of Chicago Press, 1994), especially the essays in the section "Secrets and Posterity: The Theory of the Transgenerational Phantom" (165–205).

37. Rashkin, *Family Secrets and the Psychoanalysis of Narrative*, 18, 156.

38. I say I will be employing "*something like* a cryptonomy" in my reading of the palimpsest narratives because I am dealing with only a few features of the work of Abraham and Torok; others are not particulary useful for my purposes, and some are suspect in my eyes. Readers who wish to see a more thorough, sustained, and comprehensive application of cryptonomy to literary texts should consult Abraham and Torok's *The Wolf Man's Magic Word*, Rashkin's *Family Secrets and the Psychoanalysis of Narrative*, and, especially, Abraham, "The Phantom of Hamlet or the Sixth Act: Preceded by the Intermission of 'Truth,'" *diacritics* 18, no. 4 (Winter 1988): 2–19. For a fuller discussion of "The Phantom of Hamlet" in terms of its potential as literary theory and its place in Abraham and Torok's ouevre, see Rashkin, "Tools for a New Psychoanalytic Literary Criticism: The Work of Abraham and Torok," *diacritics* 18, no. 4 (Winter 1988): 31–52; and Rand, "Family Romance or Family History?: Psychoanalysis and Dramatic Invention in Nicolas Abraham's 'The Phantom of Hamlet,'" *diacritics* 18, no. 4 (Winter 1988): 20–30.

39. Ione, *Pride of Family*, 75, 131, 212, 213.

40. Rudolph J. Vecoli, "Ethnicity: A Neglected Dimension of American History," in *The State of American History*, ed. Herbert J. Bass (Chicago: Quadrangle, 1970), 70–88. Irving Howe, "The Limits of Ethnicity," *New Republic* (June 25, 1977): 17–19. Michael Novak, *Unmeltable Ethnics: Politics and Culture in American Life* (1972; New Brunswick, N.J.: Transaction Publishers, 1996), 3–57. Nathan Glazer, "Universalisation of Ethnicity," *Encounter* 2 (1975): 16.

41. Daniel Bell, "Ethnicity and Social Change," in *Ethnicity: Theory and Experience*, eds. Nathan Glazer and Daniel Patrick Moynihan (Cambridge, Mass.: Harvard University Press, 1975), 157, 169. Gunnar Myrdal, "The Case against Romantic Ethnicity," *Center Magazine* (July/August 1974): 26–30.

Herbert Gans, "Foreword" to Neil C. Sandberg, *Ethnic Identity and Assimilation* (New York: Praeger, 1974). Abner Cohen, *Customs and Politics in Urban Africa* (Berkeley: University of California Press, 1969), 191–92. I am drawing heavily here on Werner Sollor's superb bibliographical survey, "Theory of American Ethnicity, or: S ETHNIC?/TI AND AMERICANITI, DE OR UNITED (W) STATES S SI AND THEOR?," *American Quarterly* 33 (1981): 257–83.

42. Nathan Glazer, "Blacks and Ethnic Groups: The Difference and the Political Difference It Makes," *Social Problems* 18 (1971): 447. Pierre L. van den Berghe, *Race and Racism: A Comparative Perspective* (New York: Wiley, 1967), 9–10. David Theo Goldberg, *Racist Culture* (Oxford: Blackwell, 1993), 75–76. (This debate is fully summarized in Werner Sollors, "Foreword: Theories of American Ethnicity," in *Theories of Ethnicity: A Classical Reader*, ed. Sollors [New York: New York University Press, 1996], xxix–xxxv.) Stuart Hall, *Critical Dialogues in Cultural Studies*, ed. David Morley and Kuan-Hsing Chen (New York: Routledge, 1996), 446.

43. Sollors, *Beyond Ethnicity: Consent and Descent in American Culture* (New York: Oxford University Press, 1986), 37. Omi and Winant, *Racial Formation in the United States*, 21–24.

44. Sollors, *Beyond Ethnicity*, 37. Manning Marable, "Clarence Thomas and the Crisis of Black Political Culture," in *Race-ing Justice, En-gendering Power: Essays on Anita Hill, Clarence Thomas, and the Construction of Social Reality*, ed. Toni Morrison (New York: Pantheon, 1992), 82.

45. Jim Sleeper, in "Race and Racism: American Dilemmas Revisited," *Salmagundi* 104–5 (Fall 1994–Winter 1995): 125. Sleeper, *Liberal Racism* (New York: Viking, 1997), 182. See Winthrop D. Jordan, *White over Black: American Attitudes toward the Negro, 1550–1812* (1968; New York: Norton, 1977). George Fredrickson, *The Black Image in the White Mind: The Debate on Afro-American Character and Destiny, 1817–1914* (1971; Middletown, Conn.: Wesleyan University Press, 1987).

46. *Civil Rights Issues of Euro-Ethnic Americans in the United States: Opportunities and Challenges. A Consultation Sponsored by the United States Commission on Civil Rights, Chicago, Illinois, December 3, 1979* (Washington, D.C., 1980), quoted in Philip Gleason, "Identifying Identity: A Semantic History," *Journal of American History* 69 (1983): 910–31, reprinted in *Theories of Ethnicity: A Classical Reader*, 470. Barbara Fields, in "Race and Racism," 34.

47. Jordan, *White over Black*, 95. Nell Irvin Painter, "Soul Murder and Slavery: Toward a Fully Loaded Cost Accounting," in *U.S. History as Women's History: New Feminist Essays*, ed. Linda K. Kerber, Alice Kessler-Harris, and Kathryn Kish Sklar (Chapel Hill: University of North Carolina Press, 1995), 129. Fields, "Slavery, Race and Ideology in the United States of America," *New Left Review* 181 (1990): 117.

48. P. Binzen, *Whitetown, USA* (New York: Random House, 1970). David T. Wellman, *Portraits of White Racism* (New York: Cambridge University Press, 1977). Judy H. Katz, *White Awareness: Handbook for Anti-Racism Training* (Norman: University of Oklahoma Press, 1978). David Roediger, *The*

dering the Black Critical 'I,'" *Calalloo* 16 (1993): 566–70; and Sally Robinson, *Engendering the Subject: Gender and Self-Representation in Contemporary Women's Fiction* (Albany: State University of New York Press, 1991), 24–27, 135–87. For a study of the ways *Corregidora* adopts while challenging the dictates of Black Aesthetic theory, especially those ideas about the value of oral forms, see Madhu Dubey, *Black Women Novelists and the Nationalist Aesthetic* (Bloomington: Indiana University Press, 1994), 72–88.

5. Recent studies of African American women's writing as engaged in history include Susan Willis, *Specifying: Black Women Writing the American Experience* (1987; London: Routledge, 1990); Barbara Christian, "'Somebody Forgot to Tell Somebody Something': African-American Women's Historical Novels," in *Wild Women in the Whirlwind: Afra-American Culture and the Contemporary Literary Renaissance*, ed. Joanne M. Braxton and Andrée Nicola McLaughlin (New Brunswick, N.J.: Rutgers University Press, 1990), 326–41; Kubitschek, *Claiming the Heritage*; and Melissa Walker, *Down from the Mountaintop: Black Women's Novels in the Wake of the Civil Rights Movement, 1966–1989* (New Haven, Conn.: Yale University Press, 1991).

6. Claudia C. Tate, "An Interview with Gayl Jones," *Black American Literature Forum* 13 (1979): 143. Rowell, "An Interview with Gayl Jones," 45.

7. Tate, "Interview with Gayl Jones," 143. Michael S. Harper, "Gayl Jones: An Interview," in *Chant of Saints: A Gathering of Afro-American Literature, Art, and Scholarship*, ed. Michael S. Harper and Robert B. Stepto (Urbana: University of Illinois Press, 1979), 368. Harper, "History as Rat Poison: Gailgone: Gail's Song," in *History Is Your Own Heartbeat* (Urbana: University of Illinois Press, 1971), 88. Jones, "Wild Figs and Secret Places," in *The Hermit-Woman*, 21.

8. Kristina Minister, "Rehearsing for the Ultimate Audience," *Performance, Culture, and Identity*, ed. Elizabeth C. Fine and Jean Haskell Speer (Westport, Conn.: Praeger Publishers, 1992), 269.

9. Pauli Murray, *Proud Shoes: The Story of an American Family* (1956; New York: Harper & Row, 1987), xvi. Trinh T. Minh-ha, *Woman, Native, Other: Writing Postcoloniality and Feminism* (Bloomington: Indiana University Press, 1989), 123.

10. Jones, *Liberating Voices*, 105: "In storytelling the oral tradition reinforces, complements, and acts on the reality."

11. Trinh, *Woman, Native, Other*, 133, 134, 148. Mikhail Bakhtin, *The Dialogic Imagination: Four Essays*, trans. Caryl Emerson and Michael Holquist, ed. Michael Holquist (Austin: University of Texas Press, 1981), 286, 343, 345, 346. Although, as Bakhtin says, "Dialogic relations . . . . are possible only between complete utterances of various speaking subjects," the "speaking subjects" need not be contemporaries. Dialogic relations, he continues, "do not in any way coincide with relations among rejoinders of real dialogue." Utterances can be dialogic even if they are "separated from one another both in time and in space." Bakhtin, "The Problem of the Text in Linguistics, Philology, and the Human Sciences: An Experiment in Philosophical Analysis," in

Wages of Whiteness: Race and the Making of the American Working Class (New York: Verso, 1991). Eric Lott, *Love and Theft: Blackface Minstrelsy and the American Working Class* (New York: Oxford University Press, 1995). Ruth Frankenberg, *White Women, Race Matters: The Social Construction of Whiteness* (Minneapolis: University of Minnesota Press, 1993). Vron Ware, *Beyond the Pale: White Women, Racism and History* (New York: Verso, 1992).

49. Jones, *Corregidora* (1975; Boston: Beacon, 1986), 11, 45. David Bradley, *The Chaneysville Incident* (1981; New York: Harper & Row, 1990), 223. Richard Dyer, "White," *Screen* 29 (1988): 44.

50. James Baldwin, *No Name in the Street* (New York: Dial Press, 1972), reprinted in Baldwin, *The Price of the Ticket: Collected Nonfiction, 1948–1985* (New York: St. Martin's, 1985), 547.

51. Coontz, *The Way We Never Were*, 115. Also see Coontz, *The Social Origins of Private Life: A History of American Families, 1600–1900* (New York: Verso, 1988); and Coontz, *The Way We Really Are: Coming to Terms with America's Changing Families* (New York: Basic, 1997).

52. Cf. Raymond T. Smith, "Family," in *International Encyclopedia of the Social Sciences*, ed. David L. Sills (New York: Macmillan, 1968), 5:301–12; and Fred Eggan, Jack Goody, and Julian Pitt-Rivers, "Kinship," in *International Encyclopedia of the Social Sciences*, 8:390–413.

53. Philip A. Bruce, *The Plantation Negro as a Freeman* (New York: Putnam's, 1889). See Coontz, *The Way We Never Were*, 111; and Sundquist, *To Wake the Nations*, 394. Patricia J. Williams, *The Rooster's Egg* (Cambridge, Mass.: Harvard University Press, 1995), 7–8, notes the recent resurgence of the Moynihan Report.

54. Frances Harper, *Iola Leroy* (1892), in *The African American Novel in the Age of Reaction*, ed. William Andrews (Mentor, 1992). Pauline Hopkins, *Contending Forces* (1900; New York: Oxford University Press, 1988). Charles Chesnutt, *Marrow of Tradition* (1901) in *The African American Novel in the Age of Reaction*. Hopkins, *Of One Blood* (1902), in Hopkins, *The Magazine Novels* (New York: Oxford University Press, 1988).

55. For critical studies of other African American fiction that challenges the cultural nationalism of the Black Power movement, see Elliott Butler-Evans, *Race, Gender, and Desire: Narrative Strategies in the Fiction of Toni Cade Bambara, Toni Morrison, and Alice Walker* (Philadelphia: Temple University Press, 1989); and Madhu Dubey, *Black Women Novelists and the Nationalist Aesthetic* (Bloomington: Indiana University Press, 1994). For a historical study of the Black Power movement as a whole, see William L. Van Deburg, *New Day in Babylon: The Black Power Movement and American Culture, 1965–1975* (Chicago: University of Chicago Press, 1992). For a contemporary analysis of the development of cultural nationalist ideas about black identity, see George Napper, *Blacker than Thou: The Struggle for Campus Unity* (Grand Rapids, Mich.: William B. Eerdmans, 1973).

56. Consider Pauli Murray's use of generational memory. Murray asserts that in "telling [her] grandmother's story [she] had to embrace *all* the tangled

roots from which [she] had sprung, and to accept without evasion [her] own slave heritage, with all its ambivalence and paradoxes." Her own text of her grandmother's story became a "resolution of a search for identity and the exorcism of ghosts of the past." Tamara Hareven points out that a "sense of history does not depend on the depth of generational memory, but identity and consciousness do, because they rest on the linkage of the individual's life history and family history with specific historical moments." Mikhail Bakhtin notes that "generations . . . introduce the continuity of lives taking place at various times." If the "linkages" are not being made, if the "contiguity" is not recognized, then the "generational memory" is inutile at best and dysfunctional at worst. Elizabeth Stone comments on the ways generational connections assume value in narratives of family: "Family stories, whatever else they are, can be little moments of history or slices of sociology. As to our personal questions about who we might become, family stories obligingly offer us our own taslismans and mentors. . . . Eventually we come of age and tell the story of our own lives in which the past has become our prologue: we have our own family and invent an ethos for it. This is the stage of transformations, willed or unwilled, the point at which we make our own meanings. Our meanings are almost always inseparable from stories, in all realms of life. And once again family stories, invisible as air, weightless as dreams, are there for us. To make our own meanings out of our myriad stories is to achieve balance — at once a way to be part of and apart from our familes, a way of holding on and letting go." Murray, *Proud Shoes*, xvi. Tamara K. Hareven, "The Search for Generational Memory: Tribal Rites in Industrial Society," *Daedalus* 107.4 (Fall 1978): 137. Mikhail Bakhtin, *Speech Genres and Other Late Essays*, trans. Vern W. McGee, ed. Caryl Emerson and Michael Holquist (Austin: University of Texas Press, 1986), 18. Elizabeth Stone, *Black Sheep and Kissing Cousins: How Our Family Stories Shape Us* (1988; New York: Penguin, 1989), 243–44.

CHAPTER TWO

The title of this chapter is adapted from Gayl Jones's poem "Fiction Study," in *The Hermit-Woman* (Detroit: Lotus Press, 1983), 18.

1. Gayl Jones, "Xarque," in *Xarque and Other Poems* (Detroit: Lotus Press, 1985), 24. Jones, *Song for Anninho* (Detroit: Lotus Press, 1981), 32–33.

2. Charles H. Rowell, "An Interview with Gayl Jones," *Callaloo* 5 (1982): 42. Jones, *Liberating Voices: Oral Tradition in African American Literature* (Cambridge, Mass.: Harvard University Press, 1991), 125, 132.

3. James A. Hijiya, "Roots: Family and Ethnicity in the 1970s," *American Quarterly* 30 (1978): 549.

4. The earliest critics have studied how *Corregidora* 1) exhibits pan-African themes; 2) allegedly represents black men in an unflattering way; and 3) traces the ways disempowerment creates either victimization or significant sources

of covert power. See: 1) Roseann Pope Bell, "Gayle [*sic*] Jone Whirlwind," *Studia Africana* 1 (1977): 99–107; 2) Ralph Reckl *tury Black American Women in Print*, ed. Lola E. Jones (Acto Publishing Group, 1991), 57–65; Richard K. Barksdale, "Cas ism in Recent Black Fiction," in *Praisesong of Survival: Lea 1957–1989* (Urbana: University of Illinois Press, 1992), 148–57 Ward Jr., "Escape from Trublem: The Fiction of Gayl Jones," 95–104; Keith E. Byerman, *Fingering the Jagged Grain: Tradi Recent Black Fiction* (Athens: University of Georgia Press, 19

Later critics discern how the novel 1) deals with history by ternarrative; 2) shows the effects of history in the reproduc 3) talks about the historical formation of the mother-daug 4) in a related way, represents a tradition of matrilineal de: American women's writing. See: 1) Stelamaris Coser, *Bridg The Literature of Paule Marshall, Toni Morrison, and Gayl Jon* Temple University Press, 1994), 120–63; 2) Bruce Simon, "T tition: Gayl Jones's *Corregidora*," in *Race Consciousness: African ies for the New Century*, ed. Judith Jackson Fossett and Jeffrey York: New York University Press, 1997), 93–112; 3) Missy D *Claiming the Heritage: African-American Women Novelists an* son: University Press of Mississippi, 1991), 146–55; and 4) Jo Sung Back in Return': Literary (Re)vision and Transformatio *Corregidora*," *College English* 52 (1990): 787–98; Madhu Dul and the Matrilineal Metaphor of Tradition," *Signs* 20 (199 Françoise Lionett, "Geographies of Pain: Captive Bodies and the Fictions of Myriam Warner-Vieyra, Gayl Jones, and Bess loo 16 (1993): 132–52.

The dominant trends in the critical work have been intent the novel is about the reclamation of identity through 1) th blues; 2) the use of voice more generally; and 3) the reasse: women's sexual self-representations. See the following: 1) G "The 1975 Black Literary Scene: Significant Developments," 106–9; Claudia C. Tate, "*Corregidora*: Ursa's Blues Medley," *Literature Forum* 13 (1979): 139–41; Janice Harris, "Gayl Jone *Frontiers* 3 (1981): 1–5; 2) Melvin Dixon, "Singing a Deep Son Evidence in the Novels of Gayl Jones," in *Black Women Writ A Critical Evaluation*, ed. Mari Evans (Garden City: Ancho 236–48; and Dixon, *Ride Out the Wilderness: Geography and I American Literature* (Urbana: University of Illinois Press, 198 3) Amy S. Gottfried, "Angry Arts: Silence, Speech, and Song *Corregidora*," *African American Review* 28 (1994): 559–70; I mann, "'This Woman Can Cross Any Line': Power and Aut temporary Women's Fiction," in *Engendering the Word: Femini chosexual Poetics*, ed. Temma F. Berg (Urbana: University of 1989), 113–16; Ann duCille, "Phallus(ies) of Interpretation: T

Speech Genres and Other Late Essays, trans. Vern McGee, ed. Emerson and Holquist (Austin: University of Texas Press, 1986), 117, 124.

12. Jones, *Liberating Voices*, 178: "The freed voice is the voice involved in the search for self and other, but that is self-defining."

13. Cf. Tate, "*Corregidora*: Ursa's Blues Medley," 139–41; Harris, "Gayl Jones' *Corregidora*," 1–5; Dixon, "Singing a Deep Song," 236–48.

14. Rowell, "An Interview with Gayl Jones," 45. Harper, "Gayl Jones: An Interview," 359. Jones notes: "I think most of the italicized dialogue between Ursa and Mutt is ritualistic. . . . What I mean by 'ritualized dialogue' is that either the language isn't the same that we would use ordinarily, or the movement between the people talking isn't the same."

15. Nicholas Rand, "Psychoanalysis with Literature: An Abstract of Nicolas Abraham and Maria Torok's *The Shell and the Kernel*," *Oxford Literary Review* 12 (1990): 60–61. Nicolas Abraham, "Notes on the Phantom: A Complement to Freud's Metapsychology," *Critical Inquiry* 13 (Winter 1987): 287, 289. Nicolas Abraham and Maria Torok, *The Shell and the Kernel: Renewals of Psychoanalysis*, trans. and ed. Rand (Chicago: University of Chicago Press, 1994), 140n.

16. Roseann P. Bell, "Gayl Jones Takes a Look at '*Corregidora*'—An Interview," in *Sturdy Black Bridges: Visions of Black Women in Literature*, ed. Bell, Bettye J. Parker, and Beverly Guy-Sheftall (Garden City, N.Y.: Anchor Books, 1979), 285. For readings of the final scene and its "reconciliation," see duCille, "Phallus(ies) of Interpretation," 569; Faith Pullin, "Landscapes of Reality: The Fiction of Contemporary Afro-American Fiction," *Black Fiction: New Studies in the Afro-American Novel Since 1945*, ed. A. Robert Lee (New York: Barnes and Noble, 1980), 201; Barksdale, "Castration Symbolism in Recent Black Fiction," 156; and Ward, "Escape from Trublem," 99. Dixon, *Ride Out the Wilderness*, 112; Byerman, *Fingering the Jagged Grain*, 180–81; and Lindemann, "'This Woman Can Cross Any Line,'" 116.

17. Michel Foucault, "The Concern for Truth," in his *Politics, Philosophy, Culture: Interviews and Other Writings, 1977–1984*, ed. Lawrence D. Kritzman (New York: Routledge, 1988), 262. For a fuller, and substantially different, definition of "genealogy," see Foucault, "Nietzsche, Genealogy, History," in his *Language, Counter-Memory, Practice: Selected Essays and Interviews*, ed. Donald F. Bouchard, trans. Bouchard and Sherry Simon (Oxford: Basil Blackwell, 1977), 139–64.

18. On resistance in *Corregidora*, see Robinson, *Engendering the Subject*, 163–65.

19. Eugene D. Genovese, *Roll, Jordan, Roll: The World the Slaves Made* (New York: Random House, 1974), 591, 597–98. Barbara Fields, "Slavery, Race and Ideology in the United States of America," *New Left Review* 181 (1990): 103.

20. Padre Fernao Cardim, *Treatises*, quoted in Gilberto Freyre, *The Masters and the Slaves: A Study in the Development of Brazilian Civilization*, trans. Samuel Putnam (1946; abridged from the second English-language edition;

New York: Alfred A. Knopf, 1964), 55–56. Carl Degler, *Neither Black nor White: Slavery and Race Relations in Brazil and the United States* (1971; Madison: University of Wisconsin Press, 1986), 70. André Joao Antonil, *Cultura e opulência do Brasil por suas drogas e minas* (São Paulo: Companhia Melhoramentos, 1922), 91–97, reprinted in Robert Edgar Conrad, *Children of God's Fire: A Documentary History of Black Slavery in Brazil* (Princeton, N.J.: Princeton University Press, 1983), 56–57. "Relatorio do Chefe de Policia da Corte," in *Relatorio apresentado á Assembléa Geral Legislativa na Terceira Sessao da Decima Quarta Legislatura pelo Ministro e Secretario de Estado dos Neocios de Justiça Sayao Lobato* (Rio de Janeiro, 1871), 21–22, reprinted in Conrad, *Children of God's Fire*, 130–32.

For documents on the commodification of women's bodies in Brazilian slavery, see "A Master Abuses His Adolescent Slave Girl: A Court Case of 1882–1884," in *O Direito* (Rio de Janeiro) 35 (1884): 103–18, reprinted in Conrad, *Children of God's Fire*, 278; and *Class B. Correspondence on the Slave Trade . . . From April 1, 1856, to March 31, 1857* (London, 1857), 246, reprinted in Conrad, *Children of God's Fire*, 352–53. For discussions of prostitution in Brazilian slavery, see José Honório Rodrigues, *Brazil and Africa*, trans. Richard A. Mazzara and Sam Hileman (Berkeley: University of California Press, 1965), 52–57; and A. J. R. Russell-Wood, *The Black Man in Slavery and Freedom in Colonial Brazil* (New York: St. Martin's, 1982), 57–58. For general discussions of slavery in Brazil, see Katia M. De Queirós Mattoso, *To Be a Slave in Brazil, 1550–1888*, trans. Arthur Goldhammer (1979; New Brunswick, N.J.: Rutgers University Press, 1986); and Emilia Viotti da Costa, *The Brazilian Empire: Myths and Histories* (Chicago: University of Chicago Press, 1985), 125–71.

21. William L. Andrews, *To Tell a Free Story: The First Century of Afro-American Autobiography, 1760–1865* (Urbana: University of Illinois Press, 1986), 252.

22. Darlene Clark Hine, "Female Slave Resistance: The Economics of Sex," *Western Journal of Black Studies* 3 (1979): 7.

23. Cf. Ward, "Escape from Trublem," 99–100: "Ursa never rebels, never seeks alternatives, never breaks free of the constrictive role ordained by others."

24. At issue in readings of the final scene is the unavoidable question regarding fellatio as an act and metaphor for reconciliation, which, the sociological literature tells us, has been subject to a great deal of cover-up because of the "long-standing taboos in our culture on mouth-genital activity" (Kinsey). While some women feel "uncomfortable" or "a little sick" in the performance, and others worry about being thought "cheap" and consider it something only "bad girls" do, there are others who express tentative feelings of pleasure ("Sometimes I enjoy it, I guess"), and some, according to Kinsey, "who may be much aroused by it" and "may even reach orgasm as they manipulate the male genitalia orally." Others have expressed feelings that they are "exerting power" in the act. See Alfred C. Kinsey, Wardell B. Pomeroy, and

Clyde E. Martin, *Sexual Behavior in the Human Male* (Philadelphia: W. B. Saunders Company, 1948), 577. Lillian Breslow Rubin, *Worlds of Pain: Life in the Working-Class Family* (New York: Basic Books, 1976), 140–41. Sharon Thompson, "Search for Tomorrow: On Feminism and the Reconstruction of Teen Romance," in *Pleasure and Danger: Exploring Female Sexuality*, ed. Carole S. Vance (1984; London: Pandora, 1989), 372. Kinsey, Pomeroy, Martin, and Paul H. Gebhard, *Sexual Behavior in the Human Female* (Philadelphia: W. B. Saunders Company, 1953), 257–58. John D'Emilio and Estelle B. Freedman, *Intimate Matters: A History of Sexuality in America* (New York: Harper & Row, 1988), 337. For a feminist critique of feminist condemnations of fellatio, see Esther Newton and Shirley Walton, "The Misunderstanding: Toward a More Precise Sexual Vocabulary," in *Pleasure and Danger*, 250, 243; cf. Sharon Olds, "The Sisters of Sexual Treasure," in *Pleasure and Danger*, 427.

While it is useful for us to have an idea of how sociologists and other people ascribe moral values or express personal taste regarding oral sex, it is far more important for us to ask the question of what fellatio means or can mean for Ursa. Alongside the social significance of fellatio there resides the question of its symbolic value. After all, it is difficult to think of any other sexual act that places the woman so clearly in a position in which it is difficult for her to speak, nor one that appears so problematically to valorize only the penis. In order to determine whether the final sexual act between Ursa and Mutt is either an act of submission or empowerment, it is absolutely imperative that we attend to Ursa's own stated and implied motives in performing fellatio. For this final scene is arguably a resolution of the entire range of topics that have occupied Ursa throughout the course of the narrative. First, here she is establishing new terms of desire and demonstrating an ability to discern her partner's desire without confusion. At the outset of this final sexual adventure, she comments: "I knew what he wanted. I wanted it too" (184). When compared to the earlier scenes of sexual *méconnaissance* in which each partner attempted to act against what he or she thought the other partner desired (154–57), this final sexual encounter takes on attributes of honesty and forthright recognition of the yearnings of both self and other. So, fellatio for Ursa is here a symbol of a newly cognizant sense of what she wants as well as her ability to align her desire and Mutt's. Second, in this scene we get a sense of how Ursa uses sexuality to develop her identity; in other words, this final sexual act is about the same thematic as Ursa's engagement with the blues. While we have only one scene in which Mutt asks Ursa to perform fellatio on him — and, in fact, she hardly lets him complete the request before she declines (151–52) — we have numerous scenes in which Mutt is remarkably insistent on making Ursa's vagina the source and almost the exclusive source of pleasure for him. It bothers Ursa that Mutt talks about "*his* pussy" because it betrays the way he is thinking of her as property as well as the way he is fetishizing her vagina. Using precisely the classic strategy for establishing the fetish, that is, denying the physical subject, commodifying one given aspect of that subject, and then alienating that aspect from the whole subject, Mutt makes Ursa think of her body as a disjointed and alien thing. "Let me in between your legs," Mutt implores Ursa. "It ain't a pussy down there, it's a whole world" (45). Moreover, to add to this fetishizing process, all the men, especially Mutt, make Ursa think of penetrative sex as either a cure for the blues or a replacement of them. "[A]in't nothing better for the blues than a good . . . ," remarks Mutt (97). "Next best thang to the blues is a good screw," adds one of the patrons at the Spider (168). The blues, which has been for Ursa a means to gain an identity that is integral, "which brings a sense of wholeness to the individual," has become as displaced as her vagina, the object of these men's comments. In response to this fetishizing of her song and vagina, Ursa says to Mutt, most poignantly: "I sang to you out of my whole body" (46). Her comment about singing as a means of giving herself an integrity, a wholeness, denied her by his objectifying and fetishizing of her vagina, ought to alert us to the potential significance of Ursa's performing fellatio on Mutt in their final sexual encounter. By having sex that is not based on the one part of her body Mutt had fetishized, Ursa is again informing Mutt of the "wholeness" of her body. Given the past sexual history of this couple, and given the meanings Ursa is investing in oral sex as something she desires and something she can use to inform Mutt of her completeness, we can say that fellatio for Ursa is not simply a symbol of her acquiescing to some sort of phallic order or her submitting herself to an act that she *now* considers distasteful. For other readings of the significance of fellatio in the final scene, see duCille, "Phallus(ies) of Interpretation," 568–70; Dixon, *Ride Out the Wilderness*, 118–19; and Robinson, *Engendering the Subject*, 183–84.

25. duCille, "Phallus(ies) of Interpretation," 568.

26. Barbara Bush, *Slave Women in Caribbean Society, 1650–1838* (Bloomington: Indiana University Press, 1990), 114.

27. According to Gram, Great Gram performed this resistant act no earlier than 1888, since Gram herself was born around the time of abolition and Great Gram came back for Gram in 1906, when she (Gram) was about eighteen years old (78–79).

28. R. K. Kent, "Palmares: An African State in Brazil," *Journal of African History* 6 (1965): 166, 169, 173. Kent discusses the early history of Palmares, discovering a 1597 reference to a group of Africans in the mountain areas, although he proposes 1605–6 as the latest possible date for the foundation of Palmares (163–65). For other suggested dates of the origin of Palmares, see Eugene Genovese, *From Rebellion to Revolution: Afro-American Slave Revolts in the Making of the New World* (1979; New York: Random House, 1981), 60, 61–62; and Stuart B. Schwartz, "The Mocambo: Slave Resistance in Colonial Bahia," *Journal of Social History* 3, no. 4 (1970): 313. Roger Bastide, *Les religions Africaines au Brésil* (Paris: Presses Universitaires de France, 1960); translated and reprinted as "The Other *Quilombos*," in *Maroon Societies: Rebel Slave Communities in the Americas*, ed. Richard Price (1973; 2d ed.; Baltimore, Md.: Johns Hopkins University Press, 1979), 198. Ernesto Ennes, *As guerras nos Palmares* (Coleçao Brasiliana, Vol. 127. São Paulo: Companhia Editora Nacional, 1938),

excerpted and translated in Ennes, "The Conquest of Palmares," in *The Ban-deirantes: The Historical Role of the Brazilian Pathfinders*, ed. Richard Morse (New York: Alfred A. Knopf, 1965), 115. Kent, "Palmares: An African State in Brazil," 169. For studies of the fall of Palmares, see Ennes, "The Palmares 'Re-public' of Pernambuco: Its Final Destruction, 1697," *The Americas* 5 (Octo-ber 1948): 200–216; Ennes, "The Conquest of Palmares"; Kent, "Palmares: An African State in Brazil," 169–74; Genovese, *From Rebellion to Revolution*, 60–64; and the excerpts in Conrad, *Children of God's Fire: A Documentary His-tory of Black Slavery in Brazil*, 366–77. Arthur Ramos, quoted in Kent, "Pal-mares," 170. "From Brazil's Misty Past, a Black Hero Emerges," *New York Times* (November 30, 1994).

29. Paule Marshall, *Daughters* (New York: Atheneum, 1991), 94.

30. Gayl Jones, "The Ancestor: A Street Play," *Greenfield Review* 4 (Fall 1975): 89, 91, 93, 96. Jones, *Song for Anninho*, 9, 19, 32, 43, 66. Jones, *Xarque*, 11, 43.

31. Cf. Barbara Omolade, "Hearts of Darkness," in *Powers of Desire: The Politics of Sexuality*, ed. Ann Snitow, Christine Stansell, and Sharon Thomp-son (New York: Monthly Review, 1983), 363: "All black sexuality is underlined by a basic theme: where, when, and under what circumstances could / would black men and black women connect with each other intimately and privately when all aspects of their lives were considered the dominion of the public, white master / lover's power?"

32. See Eugene Genovese, "The Influence of the Black Power Movement on Historical Scholarship: Reflections of a White Historian," *Daedalus* 1 (Spring 1970): 473–94.

33. Cf. Dubey, *Black Women Novelists and the Nationalist Aesthetic*, 72, 84.

34. Philip Brian Harper, "Nationalism and Social Division in Black Arts Poetry of the 1960s," *Critical Inquiry* 19 (Winter 1993): 239, 250–51. Stephen Henderson, *Understanding the New Black Poetry: Black Speech and Black Music as Poetic References* (New York: William Morrow, 1973), 183. Also see George Napper, *Blacker than Thou: The Struggle for Campus Unity* (Grand Rapids, Mich.: William B. Eerdman's, 1973).

35. Ron Karenga, "Black Cultural Nationalism," in *The Black Aesthetic*, ed. Addison Gayle Jr. (Garden City, N.Y.: Doubleday, 1971), 38.

36. Jones, *Liberating Voices*, 191, 160.

37. Foucault, "Nietzsche, Genealogy, History," 162.

38. Ann duCille, "The Unbearable Darkness of Being: 'Fresh' Thoughts on Race, Sex, and the Simpsons," in *Birth of a Nation'hood: Gaze, Script, and Spectacle in the O. J. Simpson Case*, ed. Toni Morrison and Claudia Brodsky La-cour (New York: Pantheon Books, 1997), 301.

39. See A. Leon Higginbotham, *In the Matter of Color: Race and the Amer-ican Legal Process: The Colonial Period* (New York: Oxford University Press, 1978); and Winthrop D. Jordan, *White over Black: American Attitudes toward the Negro, 1550–1812* (1968: New York: W. W. Norton, 1977).

40. William Wells Brown, *Clotel: Or, the President's Daughter* (1853; New

York: Carol Publishing, 1969), 66–68. My thinking on the ways sexuality, desire, and the enracing of experience are imbricated and structured along lines of power profited greatly from the work of Catharine A. MacKinnon, especially her chapter on sexuality in *Toward a Feminist Theory of the State* (Cambridge, Mass.: Harvard University Press, 1989), 126–54, and the black feminist critiques of MacKinnon's work, especially Angela P. Harris, "Race and Essentialism in Feminist Legal Theory," *Stanford Law Review* 42 (1990), reprinted in *Critical Race Feminism: A Reader*, ed. Adrien Katherine Wing (New York: New York University Press, 1997), 11–18.

41. For critiques of that critical trend, see duCille, "Phallus(ies) of Interpretation"; and Deborah E. McDowell, "Reading Family Matters," in her *"The Changing Same": Black Women's Literature, Criticism, and Theory* (Bloomington: Indiana University Press, 1995), 118–37.

42. Jones, *Liberating Voices*, 74, 39, 107.

43. See duCille, "Pallus(ies) of Interpretation," 568; Tate, "*Corregidora*: Ursa's Blues Medley," 140; Lindemann, "'This Woman Can Cross Any Line,'" 115; and Dixon, *Ride Out the Wilderness*, 110–13, 116–17.

44. The phrase "whole and consummate being" is from N. Scott Momaday, *House Made of Dawn* (1968; New York: Harper & Row, 1989), 94, and is one of Jones's favorite phrases, which she uses throughout her critical study and in her various interviews; cf. Jones, *Liberating Voices*, 1, 162, 178. Jones, ibid., 71; cf. Sherley Anne Williams, "The Blues Roots of Contemporary Afro-American Poetry," in Harper and Stepto, *Chant of Saints*, 125.

45. Hortense J. Spillers, "Interstices: A Small Drama of Words," in Vance, *Pleasure and Danger*, 86–88. Hazel Carby, "'It Jus Be's Dat Way Sometime': The Sexual Politics of Women's Blues," in *Unequal Sisters: A Multicultural Reader in U.S. Women's History*, ed. Ellen Carol DuBois and Vicki L. Ruiz (New York: Routledge, 1990), 239, 241. Hortense Spillers speculates on whether it might not be valid to say that "Black women have learned as much (probably more) that is positive about their sexuality through the practicing activity of the singer as they have from the polemicist." Michele Russell testifies that Bessie Smith had precisely that effect on her. "With her, Black women in American culture could no longer just be sexual objects. She made us sexual subjects, the first step in taking control." Likewise, Hazel Carby notes that the blues allowed a blues singer to reconstruct herself as a "sexual subject" and an "empowered presence." For other black feminist commentary on blues and black women's sexuality, see Ann duCille, "Blues Notes on Black Sexuality: Sex and the Texts of Jessie Fauset and Nella Larsen," *Journal of the History of Sexuality* 3 (1993): 418–44; and Michele Russell, "Slave Codes and Liner Notes," in *All the Women Are White, All the Blacks Are Men, But Some of Us Are Brave: Black Women's Studies*, ed. Gloria T. Hull, Patricia Bell Scott, and Barbara Smith (New York: Feminist Press, 1982), 131.

46. Dixon, *Ride Out the Wilderness*, 116.

47. Ralph Ellison, *Shadow and Act* (New York: Random House, 1964), 219, 244, 245, 246. Jones, *Liberating Voices*, 49, 53, 74, 93, 121, 122. Rowell, "An In-

terview with Gayl Jones," 45. Houston Baker, *Blues, Ideology, and Afro-American Literature* (Chicago: University of Chicago Press, 1984), 5, 194. On the blues as an "aesthetic-ethical" model, see Cheryl A. Wall, "Introduction: Taking Positions and Changing Words," in *Changing Our Own Words: Essays on Criticism, Theory, and Writing by Black Women*, ed. Cheryl A. Wall (New Brunswick, N.J.: Rutgers University Press, 1989), 8; Williams, "The Blues Roots of Contemporary Afro-American Poetry," 123–35; and Williams, "Returning to the Blues: Esther Phillips and Contemporary Blues Culture," *Callaloo* 14 (1991): 816–28.

CHAPTER THREE

The title of this chapter is taken from David Bradley, *The Chaneysville Incident* (1981; New York: Harper & Row, 1990), 428.

1. Susan L. Blake and James A. Miller, "The Business of Writing: An Interview with David Bradley," *Callaloo* 7 (1984): 26.

2. Peter Stallybrass and Allon White, *The Politics and Poetics of Transgression* (Ithaca, N.Y.: Cornell University Press, 1986), 194.

3. Bedford County Heritage Commission, *The Kernel of Greatness: An Informal Bicentennial History of Bedford County* (State College, Pa.: Himes Printing Co., 1971), 73: "On the Lester Imes farm below Chaneysville one can still find the markers for twelve or thirteen graves of runaway slaves. Mr. Imes relates that when the slaves realized their pursuers were closing in on them, they begged to be killed rather than go back to the Southland and more servitude. Someone obliged." Harriette M. Bradley is one of the authors of this book and wrote this section.

4. Hazel Carby, "Ideologies of Black Folk: The Historical Novel of Slavery," in *Slavery and the Literary Imagination*, ed. Deborah E. McDowell and Arnold Rampersad (Baltimore, Md.: Johns Hopkins University Press, 1989), 139, notes that Bradley is rewriting some of the conventions of the narrative of slavery. "In formal terms, the narrative of slavery has three conventional conclusions: escape, emancipation, or death." Slave narratives conclude with escape, historical sagas like *Jubilee* represent emancipation, and novels about slave rebellions end in the rebel's death. In what Carby considers "the most interesting revision of the form of the historical novel, David Bradley's *Chaneysville Incident*, escape leads to death, and death itself is also a form of escape."

5. Bradley, *Chaneysville Incident*, 21, 428. Hereafter all quotations will be taken from this edition and noted parenthetically in the text.

6. Kenneth Burke, "Thanatopsis for Critics: A Brief Thesaurus of Deaths and Dyings," *Essays in Criticism* 2 (1952): 369.

7. G. W. F. Hegel, *Phenomenology of Spirit*, trans. A. V. Miller (Oxford: Oxford University Press, 1977), 270. Phillipe Ariès, *The Hour of Our Death*,

trans. Helen Weaver (New York: Random House, 1982), 602–14, 22. See the essays in Joachim Whaley, *Mirrors of Mortality: Studies in the Social History of Death* (New York: St. Martin's Press, 1981).

8. Frederic Jameson, *The Political Unconscious: Narrative as a Socially Symbolic Act* (Ithaca, N.Y.: Cornell University Press, 1981), 261.

9. Ariès, *The Hour of Our Death*, 572, 602–14. Vladimir Jankélévitch, *La Mort* (Paris: Flammarion, 1966), 202, quoted in ibid., 571–72.

10. Kenneth Burke, *Language as Symbolic Action: Essays on Life, Literature, and Method* (Berkeley: University of California Press, 1966), 7, 9, 455, 477. G. W. F. Hegel, *Lectures on the Philosophy of Religion: The Lectures of 1827*, trans. R. F. Brown, P. C. Hodgson, J. M. Stewart, and H. S. Harris (Berkeley: University of California Press, 1988), 311.

11. Jameson, *The Political Unconscious*, 13. Didier Coste, *Narrative as Communication* (Minneapolis: University of Minnesota Press, 1989), 10–11. Walter Benjamin, "The Storyteller: Reflections on the Works of Nikolai Leskov," in *Illuminations: Essays and Reflections*, trans. Harry Zohn, ed. Hannah Arendt (New York: Schocken, 1969), 94, 101. I have used Jameson's translation of the first quotation from Benjamin (see *The Political Unconscious*, 154).

12. Hegel, *Phenomenology of Spirit*, 271.

13. Margaret Washington Creel, "Gullah Attitudes toward Life and Death," *Africanisms in American Culture*, ed. Joseph E. Holloway (Bloomington: Indiana University Press, 1990), 80, 82. Melville Herskovits, *The Myth of the Negro Past* (1941; Boston: Beacon, 1990), 63. M. Fortes and G. Dieterlen, eds., *African Systems of Thought* (London: Oxford University Press, 1965), 16, quoted in Robert L. Hall, "African Religious Retentions in Florida," in *Africanisms in American Culture*, 111. Charles Joyner, *Down by the Riverside: A South Carolina Slave Community* (Urbana and Chicago: University of Illinois Press, 1984), 138. Herskovits, *The Myth of the Negro Past*, 198. I have profited from the general anthropological essays in *Mortality and Immortality: The Anthropology and Archaeology of Death*, ed. S. C. Humphreys and Helen King (London: Academic Press, 1981); and the specific studies in African American mortuary practices in *The Last Miles of the Way: African-American Homegoing Traditions, 1890–Present*, ed. Elaine Nichols (Columbia, S.C.: Commissioners of the South Carolina State Museum, 1989). Herskovits offers as evidence of the American survival of this African cultural belief a description of an African American family reunion in 1930, which concluded with a "visit to the family burying-ground where there is a tombstone bearing the names of the founder and his wife and the date of their birth and death." Many European American families have family reunions, but it is doubtful, adds Herskovits, whether many end with a similar visit to the graves of the ancestors (199). Cf. Ariès, *The Hour of Our Death*, 288–93, 455–56, for a brief history of European attitudes toward burial and visitation rites.

14. Orlando Patterson, *Slavery and Social Death: A Comparative Study* (Cambridge, Mass.: Harvard University Press, 1982), 5, 62–65. Herbert Gut-

man, *The Black Family in Slavery and Freedom, 1750–1925* (New York: Random House, 1976), 222. Joyner, *Down by the Riverside*, 137.

15. Charles Ball, *Fifty Years in Chains: Or, the Life of an American Slave* (New York: Dover Publications, 1970), 263, 265. (This slave narrative was originally published under this title in 1858; in 1837, it had been published as *Slavery in the United States: A Narrative of the Life and Adventures of Charles Ball, a Black Man*.) Eugene Genovese, *Roll, Jordan, Roll: The World the Slaves Made* (New York: Random House, 1974), 195, 201. Hall, "African Religious Retentions in Florida," 113. Sylvia R. Frey, *Water from the Rock: Black Resistance in a Revolutionary Age* (Princeton, N.J.: Princeton University Press, 1991), 301. On "second burials," see Herskovits, *The Myth of the Negro Past*, 202; Genovese, *Roll, Jordan, Roll*, 198; Mechal Sobel, *The World They Made Together: Black and White Values in Eighteenth-Century Virginia* (Princeton, N.J.: Princeton University Press, 1987), 217–18; Albert J. Raboteau, *Slave Religion: The "Invisible Institution" in the Antebellum South* (New York: Oxford University Press, 1978), 230–31; and Frey, *Water from the Rock*, 303–4.

16. Toni Morrison, *Song of Solomon* (1977; New York: NAL, 1978), 341. Reynolds Price, Review of *Song of Solomon*, *New York Times Book Review* (September 11, 1977), 48. Keith E. Byerman, *Fingering the Jagged Grain: Tradition and Form in Recent Black Fiction* (Athens: University of Georgia Press, 1985), 207. Trudier Harris, *Fiction and Folklore: The Novels of Toni Morrison* (Knoxville: University of Tennessee Press, 1991), 106–7. Gay Wilentz, *Binding Cultures: Black Women Writers in Africa and the Diaspora* (Bloomington: Indiana University Press, 1992), 98. Morrison, *Song of Solomon*, 333. Morrison, "Foreword," *The Harlem Book of the Dead*, by Camille Billops (New York: Morgan & Morgan, 1978): "It's true what Africans say: 'The Ancestor lives as long as there are those who remember.'" For a fuller discussion of the role of African belief in immortality in Bradley's novel, see Ralph Reckely Sr., "The Quest for Immortality in David Bradley's *The Chaneysville Incident*," *MAWA Review* 1, nos. 2–3 (Summer–Fall 1982): 56–59.

17. Bradley, *Chaneysville Incident*, 368; Morrison, *Song of Solomon*, 18. Sandi Russell, *Render Me My Song: African-American Women Writers from Slavery to the Present* (London: Pandora, 1990), 104. Cf. Valerie Smith, *Self-Discovery and Authority in Afro-American Narrative* (Cambridge, Mass.: Harvard University Press, 1987), 151. B. Allen, Review of *The Chaneysville Incident*, *Christian Science Monitor* 74 (June 1982): 62. Jane Campbell, *Mythic Black Fiction: The Transformation of History* (Knoxville: University of Tennessee Press, 1986), 136–53.

18. Cf. Klaus Ensslen, "Fictionalizing History: David Bradley's *The Chaneysville Incident*," *Callaloo* 11, no. 2 (Spring 1988): 285: "The tracking and trailing of the buck, with clear emphasis on intuition, can be understood as a parallel symbolic action to John's attempt at making tracks into, and making sense of, the interconnected pattern of his personal, family, and group history"; and Martin J. Gliserman, "David Bradley's *The Chaneysville Incident*:

The Belly of the Text," *American Imago* 43.2 (Summer 1986): 112, who comments that John "must learn to see the data and get beyond it, as he does as a hunter."

19. Bradley notes that he himself came to much the same kind of knowledge as he was doing the research for *The Chaneysville Incident*. "It was during his research for the book that Bradley began to remember incidents in his childhood that he had apparently suppressed before: what it was like for blacks to live on Gravel Hill [in Bedford, Pa.] (known by whites in town as 'Niggers Knob,' 'Boogie Bend,' or 'Spade Hollow')." See Patricia Holt, "PW Interviews: David Bradley," *Publisher's Weekly* (April 10, 1981): 12.

20. Garrett Stewart, "A Valediction for Bidding Mourning: Death and the Narratee in Brontë's *Vilette*," in *Death and Representation*, ed. Sarah Webster Goodwin and Elisabeth Bronwen (Baltimore, Md.: Johns Hopkins University Press, 1993), 55.

21. Lucille Clifton, *generations: a memoir* (1976); reprinted in *good woman: poems and a memoir, 1969–1980* (Brockport, N.Y.: BOA Editions, 1987), 265, 275. Marilyn Nelson Waniek, *The Homeplace* (Baton Rouge and London: Louisiana State University Press, 1990), 5, 52.

22. Nicolas Abraham and Maria Torok, *The Shell and the Kernel: Renewals of Psychoanalysis*, trans. and ed. Nicholas T. Rand (Chicago: University of Chicago Press, 1994), 22, 130, 167, 168, 175.

23. Esther Rashkin, *Family Secrets and the Psychoanalysis of Narrative* (Princeton, N.J.: Princeton University Press, 1992), 9, 18; cf. 157. Nicholas T. Rand, "Family Romance or Family History?: Psychoanalysis and Dramatic Invention in Nicolas Abraham's 'The Phantom of Hamlet,'" *diacritics* 18, no. 4 (Winter 1988): 25. See Abraham, "The Phantom of Hamlet or The Sixth Act: Preceded by The Intermission of 'Truth,'" *diacritics* 18.4 (Winter 1988): 2–19; cf. Rashkin, "Tools for a New Psychoanalytic Literary Criticism: The Work of Abraham and Torok," *diacritics* 18, no.4 (Winter 1988): 31–52.

24. It is worth noting that Judith Powell is a professional psychoanalyst.

25. Blake and Miller, "The Business of Writing," 25, 30–31.

26. Trudier Harris, *Exorcising Blackness: Historical and Literary Lynching and Burning Rituals* (Bloomington: Indiana University Press, 1984), 182. Blake and Miller, "The Business of Writing," 30–31. It should be noted that John's learning to use his imagination does not mean he renounces history as a discipline with its own standards of verification, nor does his performance of an imaginative narrative signify his rejection of factual data. Indeed, when one of his interviewers suggests to Bradley that "John as a historian has to learn how to get rid of all that academic apparatus that stands between him and his ability to imagine, [and] imaginatively re-create history," Bradley responds by arguing that John "has to learn to do both things at once." John must be attentive to whatever academic or disciplinary apparatus is available because John still has some residual respect for "historical facts." Yet John must also be able to apply his imagination to these facts in order to animate them for his own life. As Bradley puts it in the interview: "You know, in the

funeral chapter, what he's talking about is not choosing one or the other [history or imagination] but applying both of them. It's the fact that he knows all these things that allows him to imagine. And the fact of imagining does involve the use of names and places and people that he knows. I mean, he doesn't . . . he still doesn't make anything up." It is also worth noting the degree of ambiguity in those so-called facts. Whatever relationship Richard Iiames might have to Joseph Powell, we need to remember that we are not certain whether Judith's family can trace their line back from Joseph to John Powell. John Washington refers to "her *maybe* however-many-great-whatever Thomas" (242, my italics).

27. Gloria Naylor and Toni Morrison, "A Conversation," *Southern Review* 21 (1985): 584–85.

28. Blake and Miller, "The Business of Writing," 35. Kay Bonetti, "An Interview with David Bradley," *Missouri Review* 15 (1992): 87.

29. Bonetti, "Interview with David Bradley," 78.

30. Blake and Miller, "The Business of Writing," 35.

31. It is plausible that by incorporating Iiames into the narrative of the Washington family, John effectively replaces in his biological family the one person who attempts to murder the memory of his own father by destroying his father's story—Lamen—and he replaces him in his symbolic family with a person who attempts to resuscitate the stories of those who are dead by burying them properly. The final refraction in this narrative that had made refraction a strategy for coming to terms with death and history is John's act of effectively disclaiming his biological grandfather—a professional mortician—and claiming as a symbolic ancestor Richard Iiames, someone who buries the dead in order to ensure that their story survives.

32. Bonetti, "Interview with David Bradley," 74, 82.

33. It is important to point out that in burning the cards John does not renounce "history"—either as what he does professionally or as a structure for organizing past events in a coherent order. He does not signal to Judith that he is now ready to "forget" about the past in order to get on with their lives. In order to emphasize that John does not renounce the study of the past or even the documents needed to study the past, Bradley has John destroy only some of the implements and records of historical research. Even though John burns "the pens and inks and pencils, the pads and the cards," he nonetheless saves the "books and pamphlets and diaries and maps" and leaves these things in the cabin "ready for the next man who would need them" (431). Most important, he takes with him the folio that contains his father's and his great-grandfather's diaries and documents (431). Some critics have generated readings on the end of the novel based on a misreading of what John does with this important folio. See Michael Cooke, *Afro-American Literature in the Twentieth-Century: The Achievement of Intimacy* (New Haven, Conn.: Yale University Press, 1984) 215, 216; and Cathy Brigham, "Identity, Masculinity, and Desire in David Bradley's Fiction," *Contemporary Literature* 36, no. 2 (1995): 312; and, for a corrective reading, John F. Callahan, *In the African-*

American Grain: Call and Response in Twentieth-Century Black Fiction (1987; Middletown, Conn.: Wesleyan University Press, 1988), 261.

34. Campbell, *Mythic Black Fiction*, 150. Ensslen, "Fictionalizing History," 286, 293. Callahan, *In the African-American Grain*, 261. Harris, *Exorcising Blackness*, 182.

35. Albert E. Stone, *The Return of Nat Turner: History, Literature, and Cultural Politics in Sixties America* (Athens: University of Georgia Press, 1992), 371, 372. Brigham, "Identity, Masculinity, and Desire in David Bradley's Fiction," 312–13. My reading is that the novel does endorse suicide as something appropriate for C. K. Washington and Moses Washington, but proposes instead a symbolic suicide as something appropriate for John.

36. My study of an act signifying a symbolic suicide was indirectly aided by Derrida's interesting study of the distinctions Hegel and de Saussure made between "symbol" and "sign," particularly his tracing of the difference Hegel marks between "symbol" and "sign" to the "funerary monument." Jacques Derrida, "The Pit and the Pyramid: Introduction to Hegel's Semiology," in *Margins of Philosophy*, trans. Alan Bass (Chicago: University of Chicago Press, 1982), 82–83.

37. Shoshana Felman and Dori Laub, *Testimony: Crises of Witnessing in Literature, Psychoanalysis, and History* (New York: Routledge, 1992), 135. Boris Pasternak, *An Essay in Autobiography*, trans. Manya Haran (London and New York: Collins Harvill, 1959), 91–93, quoted in A. Alvarez, *The Savage God: A Study of Suicide* (1971; New York: Bantam Books, 1973), 239. Alvarez, *The Savage God*, 272. Antonin Artaud, *Antonin Artaud: Selected Writings*, ed. Susan Sontag, trans. Helen Weaver (1976; Berkeley: University of California Press, 1988), 103, 105. It is worth noting that Artaud often contradicted himself and remained ambivalent about suicide — symbolic or material — for most of his life. He could claim, without any indication of conscious irony, that while the "state of suicide is to [him] incomprehensible," it was nonetheless apparently "the fabulous and remote victory of men who think well" (102). In his study of Van Gogh, for example, he notes that "in the case of suicide, there must be an army of evil beings to cause the body to make the gesture against nature, that of taking its own life" (511). In the same work, however, he also contends that Van Gogh "did not die of a state of delirium properly speaking" (487). Artaud also liked to speak about how individuals "are suicided." He mentions that society has "suicided me, so to speak" (103) and that Van Gogh was "suicided" by the "collective consciousness of society" (487).

38. It is also worth noting that certain African cultures, like the BaKango, believed in concepts like "symbolic death" involving a "journey into the world of the ancestors (i.e. death) and [a] subsequent return." See Creel, "Gullah Attitudes toward Life and Death," 80–82.

39. I have elsewhere offered a fuller discussion of what I am calling "imbrication" and what I have elsewhere called "texturalization"—which is the process by which the reader's desire is wrought out of his or her being involved or imbricated into a story through an act of narrative identification. See

Ashraf H. A. Rushdy, "Cartesian Mirror / Quixotic Web: Toward a Narrativity of Desire," *Mosaic: A Journal for the Interdisciplinary Study of Literature* 26, no. 2 (Spring 1993): 83–110. My work, there and here, is indebted to Teresa de Lauretis's theory of "narrativity." See de Lauretis, *Technologies of Gender: Essays on Theory, Film, and Fiction* (Bloomington: Indiana University Press, 1987), 108–18.

40. Blake and Miller, "The Business of Writing," 33. Bonetti, "Interview with David Bradley," 80.

CHAPTER FOUR

The title of this chapter is taken from Barbara Chase-Riboud, *Echo of Lions* (New York: William Morrow, 1989), 368.

1. Octavia Butler, *Kindred* (1979; Boston: Beacon Press, 1988), 28. All quotations from *Kindred* will hereafter be taken from this edition and cited parenthetically in the body of the text.

2. Randall Kenan, "An Interview with Octavia E. Butler," *Callaloo* 14 (1991): 497. Stokely Carmichael, "A Declaration of War," in *The New Left: A Documentary History*, ed. Massimo Teodori (Indianapolis: Bobbs-Merrill, 1969), 277. Chicago Office of SNCC, "We Must Fill Ourselves with Hate for All White Things," in *Black Protest Thought in the Twentieth Century*, ed. August Meier, Elliot Rudwick, and Francis Broderick (2d ed.; Indianapolis: Bobbs-Merrill, 1971), 489. Imamu Amiri Baraka, *Raise Race Rays Raze: Essays since 1965* (New York: Random House, 1971), 160.

3. Frances M. Beal, "Black Women and the Science Fiction Genre: Black Scholar Interview with Octavia Butler," *Black Scholar* 17, no. 2 (March/April 1986): 15. Kenan, "An Interview with Octavia E. Butler," 496, 497. Charles H. Rowell, "An Interview with Octavia Butler," *Callaloo* 20, no. 1 (1997): 51.

4. Rowell "An Interview with Octavia Butler," 51. Itabari Njeri, "Sushi and Grits: Ethnic Identity and Conflict in a Newly Multicultural America," in *Lure and Loathing: Essays on Race, Identity, and the Ambivalence of Assimilation*, ed. Gerald Early (New York: Allen Lane, 1993), 34.

5. Pauli Murray, *Proud Shoes: The Story of an American Family* (1956; New York: Harper & Row, 1978), 88, 158.

6. Dorothy Spruill Redford with Michael D'Orso, *Somerset Homecoming: Recovering a Lost Heritage* (New York: Doubleday, 1988), 29. Jan Willis, "Mayer" (manuscript), 6, 7, 19, 21–22. Again, I would like to thank my colleague and friend Jan Willis for allowing me to quote from her powerful and beautiful family history.

7. Redford, *Somerset Homecoming*, 61, 202, 219. Willis, "Mayer," 3, 22.

8. Redford, *Somerset Homecoming*, 33. Willis, "Mayer," 20. David Chioni Moore, "Routes: Alex Haley's *Roots* and the Rhetoric of Genealogy," *Transition* 64 (1994): 14, 15, 21.

9. Murray, *Proud Shoes*, xvi.

10. Willis, "Mayer," 18–19. Willis, "January 21, 1995" (manuscript), 32.

11. Kenan, "Interview with Octavia E. Butler," 496. Beal, "Black Women and the Science Fiction Genre," 14. Larry McCaffery, *Across the Wounded Galaxies: Interviews with Contemporary Science Fiction Writers* (Urbana: University of Illinois Press, 1990), 65–66. For discussions of the genre of *Kindred*, see Robert Crossley, "Introduction," in Butler, *Kindred*, ix–xxvii; Susan Willis, *Specifying: Black Women Writing the American Experience* (Madison: University of Wisconsin Press, 1987); Thelma J. Shinn, "The Wise Witches: Black Women Mentors in the Fiction of Octavia E. Butler," in *Conjuring: Black Women, Fiction, and Literary Tradition*, ed. Marjorie Pryse and Hortense J. Spillers (Bloomington: Indiana University Press, 1985), 203–15; Charles Johnson, *Being and Race: Black Writing since 1970* (Bloomington: Indiana University Press, 1988); and Ruth Salvaggio, "Octavia Bulter," in Marleen S. Barr et al., *Suzy McKee Charnas, Octavia Butler, Joan D. Vinge* (Mercer Island, Wash.: Starmont, 1986). For studies of *Kindred* in light of Butler's science-fiction writing, see Amanda Boulter, "Polymorphous Futures: Octavia E. Butler's *Xenogenesis* Trilogy," in *American Bodies: Cultural Histories of the Physique*, ed. Tim Armstrong (New York: New York University Press, 1996), 17–85; Frances Bonner, "Difference and Desire: Slavery and Seduction: Octavia Butler's *Xenogenesis*," *Foundation* 48 (1990): 50–62; Sandra Y. Govan, "Homage to Tradition: Octavia Butler Renovates the Historical Novel," *Melus* 13 (1986): 79–96; and Stephanie A. Smith, "Morphing, Materialism, and the Marketing of *Xenogenesis*," *Genders* 18 (1993): 67–86. For studies of Butler's other science-fiction novels, see Govan, "Connections, Links, and Extended Networks: Patterns in Octavia Butler's Science Fiction," *Black American Literature Forum* 18 (1984): 82–87; Salvaggio, "Octavia Butler and the Black Science-Fiction Heroine," *Black American Literature Forum* 18 (1984): 78–81; Judith Lee, "'We Are All Kin': Relatedness, Mortality, and the Paradox of Human Immortality," in *Immortal Engines: Life Extension and Immortality in Science Fiction and Fantasy*, ed. George Slusser, Gary Westfahl, and Eric S. Rabkin (Athens: University of Georgia Press, 1996), 170–82; Robin Roberts, "'No Woman Born': Immortality and Gender in Feminist Science Fiction," in *Immortal Engines*, 135–44; Hoda M. Zaki, "Utopia, Dystopia, and Ideology in the Science Fiction of Octavia Butler," *Science-Fiction Studies* 17 (1990): 239–51; and Donna Haraway, *Primate Visions: Gender, Race, and Nature in the World of Modern Science* (New York: Routledge, 1989), 376–82.

12. Kenan, "Interview with Octavia E. Butler," 498.

13. Gayl Jones, *Corregidora* (1975; Boston: Beacon, 1986), 46. Michel Foucault, "Nietzsche, Genealogy, History," in *Language, Counter-Memory, Practice: Selected Essays and Interviews*, ed. Donald F. Bouchard, trans. Bouchard and Sherry Simon (Oxford: Basil Blackwell, 1977), 148.

14. Octavia Butler, *Wild Seed* (1980; New York: Popular Library, 1988), 224.

15. On the question of how slave women's bodies are used for the inscrip-

tion of history, Mae Henderson insightfully notes about *Beloved* that Sethe's challenge is "to configure the history of her body's text" into *history* because her "scars function as an archeological site or memory trace" made invisible or repressed in the written historical record. Even more so than *Beloved*, as Henderson elsewhere notes, *Dessa Rose* represents the body as the site on which "an attempt [is made] to inscribe the sign *slave* in an area that marks her as *woman*." See Henderson, "Toni Morrison's *Beloved*: Re-membering the Body as Historical Text," in *Comparative American Identities: Race, Sex, and Nationality in the Modern Text*, ed. Hortense Spillers (New York: Routledge, 1991), 69, 68; and Henderson, "Speaking in Tongues: Dialogics, Dialectics, and the Black Woman Writer's Literary Tradition," in *Changing Our Own Words: Essays on Criticism, Theory, and Writing by Black Women*, ed. Cheryl A. Wall (New Brunswick, N.J.: Rutgers University Press, 1989), 26.

16. bell hooks, "Representing Whiteness in the Black Imagination," in *Cultural Studies*, ed. Lawrence Grossberg, Cary Nelson, and Paula Treichler (New York: Routledge, 1992), 342, 345. Barbara Christian, "'Somebody Forgot to Tell Somebody Something': African-American Women's Historical Novels," in *Wild Women in the Whirlwind: Afra-American Culture and the Contemporary Literary Renaissance*, eds. Joanne Braxton and Andrée Nicola McLaughlin (New Brunswick, N.J.: Rutgers University Press, 1990), 341.

17. Alexander Crummell, *Africa and America: Addresses and Discourses* (Springfield, Mass.: Willey & Co., 1891), 26, 46.

18. Wahneema Lubiano, "Black Nationalism and Black Common Sense: Policing Ourselves and Others," in *The House That Race Built: Black Americans, U.S. Terrain*, ed. Lubiano (New York: Pantheon, 1997), 239–45. Jimmy Garrett, "We Own the Night: A Play of Blackness," in *Black Fire: An Anthology of Afro-American Writing*, ed. LeRoi Jones and Larry Neal (New York: William Morrow, 1968), 539, 540.

19. Rhonda M. Williams, "Living at the Crossroads: Explorations in Race, Nationality, Sexuality, and Gender," in Lubiano, *The House That Race Built*, 141, 144.

20. Ibid., 145.

21. Lubiano, "Black Nationalism," 246, 250–51.

22. Paul Gilroy, *The Black Atlantic: Modernity and Double Consciousness* (Cambridge, Mass.: Harvard University Press, 1993), 191. Gilroy, *Small Acts: Thoughts on the Politics of Black Cultures* (London: Serpent's Tail, 1993), 190.

23. Gilroy, *Black Atlantic*, 99, 203, 207; Gilroy, *Small Acts*, 194, 207, 205.

24. Cf. hooks, *Killing Rage: Ending Racism* (New York: Henry Holt, 1995), 71.

25. Angela Davis, "Reflections on the Black Woman's Role in the Community of Slaves," *Black Scholar* (December 1971): 15.

26. Stephen W. Potts, "'We Keep Playing the Same Record': A Conversation with Octavia E. Butler," *Science-Fiction Studies* 23 (1996): 333.

27. For studies on the resolution or irresolution at the end of *Kindred*, see Missy Dehn Kubitschek, *Claiming the Heritage: African-American Women*

Novelists and History (Jackson: University Press of Mississippi, 1991), 47, 50–51; and Dorothy Allison, "The Future of Female: Octavia Butler's Mother Lode," in *Reading Black, Reading Feminist: A Critical Anthology*, ed. Henry Louis Gates Jr. (New York: Meridian, 1990), 476.

28. Orlando Patterson, *Slavery and Social Death: A Comparative Study* (Cambridge, Mass.: Harvard University Press, 1982), 7. Barbara Chase-Riboud, *Echo of Lions* (New York: William Morrow, 1989), 367.

29. Ralph Ellison, *Going to the Territory* (New York: Random House, 1986), 303.

30. Richard Sennett, *The Fall of Public Man* (New York: Basic Books, 1977), 220. Stephanie Coontz, *The Way We Never Were: American Families and the Nostalgia Trap* (New York: Basic Books, 1992), 114–15. Robert Bellah et al., *Habits of the Heart: Individualism and Commitment in American Life* (New York: Harper & Row, 1986), 71–72.

31. Moore, "Routes," 15. George Schuyler, *Black No More* (1931; Boston: Northeastern University Press, 1989), [iii].

32. Njeri, "Sushi and Grits," 38.

33. See, for example, Theodore W. Allen, *The Invention of the White Race*, vol. 1, *Racial Oppression and Social Control* (London: Verso, 1994), and vol. 2, *The Origin of Racial Oppression in Anglo-America* (1997); Ian F. Haney López, *White by Law: The Legal Construction of Race* (New York: New York University Press, 1996); A. Leon Higginbotham Jr., *In the Matter of Color: Race and the American Legal Process: The Colonial Period* (New York: Oxford University Press, 1978); and Barbara J. Flagg, "Fashioning a Title VII Remedy for Transparently White Subjective Decisionmaking," *Yale Law Journal* 104 (1995).

34. David R. Roediger, *The Wages of Whiteness: Race and the Making of the American Working Class* (London: Verso, 1991); Roediger, *Towards the Abolition of Whiteness: Essays on Race, Politics, and Working Class History* (London: Verso, 1994); and Eric Lott, *Love and Theft: Blackface Minstrelsy and the American Working Class* (New York: Oxford University Press, 1993).

35. Cheryl I. Harris, "Whiteness as Property," in *Critical Race Theory: The Key Writings That Formed the Movement*, ed. Kimberlé Crenshaw, Neil Gotanda, Gary Peller, and Kendall Thomas (New York: New Press, 1995); and George Lipsitz, "The Possessive Investment in Whiteness: Racialized Social Democracy and the 'White' Problem in American Studies," *American Quarterly* 47 (1995): 369–87.

36. Eugene D. Genovese, *Roll, Jordan, Roll: The World the Slaves Made* (New York: Random House, 1974), 506.

37. Cf. Richard Dyer, "White," *Screen* 29 (1988): 44: "White power secures its dominance by seeming not to be anything in particular." For another reading of race in *Kindred*, see Diana R. Paulin, "De-Essentializing Interracial Representations: Black and White Border-Crossings in Spike Lee's *Jungle Fever* and Octavia Butler's *Kindred*," *Cultural Critique* 36 (1997): 165–93.

38. Lipsitz, "The Possessive Investment in Whiteness," 384.

39. Redford, *Somerset Homecoming*, 56.

40. Ibid., 219.

41. Charles Rowell, "This Louisiana Thing That Drives Me: An Interview with Ernest J. Gaines," *Callaloo* 1 (May 1978): 39–51. Octavio Paz, "The Tree of Life," in Paz, *Convergences: Essays on Art and Literature* (New York: Harcourt, Brace, Jovanovich, 1987). I have greatly benefited in my thinking about these issues from reading the essays in *History and Memory in African-American Culture*, ed. Geneviève Fabre and Robert O'Meally (New York: Oxford University Press, 1994); and Michael Kammen, *Mystic Chords of Memory: The Transformation of Tradition in American Culture* (1991; New York: Random House, 1993).

CHAPTER FIVE

The title of this chapter is taken from Gayl Jones, *Song for Anninho* (Detroit: Lotus Press, 1981), 79.

1. Nicholas Lemann, *The Promised Land: The Great Black Migration and How It Changed America* (New York: Random House, 1991), 160. Studs Terkel, *Division Street: America* (1967; New York: New Press, 1993), 214–15. Terkel, *Race: How Blacks and Whites Think and Feel about the American Obsession* (New York: New Press, 1992), 30, 34, 67, 77, 170. Orlando Bagwell, "Journal Entry, October 11, 1996, 9:00 A.M., EL MINA CASTLE," in Charles Johnson, Patricia Smith, and WGBH Series Research Team, *Africans in America: America's Journey through Slavery* (New York: Harcourt, Brace & Company, 1998), x. Shelby Steele, *The Content of Our Character: A New Vision of Race in America* (1990; New York: HarperCollins, 1991), 150.

2. Pamela Woolford, "Filming Slavery: A Conversation with Haile Gerima," *Transition* 64 (1994): 103. Stephen Steinberg, *Turning Back: The Retreat from Racial Justice in American Thought and Policy* (Boston: Beacon, 1995), 208–9. Dorothy Spruill Redford with Michael d'Orso, *Somerset Homecoming: Recovering a Lost Heritage* (New York: Doubleday, 1988), 56. James Baldwin, *The Price of the Ticket: Collected Nonfiction, 1948–1985* (New York: St. Martin's, 1985), 562.

3. Christopher Lasch, *The Minimal Self: Psychic Survival in Troubled Times* (New York: Norton, 1984), 60, 65–66, 96, 162. For a different assessment of nostalgia in America during the seventies, see Michael Kammen, *Mystic Chords of Memory: The Transformation of Tradition in American Culture* (New York: Random House, 1991), 619–54.

4. George Lipsitz, *Time Passages: Collective Memory and American Popular Culture* (Minneapolis: University of Minnesota Press, 1990), 213. "Countermemory," for most of us, is a term we associate with Foucault's skeptical analysis of historical writing. Lipsitz distinguishes his definition of "countermemory" from Foucault's by noting that while Foucault attempts to proscribe all "totalizing narratives" absolutely, he (Lipsitz) thinks such an absolute pro-

scription would obscure "real connections, causes, and relationships" and potentially lead to a history in which common experiences are atomized into "accidents and endlessly repeated play" (214). Cf. Michel Foucault, *Language, Counter-Memory, Practice: Selected Essays and Interviews*, ed. Donald F. Bouchard, trans. Bouchard and Sherry Simon (Oxford: Basil Blackwell, 1977), 113–96.

5. Jesse Hamlin, "Marsalis Fields a Monumental Work," *San Francisco Chronicle* (January 26, 1997): 36. Howard Reich, "Marsalis' Gamble," *Chicago Tribune* (February 2, 1997): C-8. Richard Harrington, "Marsalis's 'Blood': The Spirit Moves It," *Washington Post* (February 6, 1997): B-1. Bob Young, "'Fields' Cements Marsalis' Place in Jazz," *Boston Herald* (February 10, 1997): 31. Calvin Wilson, "Opera in the Key of Marsalis," *Kansas City Star* (June 17, 1997): E-1. Jeff Bradley, "Marsalis Oratorio out on CD 'Blood on Fields' Impressed Fans, Pulitzer Jurors," *Denver Post* (June 19, 1997): E-10.

6. Sabrina Eaton, "Rep. Hall Proposes an Apology for Slavery," *Cleveland Plain Dealer* (June 13, 1997): 11A. Scott Montgomery, "In Black and White: Americans Write to Ohio Congressman about Plan to Apologize for Slavery," *St. Louis Post-Dispatch* (August 17, 1997): A-1. Frank Trejo, "Tuskegee Apology Part of Effort to Heal Old Wounds," *Dallas Morning News* (May 11, 1997): J-1. John Leo, "So Who's Sorry Now," *U.S. News and World Report* (June 30, 1997): 17. Gustav Niebuhr, "Baptist Group Votes to Repent Stand on Slaves," *New York Times* (June 21, 1995): A-2. William Montalbano, "Time to Repent History's Sins, Pope Says," *Los Angeles Times* (November 15, 1994): A-8. John F. Harris, "Clinton Says U.S. Wronged Africa," *Washington Post* (March 25, 1998): A-1. Ann Scales, "Clinton, in Senegal, Revisits Slavery's Horrors," *Boston Globe* (April 3, 1998): A-2. Clarence Page, "Slavery Regret: Why the Backlash?" *Sacramento Bee* (April 2, 1998): B-7.

7. Steven Weisenburger, *Modern Medea: A Family Story of Slavery and Child-Murder from the Old South* (New York: Hill and Wang, 1998). Johnson, Smith, and WGBH Series Research Team, *Africans in America: America's Journey through Slavery*. Ira Berlin, Marc Favreau, and Steven F. Miller, eds., *Remembering Slavery: African Americans Talk about Their Personal Experiences of Slavery and Emancipation* (New York: New Press, 1998).

8. Lipsitz, *The Possessive Investment in Whiteness: How White People Profit from Identity Politics* (Philadelphia: Temple University Press, 1998), 160.

9. Zora Neale Hurston, *Dust Tracks on a Road* (1942; New York: HarperPerennial, 1996), 229–30.

10. Nancy Pate, "Critics Honor 'Cold Mountain,' 'Slaves in the Family,'" *Columbus Dispatch* (August 7, 1998): D-10. "National Book Award Finalists Named," *New York Times* (October 15, 1998): B-9. Dinitia Smith, "Alice McDermott Wins National Book Award for Fiction," *New York Times* (November 19, 1988). *Family Name* was also named a Grand Jury Prize Award Winner at the 1997 Bermuda International Film Festival.

11. Michael J. Sandel, *Democracy's Discontent: America in Search of a Public Philosophy* (Cambridge, Mass.: Harvard University Press, 1996), 14.

12. Steven Knapp, "Collective Memory and the Actual Past," *Representations* 26 (Spring 1989): 138–39.

13. Sandel, *Democracy's Discontent*, 15–16.

14. Ibid., 16.

15. Alasdair MacIntyre, *After Virtue: A Study in Moral Theory* (1981; Notre Dame, Ind.: University of Notre Dame Press, 1984), 11–12, 32, 225.

16. Ibid., 187, 190, 211, 218, 220. MacIntyre then places this entire model of practices within what he calls a "tradition," which he hastens to define against the concept of tradition used by conservative political theorists. Unlike, say, Edmund Burke, who uses tradition to oppose the conflicts that come with the exercise of reason and glories in the stability that comes from continuity, MacIntyre holds to a notion of tradition premised on and embodying "continuities of conflicts." "A living tradition," he concludes, "is an historically extended, socially embodied argument, and an argument precisely in part about the goods which constitute that tradition." Rather than being the ultimate arbiter of conflicts, judgments, and rights, a tradition in MacIntyre's sense is rather the cultural debate about precisely those conflicts, judgments, and rights.

17. Sandel, *Democracy's Discontent*, 15.

18. Knapp, "Collective Memory and the Actual Past," 136, 140.

19. Ibid., 142–44.

20. Ibid., 129, 130, 131. See also Walter Benn Michaels, "'You who never was there': Slavery and the New Historicism, Deconstruction and the Holocaust," *Narrative* 4 (January 1996): 1–16.

21. MacIntyre, *After Virtue*, 220.

22. Knapp, "Collective Memory and the Actual Past," 142–44.

23. MacIntyre, *After Virtue*, 220–21.

24. William W. Hening, *The Statutes at Large: Being a Collection of All the Laws of Virginia, from the First Session of the Legislature in the Year 1619* (Charlotteville: Published for the Jamestown Foundation of the Commonwealth of Virginia by the University Press of Virginia, 1969).

25. Henry Louis Gates, *The Signifying Monkey: A Theory of African-American Literary Criticism* (New York: Oxford University Press, 1988), 218. Hazel Carby, "Ideologies of Black Folk: The Historical Novel of Slavery," in *Slavery and the Literary Imagination*, ed. Deborah McDowell and Arnold Rampersad (Baltimore, Md.: Johns Hopkins University Press, 1987), 126. Lipsitz, *The Possessive Investment in Whiteness*. Cheryl I. Harris, "Whiteness as Property," in *Critical Race Theory: The Key Writings That Formed the Movement*, ed. Kimberlé Crenshaw, Neil Gotanda, Gary Peller, and Kendall Thomas (New York: New Press, 1995), 276–91.

26. Nell Irvin Painter, "Soul Murder and Slavery: Toward a Fully Loaded Cost Accounting," in *U.S. History as Women's History: New Feminist Essays*, ed. Linda K. Kerber, Alice Kessler-Harris, and Kathryn Kish Sklar (Chapel Hill: University of North Carolina Press, 1995), 146.

27. Edward Ball, *Slaves in the Family* (New York: Farrar, Strauss, and

Giroux, 1998), 7–8. *Family Name*, directed by Macky Alston, written by Alston and Kay Gayner, photographed by Eliot Rockett, edited by Sandra Marie Christie and Christopher White (Opelika Pictures, 1997).

28. Ibid., 13–14, 63.

29. Ibid., 108–10. Barbara Chase-Riboud, *Sally Hemings* (New York: Viking Press, 1979), 286. I have discussed this idea of the dialectic between hate and love in slave-master sexual relations more fully in my "'I Write in Tongues': The Supplement of Voice in Barbara Chase-Riboud's *Sally Hemings*," *Contemporary Literature* 35, no. 1 (Spring 1994): 100–135. Ball, *Slaves in the Family*, 278, 110.

30. Ball, *Slaves in the Family*, 411–15.

31. Ibid., 212–14, 410.

32. Barbara Liss, "A Family's Gnarled Roots," *Houston Chronicle*, Zest Section (March 22, 1998): 24. Drew Gilpin Faust, "Skeletons in the Family Closet," *New York Times*, Book Review Desk (March 1, 1998): 7. Benjamin Schwarz, "Roots," *Los Angeles Times*, Book Review Section (March 22, 1998): 7.

33. Kevin Thomas, "Critic's Pick: 'Family Name,'" *Los Angeles Times*, T.V. Times Section (September 13, 1998): 85.

34. David Zurawik, "Family Truths in Black and White," *Baltimore Sun* (September 15, 1998): E-1.

35. Deirdre Donahue, "A Family Tree Shows Ugly Roots," *Detroit News* (March 28, 1998): D-24. Jeffry Scott, "Slaves in the Family," *Atlanta Journal and Constitution* (February 15, 1998): M-1.

36. Ball, *Slaves in the Family*, 133.

37. Ibid., 87, 133, 214. Toni Morrison, "Introduction: Friday on the Potomac," in *Race-ing Justice, En-Gendering Power: Essays on Anita Hill, Clarence Thomas, and the Construction of Social Reality*, ed. Morrison (New York: Pantheon, 1992), xiii. It is perhaps worth comparing the actual picture of the very somber Thomas Martin with the picture of Ball and Goodson laughing comfortably together. See the pictures opposite page 91 and the pictures between pages 314–15.

38. Susan Larson, "All in the Family," *Times-Picayune* (March 21, 1998): E-1. Kenney Littlefield, "Filmmaker: What Color Is My Family Name?," *Fort Lauderdale Sun-Sentinel* (September 23, 1998): E-3. Torri Minton, "Search for What It Means to Be White," *San Francisco Chronicle* (May 8, 1998): A-1.

39. Roger Ebert, "'Family' Secrets: Roots Search Transcends Race," *Chicago Sun-Times*, WKP Movie Review Section (May 8, 1998): 312. Thomas, "Critic's Pick: 'Family Name,'" 85.

40. Littlefield, "Journey into Roots Unravels Dangerous Family Secrets," *Orange County Register* (September 13, 1998): F-36.

41. Ball, *Slaves in the Family*, 13, 14, 356, 416. The point Ball was making about his lack of inheritance was not lost on Richard Gott, who referred to Ball as "a poor white," "the son of an impoverished clergyman," and a "schol-

arship boy." Gott, "Monday Book: Digging the Roots of Evil," *The Independent*, Comment Section (July 27, 1998): 5.

42. Ball, *Slaves in the Family*, 455. Larson, "All in the Family," E-1.

43. Laura Lippman, "The Family Secret," *Baltimore Sun* (March 7, 1998): D-1. Colin Cardwell, "Sins of His Fathers," *Scotland on Sunday* (June 28, 1998): 27. Dianne Aprile, "Uneasy Legacy," *Louisville Courier-Journal* (March 24, 1998): D-1. Dierdre Glenn Paul, "America Owes Blacks an Apology — At the Very Least," *The Record*, Review and Outlook Section (July 13, 1997): 4.

44. Cardwell, "Sins of His Fathers," 27. Gott, "Monday Book," 5. Maggie Gee, "Antebellum and Uncle Tom," *Daily Telegraph*, Books Section (July 4, 1998): 2. Ball, *Slaves in the Family*, 442. Philippa Gregory, "A Family Shackled to Its History," *The Times*, Features Section (July 2, 1998). As Gregory argues, ambiguously, it was to "Ball's credit that it is on this note that he closes his remarkable book." It's not quite clear, however, what "note" she is talking about.

45. Nathan Irvin Huggins, *Black Odyssey: The African-American Ordeal in Slavery* (1977; New York: Random House, 1990), 34, 36–37.

46. Schwarz, "Roots," 7. Aprile, "Uneasy Legacy," D-1. Lippman, "The Family Secret," D-1.

47. Aprile, "Uneasy Legacy," D-1. Nicholas Tavuchis, *Mea Culpa: A Sociology of Apology and Reconciliation* (Stanford, Calif.: Stanford University Press, 1991), 113. Ball, *Slaves in the Family*, 416. For other discussions of the propriety of Ball's apologizing in media reviews, see Harris Mullen, "Research Reveals Deep Wounds," *Tampa Tribune*, Commentary Section (April 5, 1998): 4; Allen J. Share, "'Slaves in the Family' Is a Gripping Account," *Louisville Courier-Journal*, Arts Section (March 29, 1998): I-5; and Larson, "All in the Family," E-1. Margo Hammond, "Facing a History of Slave Owning," *St. Petersburg Times* (March 8, 1998): D-1. Attesting to the crucial nature of an apology, three reviews end by citing and quoting the scene where Ball apologizes to Mrs. Frayer: see Samuel G. Freedman, "History in Black and White," *Newsday* (March 15, 1998): B-9; Susan Llewelyn Leach, "Author Traces His Family Legacy Black and White," *Christian Science Monitor*, Books Section (February 26, 1998): 10; and Harry Levins, "Writer Tracks Black-White Bloodlines," *St. Louis Post-Dispatch*, Everyday Magazine Section (February 22, 1998): 5.

48. Jonathan Yardley, "The Fetters of the Past," *Washington Post*, Book World Section (February 22, 1998): X-3. Steele, *The Content of Our Character*, 119. Tavuchis, *Mea Culpa*, 5.

49. Caryl Phillips, "Relations with the Slave Trade," *Financial Times* (London), Books Section (July 25, 1998): 6. Leonard Pitts, "Facing the Yesterdays of Race," *St. Louis Post-Dispatch* (March 19, 1998): C-13. Vivian B. Martin, "White Lives Have Been Threaded through Black History," *Hartford Courant* (February 12, 1998): A-23. Mae Gentry, "Shared History Fills in

Gaps, Puts Face on Personal Tragedy," *Atlanta Journal and Constitution* (February 15, 1998): M-3.

50. Dinitia Smith and Nicholas Wade, "DNA Tests Offer Evidence That Jefferson Fathered a Child with His Slave," *New York Times* (November 1, 1998). The story of Jefferson and Hemings has been circulating in some form or other (written and oral) since Callender's first newspaper report. Notable moments in the debate include Madison Hemings's interview published in the March 13, 1873, issue of the *Pike County (Ohio) Republican* and Israel Jefferson's interview published in the December 25, 1873, issue of the same paper; both attest to the truth of Jefferson's affair with Sally Hemings. Another critical document is a letter by Henry S. Randall to James Parton (both Jefferson biographers), recounting a conversation Randall had with Jefferson's grandson Thomas J. Randolph. (The letter is dated June 1, 1868, and its substance was recorded in Parton's biography of Jefferson in 1874). Randolph denies that Jefferson had an affair with Sally Hemings — stating, "You are not bound to prove a negation" — and notes that Jefferson's nephew Peter Carr was the father of the Hemings children. For surveys of how the debate has been conducted from 1802 to the present, see Fawn Brodie, *Thomas Jefferson: An Intimate History* (1974; New York: Bantam, 1975), 12–17, 293–318, 679 (n. 28); Virginius Dabney, *The Jefferson Scandals: A Rebuttal* (Lanham, Md.: Madison Books, 1981); John Chester Miller, *The Wolf by the Ears: Thomas Jefferson and Slavery* (1977; Charlottesville: University Press of Virginia, 1991), 148–76; and Annette Gordon-Reed, *Thomas Jefferson and Sally Hemings: An American Controversy* (Charlottesville: University of Virginia Press, 1997). I have discussed these issues elsewhere in a reading of Barbara Chase-Riboud's novel on the subject; see "'I Write in Tongues': The Supplement of Voice in Barbara Chase-Riboud's *Sally Hemings*," 100–135.

51. Ball, *Slaves in the Family*, 431.

Index

Black Seventies, The, 16, 17
Blassingame, John, 14
Blockson, Charles, 15
Blood on the Fields, 131
Boyz N the Hood, 110
Bradley, David, 7, 68–98; on college experience, 88; on racism, 88–89. See also *Chaneysville Incident, The*
Bradley, Harriette Jackson, 68–69, 187 (n. 3)
Brazil, 37, 46–47, 49–53, 59
Brigham, Cathy, 95, 191 (n. 33)
Brown, William Wells, 61
Brown University, 159
Brown v. Board of Education, 18
Bruce, Philip, 31
Buddhism, 104
Burial: and familial reconstruction, 73–76, 81–82; and narrative reconstruction, 85–86
Burke, Kenneth, 70, 72
Butler, Octavia, 7, 88, on purity in social movements of 60s, 100–102, 113–14; on college experience during 60s, 100–103; series by, 113; and discourse of family, 113–18. See also *Kindred*

California, 101
Callahan, John F., 191 (n. 33)
Callender, James T., 166
Cambodia, 11
Cape Coast Castle, 162
Carby, Hazel, 146, 186 (n. 45), 187 (n. 4)
Cardim, Padre Fernao, 47
Carlyle, Thomas, 7
Carmichael, Stokely, 101
Chaneysville Incident, The, 5, 9, 21, 28, 69–98, 99, 120, 125, 131; burial sites in, 69–70, 85–87; refraction in, 70, 72, 76, 80–81, 88, 97; symbolic relations in, 70, 82–83, 87, 96–97; symbolic systems in, 70–71; cultural identities in, 71; family

secrets in, 71, 78, 83–85, 97; symbolic suicide in, 71, 94–98; versus *Song of Solomon*, 76–78; hunting in, 78–79, 81, 88, 94; belief systems about death in, 79; community narratives in, 79–80; death as unstable signifier in, 79–81, 95; and racialist thought, 89–94; slave resistance in, 90; critique of racial essentialism in, 91–94; D. Bradley on, 95; whiteness in, 120
Chase-Riboud, Barbara, 116–17, 150
Chesnutt, Charles, 9
Chosen Place, the Timeless People, The, 9
Civil Rights Commission, 26
"Civil Rights Issues of Euro-Ethnic Americans" conference, 26
Civil rights movement, 28, 30
Civil War, 103, 134
Cleaver, Eldridge, 92
Clifton, Lucille, 82
Clinton, William J., 132
Clotel, 61
Connor, Eugene "Bull," 28
Contending Forces, 32
Conyers, John, 160
Cooke, Michael, 191 (n. 33)
Coontz, Stephanie, 12, 30, 31, 117
Corregidora, 5, 9, 21, 28, 35–67, 83, 88, 99, 119, 125, 126, 131; desire in, 35, 57, 62–66; blues in, 36, 42–43, 55, 56–57, 62–66; performance in, 36, 56–57, 62–66; black women's sexuality in, 36, 58–61, 64–66; foremothers' stories in, 36–42; oral-familial tale in, 37, 41–42, 54–55, 57, 65–66; treachery of memory in, 40; formulaic discourse in, 42; "ritualized dialogue" in, 42; family secret in, 43–45, 47–49, 54–55, 57; reconciliation in, 44, 53, 64–66; intersubjectivity in, 44, 54–55, 57, 65–66; slave agency in, 45, 54; slave resistance

in, 45–46, 47–48, 53–55; Palmares in, 49–54, 65; performance of race in, 56–66; sex as weapon in, 58–59; whiteness in, 59–60; black community discourse in, 60–62; master-slave dialectic in, 66
Coutinho, Ferna de Sousa, 51
Creel, Margaret Washington, 74, 192 (n. 38)
Crummell, Alexander, 109
"Cryptonomy," 20–21, 83

Danforth, John, 155
Daughters, 52
Davis, Angela, 113
Death: and symbolic systems, 71–74, 81; in different world cultures, 71–76; and ancestral cult, 74
Deep Cover, 110
De Lauretis, Teresa, 193 (n. 39)
Derrida, Jacques, 20, 192 (n. 36)
Division Street: America, 128
"Domain," discursive, 69, 76
DuCille, Ann, 48, 186 (n. 45)
Duke, Bill, 110
Duke, David, 25
Dust Tracks on a Road, 134

Early, Gerald, 15
Elkins, Stanley, 172 (n. 23)
Ellison, Ralph, 9, 16, 17, 65, 117
Elmina Castle, 162
England, 140
Enlightenment, 3, 139, 146
Ensslen, Klaus, 189 (n. 18)
Ethnicity: theories of during 70s, 22–26; criticism of, 23–24; and slavery, 24; and social categorization, 24–26; and rugged individualism, 35

Fabre, Geneviève, 197 (n. 41)
Family: discourse of in 70s, 10–22, 29–33; as model for public life, 30–31; as trope used by abolitionists, 30–31; kinship as critique of, 31, 124–25; black nationalist model of, 109–13; and discourse of nationalism, 109–14; as trope for racial authenticity, 110–11
"Family Name," 134–35, 147–58; published family history in, 148; and responsibility for slavery, 148; family secret in, 148–49, 152, 157; family resists making of, 149; search for black family members in, 150–51; family history shared with black family members in, 151; interracial awkwardness in, 152–53; family in, 156–58; models of racial harmony in, 156–58
Family secrets, 10, 18–19, 33, 83, 108, 131, 133; in palimpsest narratives, 10; as national phenomenon, 10, 29, 127, 166; and shame about slavery, 15, 22, 127; texts containing, 19–21
Family Secrets and the Psychoanalysis of Narrative, 19
Fellatio, 45, 182–84 (n. 24)
Felman, Shoshana, 4, 95, 96
Fields, Barbara, 26–27, 46, 50
Finding Our Families, 15
Finding Your Roots, 14
Fordham, Sonya, 151
Foucault, Michel, 45, 57, 108, 197
Fourteenth Amendment, 31
France, 140
Franklin, Benjamin, 89
Frazier, E. Franklin, 128
Frederickson, George, 26
Freud, Sigmund, 6, 20
From Sundown to Sunup, 14
Fry, Ron, 15

Gaines, Ernest, 17, 127, 173 (n. 28)
Gambia, 105
Garner, Margaret, 132
Garrett, Jimmy, 110, 112
Gates, Henry Louis, 146